Exploring Leadership

Exploring Leadership

For College Students Who Want to Make a Difference

Susan R. Komives
Nance Lucas
Timothy R. McMahon

JOSSEY-BASS
A Wiley Company
www.josseybass.com

Published by

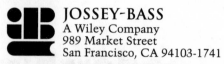

JOSSEY-BASS
A Wiley Company
989 Market Street
San Francisco, CA 94103-1741

www.josseybass.com

Jossey-Bass books and products are available through most bookstores. To contact Jossey-Bass directly, call (888) 378-2537, fax to (800) 605-2665, or visit our website at www.josseybass.com.

Substantial discounts on bulk quantities of Jossey-Bass books are available to corporations, professional associations, and other organizations. For details and discount information, contact the special sales department at Jossey-Bass.

We at Jossey-Bass strive to use the most environmentally sensitive paper stocks available to us. Our publications are printed on acid-free recycled stock whenever possible, and our paper always meets or exceeds minimum GPO and EPA requirements.

Jossey-Bass also publishes its books in a variety of electronic formats. Some content that appears in print may not be available in electronic books.

Credits are on p. 348.

Library of Congress Cataloging-in-Publication Data
Komives, Susan R., date.
    Exploring leadership : for college students who want to make a difference / Susan R.
    Komives, Nance Lucas, Timothy R. McMahon. —1st ed.
    p. cm.
    Includes bibliographical references and index.
    ISBN 0–7879–0929–7
    1. Student activities—United States. 2. Leadership—Study and teaching (Higher)—United States. 3. Interpersonal relations—United States. I. Lucas, Nance, date. II. McMahon, Timothy R., date. III. Title.
LB3605.K64 1998
378.1'98—dc21
                                                 97–33923

FIRST EDITION
PB Printing   10 9 8 7 6 5 4

Contents

Preface

What comes to mind when you hear the word leadership? Do you think of international or national figures like Golda Meir, Lee Iacocca, Bill Clinton, Wilma Mankiller, Martin Luther King Jr., Henry Cisneros, Mohandas Gandhi, Nelson Mandela, Corazon Aquino, or General Colin Powell? Our brains somehow immediately translate the word leadership to mean leader. You probably just did the same thing. You probably imagined a company president, a prime minister, your professor, your supervisor at work, or the person standing at a podium with a gavel. However, the premise of this book is that leadership is a relational process of people working together to accomplish change or to make a difference that will benefit the common good. In other words, leadership is about relationships. And you can be part of the leadership process, whether as a formal leader or as an active, committed group member.

Purpose of the Book

Chances are that you are reading this book because you want to learn more about leadership. You may be taking a leadership course, attending a workshop, learning to be a resident assistant, or just reading for your own development. Somehow, you want to be more effective in accomplishing change, making a difference, or working with others. Perhaps you have just accepted a new leadership role or selected a career in which you will be called on to assume leadership responsibilities. Maybe you have had many leadership experiences, or maybe you have never thought of yourself as a leader at all. Indeed, you may have thought of leadership as emphasizing leaders—not followers or group members.

A popular sentiment wisely reminds us that all of us are smarter than one of us. The wisdom, common purpose, inclusivity, sense of community, and personal empowerment embedded in that statement are profound. Leadership is not something possessed only by a select few people in high positions. We are all involved in the leadership process, and we are all capable of being effective leaders. *Through collaboration with others, you can make a difference from any place within a group or organization, whether as the titled leader or as an active member.*

Scope of the Book and Treatment of Topics

Our rapidly changing world needs each of us to do what we can to make a difference in our own communities. Each of us is a member of many communities—our family, neighborhood, religious group, workplace, classroom, or sports team. In this book, we will ask you to examine yourself and your communities: where you live, where you work, whom you care for, what interests you, and how you want to develop. Together, we will explore how you see yourself in relation to others and how you prefer to interact with others in group settings. Our aim in this book is to help you use your own college context and your experience as a college student as the frame within which to understand leadership. The students who helped us with this book said, "Most students skip the Preface!" We are glad you didn't do that. You will understand the book better for having read this section.

The three of us have, for years, taught leadership courses, advised students in formal leadership roles, mentored student leaders and group members, supervised student workers, sought to bring students into campus governance, served as leaders ourselves, and read and researched leadership. Each time we have taught a leadership course, we have shared a frustration that the scholarship and literature in leadership studies do not connect with most students. Business majors often find themselves in the literature because so much of it comes from their major. Psychology and sociology majors usually relate to it because the leadership field is interdisciplinary and draws heavily from their fields. But many students have trouble relating to the leadership literature, much of which is written for corporate chief executive officers (CEOs). Some students find the leader-focused approaches to be self-centered, and some say, "I'm not a leader. I just want to make a difference."

Leadership can be viewed from various frames: political science addresses power and influence; business management sees leadership as effectiveness in outcomes or emphasizes supervisor-subordinate relationships; anthropology views cultural influences and such factors as symbols and norms; history looks to the influence of key figures during significant times or when leading major social movements; and psychology or sociology looks at individuals and groups as they interact. One book cannot do justice to all these diverse perspectives, but we challenge you to explore how your field of study approaches leadership.

The primary perspectives or frames we use in this book are a combination of psychological and educational approaches; we emphasize learning about yourself and understanding yourself in the context of others. Being aware of your personal values, beliefs, and commitments builds a strong foundation for your position as a member in the world's many communities. Self-awareness is central to being able to understand others and interact effectively in groups, organizations, and communities.

We believe that you can learn to understand yourself and others, that organizations are most effective when they are learning environments, and that our rapidly changing world will require people leading together toward meaningful change. The belief that leadership is grounded in learning together must be modeled in our educational environments. Yet the world does not always work this way. You will constantly be challenged to understand how things are, see how they could be, and be a part of change if necessary.

Throughout the book, you will find quotes from students from across the country. We think you will find their attitudes and experiences interesting.

Summary of the Contents

Because personal awareness and personal development are central to learning leadership, the focus of this book is as much on you and your relationships with others as it is on understanding leadership theory, styles, practices, or applications.

We organized the book around four major themes: leadership for a changing world (Part One), with an emphasis on the Relational Leadership Model; relationships as the foundation of leadership (Part Two); the context of leadership in groups, organizations, and communities—all devoted to moral purpose (Part Three); and leadership and renewal (Part Four).

In Chapter One, we introduce the concepts in this book with specific attention to the variety among groups of students with different experiences who learn leadership for different purposes and practice it in various settings. In Chapter Two, we show how the study and understanding of leadership has evolved through recent times and how rapidly changing times lead to new leadership approaches. In Chapter Three, we present the Relational Leadership Model. This model emphasizes the nature of relationships that are the building blocks in working with others to make a difference and accomplish change.

In Part Two (Chapters Four and Five), we ask you to explore yourself, others, and yourself in relation to others. Understanding self includes understanding your values, character, and the preferences you have in interacting, deciding, and learning. Self-awareness is an essential foundation for understanding leadership and helps you respond to the differences and commonalties you have with others.

Part Three (Chapters Six, Seven, Eight, and Nine) examines the various settings in which leadership is needed, for example, in groups and teams. It also examines aspects of complex organizations and how these may raise distinct issues for the practice of relational leadership. The section explores the core elements of communities and emphasizes collaborative processes; the last chapter stresses the importance of integrity and moral purpose.

Part Four (Chapters Ten and Eleven) presents the profound need for renewal, both for groups and organizations and for individuals. These two chapters close the circle and bring you back to where you started, with the most foundational aspects of self-awareness.

Leadership Can Be Learned

This book (and perhaps the course you are taking as well) is designed to expose you to key concepts of leadership and to provide activities that will encourage you to learn leadership. You will need to practice these new skills and help your classmates and peers practice them as well. If you want to learn to play the piano, you might imagine playing with gusto, but you know it will take practice to do that. If you want to learn to play tennis, you can imagine hitting a cross-court backhand, but you know you have to hit many of them to perfect that stroke. Likewise, if you imagine a group coming to agreement after much conflict and going forward with shared vision and a sense of respectful community, then you have to learn a lot about yourself and practice the skills of listening and collaborating. You would not drop piano lessons when the first scale you learn gets boring or sell your tennis racket when you develop a sore muscle. Likewise, you do not give up on practicing leadership because you find it hard or challenging. Practicing together will help each person learn leadership.

If you are using this book as a textbook for a class, you will find it is designed to help your class become a learning community. After an introduction to leadership, the book focuses on you. Learning activities are designed to help you reflect on yourself and show you how to listen and learn from others. This will not always be easy or painless. But the classroom provides an opportunity to practice the difficult skills of building learning communities in which to experience collaborative leadership. Many students tell us they hate group projects, but unless you learn the skills required for working effectively with others and building common purpose with others, including handling frustration when things do not go well, you have not practiced collaborative leadership. Most great things were not accomplished by an individual acting alone. Even when one person is singled out for credit, there were usually many others who contributed or collaborated to make that accomplishment possible.

As you read and discuss this book, we encourage you to think about yourself. Don't distance yourself from the pages but connect with the concepts and ask, In what ways could this help me be more effective? Not everything will relate to you all the time, but think about your life right now and the many roles and responsibilities you anticipate acquiring as you go forward. We invite you to begin your leadership journey as you explore yourself in your own context. Each step of the way will enhance your sense of self-awareness and help you realize that you are leading when you are actively working with others toward a shared purpose. You do make a difference.

We are still on our own leadership journey and know this is a lifelong activity. As we change and as times change, we will always need to be sensitive to the relational process of leadership. We hope you will enhance your own abilities to be effective in this leadership journey.

January 1998

SUSAN R. KOMIVES
University of Maryland, College Park

NANCE LUCAS
University of Maryland, College Park

TIMOTHY R. MCMAHON
Western Illinois University

Acknowledgments

In the process of writing this book, we tried very hard to practice what we were preaching. Our collaborative effort constantly affirmed for us the benefits of working together in a caring and supportive manner. We became travelers in cyberspace and made great use of e-mail. We learned from each other, constantly wishing we had more time together, and in the process became our own learning community. We also learned from the many people who assisted us.

We recognize the tremendous support we have received from others and feel truly blessed to have such an array of loving and giving families, friends, and colleagues. We all offer a special appreciation to Marcy Levy Shankman for her assistance in planning and in identifying so many resources when she was a master's student at the University of Maryland, College Park (UMCP). Special thanks go to Elizabeth McGovern of The Academy of Leadership (UMCP), who so willingly moved in to manage many parts of the project in the extensive stage of revisions and researching student quotes. Several UMCP undergraduates were very helpful in providing a student voice to our book: Mike Sarich for his interviews of numerous student leaders around the country and Reena Meltzer and Carrie Goldstein for their careful and critical editing and feedback. We thank Mary Campbell for her editing assistance. The National LeaderShape Institute, through

Alice Faron, provided us access to student participants who willingly shared with us their beliefs about leadership.

Susan offers special thanks to her husband, Ralph, and son, Jeffrey, who brought their Macintosh expertise to converting and saving many documents. She is particularly grateful to her doctoral student leadership research team (Dusty Porter, Mary Kay Schneider, Gardiner Tucker, and Tracy Tyree) for their challenging ideas about leadership.

Nance thanks Tami Franklin for her unyielding support, love, and encouragement; family members and mentors who taught her about leadership through their example; best friends, Checka Leinwall and Dee Mazza, for their advice and confidence; Georgia Sorenson and the faculty, staff, and students at The James MacGregor Burns Academy of Leadership for their support and interest in our work; and her students who have influenced her teachings about leadership.

Tim thanks his parents, Jim and Irene, for all of their support; Curt Kochner for sharing ideas, laughter, and experiences in the last, best place; and Kathy Allen, Gary Althen, George Bettas, Pam Boersig, Bruce Clemetsen, Barbara Panzl, and Karen Roth for helping shape his thoughts about leadership.

We are all grateful to Jossey-Bass's Gale Erlandson and editorial assistants Rachel Livsey and David Brightman for their continued guidance, patience, and motivation.

The Authors

Susan R. Komives is associate professor of counseling and personnel services and faculty associate for the Division of Student Affairs at the University of Maryland, College Park. Previously she was vice president for student development, first at the Stephens College, then at the University of Tampa. She held other student affairs positions at Denison University and at the University of Tennessee, Knoxville. She is the former president of the American College Personnel Association (ACPA), is an ACPA Senior Scholar, and received the 1994 ACPA Esther Lloyd Jones Professional Service Award.

In 1992 Komives received an ACPA research award for her studies of leadership development from Commission III, and in 1997 she received the Association of College and University Housing Officers-International S. Earl Thompson Contribution to the Profession Award. She has delivered more than 375 keynote speeches and papers on such topics as futures forecasting, empowering leadership, transforming leadership, and student affairs administration. She is a cofounder of the National Clearinghouse for Leadership Programs (NCLP) and serves as research editor of *Concepts & Connections*, the NCLP quarterly leadership newsletter. Komives and D. B. Woodard Jr. coedited *Student Services: A Handbook for the Profession* (third edition), published by Jossey-Bass. She is a contributing editor on leadership for the ACPA magazine,

About Campus. She has taught leadership courses on three campuses and was a member of Leadership Tampa. Komives received her B.S. degree (1968) in mathematics and chemistry from Florida State University, as well as her M.S. degree (1969) in higher education administration. Her doctorate in educational administration and supervision (1973) is from the University of Tennessee.

Nance Lucas is the academy associate director and faculty director of College Park's Scholars Public Leadership Program at The James MacGregor Burns Academy of Leadership, University of Maryland, College Park. Previously, she was assistant director for leadership development in the Office of Campus Programs and the cofounder and first director of the National Clearinghouse for Leadership Programs. She was the assistant dean of students at Ohio University and co-created and coordinated the Ohio University Leadership Development Program. Lucas is a cofounder of the National Leadership Symposium and past chair of the InterAssociation Leadership Project. She is past chair of the Leadership Task Force of Commission IV of the American College Personnel Association and received the Ohio College Personnel Administration's Outstanding New Professional Award. She is a faculty member at the National LeaderShape Institute and is active in the Habitat for Humanity community service organization. She teaches leadership courses and makes numerous presentations on such topics as leadership, ethics, program evaluation, and academic excellence. A journal partner of *The Journal of Leadership Studies*, she coauthored a chapter on leadership in *The Senior Year Experience: Facilitating, Integration, Reflection, Closure, and Transition*, published by Jossey-Bass, and a foreword in *Training for Student Leaders*. Lucas received both a B.A. degree (1982) in industrial psychology and an M.A. degree (1984) in college student personnel administration from The Pennsylvania State University. She is a doctoral candidate in college student personnel administration at the University of Maryland, College Park.

Timothy R. McMahon is currently assistant professor in the Department of Counselor Education and College Student Personnel at Western Illinois University. Prior to coming to Western Illinois, he amassed fourteen years of professional experience in student affairs at The University of Iowa, Washington State University, Lakeland College, and the University of Wisconsin–River Falls. McMahon has made numerous national presentations on topics related to leadership education and has been a presenter at the National Leadership Symposium. He has also taught undergraduate leadership courses and worked with Project LEAD, a joint community college leadership development program for community members in Waverly, Iowa. McMahon's current professional interests include leadership, chaos and systems theory, and issues related to diversity. He received a B.S. degree (1973) in astronomy and an M.Ed. degree (1975) in higher education administration from the University of Illinois. He received his Ph.D. degree (1992) in college student services administration from Oregon State University.

PART ONE

Leadership for a Changing World

More than ever, today's times demand that diverse people work flexibly and respectfully together. The chapters in this section establish a foundation for understanding how leadership has been perceived over time and how today's rapidly changing world needs new approaches to leadership. This section ends with the exploration of a model of relational leadership and its elements of *inclusion, empowerment, purposefulness, ethical practices*, and its overall *process orientation*.

The leadership process is not about things—it is about people. As you read this section, challenge yourself to think how it relates to you and to those you have worked with in groups or committees. Try to see what new awareness or skill you might need to be more effective in working with others.

Chinese philosopher Lao Tzu's writings are wise guides to self and others. In *Tao of Leadership*, Heider (1985) adapts Lao Tzu's proverbs. Lao Tzu advises us:

> The superficial leader cannot see how things happen, even though the evidence is everywhere. This leader is swept up by drama, sensation and excitement. All this confusion is blinding. But the leader who returns again and again to awareness-of-process has a deep sense of how things happen. (p. 60)

The model presented in this section promotes a relational process to leadership.

1

An Introduction to Leadership

You will most likely find yourself—your interests and your attitudes—reflected on every page of this book, no matter what your age, gender, race, ethnicity, or major might be. You should find ideas that apply to your interests whether you are majoring in engineering or English, or are planning a career in journalism, education, or law. Any number of other majors pertain to leadership as well.

Your habits are also reflected here. You may like details, or you may only focus on the big picture. You may think best by speaking aloud or by turning thoughts over in your head. However you work and think best, your perspective is distinctly yours and is represented in these pages.

Your unique experiences have shaped your view of yourself as a leader or member of a group. Think of the various leadership roles you have held or observed. Think about the various ways you have led formally, led informally, or been an active participant in various groups. Think ahead to the places and relationships in which you could become more active; the possibilities are endless—your student employment position, residence hall, honor societies, student government, Greek organizations, classes, athletic teams, PTA meetings, your family, friendship groups, your off-campus work, community service settings, or your church or temple.

You draw on your personal characteristics, experiences, and the settings in which you might be involved for different leadership purposes. Some readers may want to further personal development; others may want to enhance a career skill, or still others to accomplish social change. Whatever your purpose, your journey through the leadership process will make a difference in all aspects of your life.

Chapter Overview

In this chapter, we introduce key concepts and models that will be developed throughout the book and provide an overview of what we mean by *leader, follower,* and *leadership.* We show that new views on leadership are needed—views that call for ethical collaborations—and will describe ways to understand these new views. We assert our belief that leadership develops best when organizations and the individuals in them are open to learning together.

Foundational Principles

Please critique and analyze the perspectives and frames we present in this book. You will probably agree and connect with some ideas and disagree with others. But try to figure out *why* you agree or disagree. Exercising critical thinking is a key to furthering your understanding about leadership. We encourage you to learn about leadership using different perspectives. To do that, you will need to identify the principles that are important to you and relate those beliefs to these perspectives. The foundational principles in this book are:

1. *Leadership is a concern to all of us.* As individuals and groups, we have a responsibility to contribute effectively as members of organizations, local communities, nations, and in the world community. Members of communities (work, learning, living, and ideological communities) are citizens of those various groups and have a responsibility to develop shared leadership and participatory governance.

2. *Leadership is viewed and valued differently by various disciplines and cultures.* A multidisciplinary approach to leadership develops a shared understanding of differences and commonalties in leadership principles and practices across professions and cultures.

3. *Conventional views of leadership are changing.* Leadership is not static; it must be practiced flexibly. The rapid pace of change leads people to continually seek new ways of relating to shared problems.

4. *Leadership can be exhibited in many ways.* These ways of leading can be analyzed and adapted to varying situations. Different settings might call for different types of leadership. Pluralistic, empowering leadership values the inclusion of diverse people and diverse ideas working toward common purposes.

5. *Leadership qualities and skills can be learned and developed.* Today's leaders are made, not born. Leadership effectiveness begins with self-awareness and self-understanding and grows to an understanding of others.

6. *Leadership committed to ethical action is needed to encourage change and social responsibility.* Leadership happens through relationships among people engaged in change. As a relational process, leadership requires the highest possible standards of credibility, authenticity, integrity, and ethical conduct. Ethical leaders model positive behaviors that influence the actions of others.

Leadership development is greatly enhanced when you understand how important relationships are in leadership, that is, when you see the basic relational foundation of the leadership process. Three basic principles are involved: *knowing, being,* and *doing:*

- *Knowing.* You must know—yourself, how change occurs, and how others view things differently than you do.

- *Being.* You must be—ethical, principled, open, caring, and inclusive.

- *Doing.* You must act—in socially responsible ways, consistently and congruently, as a participant in a community and on your commitments and passions.

It is unrealistic to think that certain proven behaviors are required if you are to be an effective leader or collaborator in this time of rapid change. Leadership cannot be reduced to a number of easy steps. It is realistic, however, to develop a way of thinking—a personal philosophy of leadership—and identify core values that can help you work with others toward change. In today's complex times, we need a set of principles to guide our actions.

"Leadership is an electric current of believing. The energy created from people believing in each other fuels a constant positive reaction to work together and achieve."—Lisa M. Stevens is a recent graduate of the Jepson School of Leadership Studies at the University of Richmond and was active in the Women's College Government Association and at the campus radio station.

Rapidly Changing Times

Peter Vaill (1989, 1991, 1996) describes these times as similar to swirling rapids—permanent white water. We can easily feel overwhelmed; we gasp for air as we navigate our fast-paced days with our many responsibilities. Your clock radio may awaken you to the news of airline crashes and the latest horrific crimes in your community. You go to class to learn something you hope you can apply to real life, but you often find the material irrelevant. You get to your job in the student activities office and find that the work you left unfinished yesterday is needed in fifteen minutes instead of in two days, as you had thought. And the problems go on and on and on.

We no longer have simple problems with right and wrong answers but are increasingly faced with complex dilemmas and paradoxes. For example, we may want to be civil yet affirm freedom of speech, or we want to find community and common purpose but also value individuality and individual differences.

Vaill (1989) observes that traditional approaches like simply working harder may no longer be the most effective strategy. The paradigm of hard work solving all problems is now too simplistic. Instead of working harder, we need to work smarter. Vaill (p. 29) challenges us to work

- Collectively smarter
- Reflectively smarter
- Spiritually smarter

Working collectively smarter means knowing that all of us are smarter than one of us. It means believing that coalitions can accomplish more than single groups; it means knowing that collaborative practices build more community and commitment than isolated, individual actions do.

Working reflectively smarter means taking the time to make meaning out of what is happening in order to gain perspective and understanding. Reflection keeps priorities in order; it helps new paradigms become clear and enables us to identify patterns as they emerge. Reflection helps us keep a sense of common purpose and becomes the beacon that guides us through the rapids.

Working spiritually smarter means being aware of the values, beliefs, and principles that become our rudder in white water and build our character. Instead of bouncing around with the swirl of the rapids, knowing our values and beliefs provides a rudder to guide ethical actions. Working spiritually smarter does not necessarily refer to an involvement in religion, but it does signal a personal purpose and centering that transcends unexamined action. Some envision that we are in a "spiritual renaissance" and are recognizing the value of "a renewed search for contemplative values in the flurry of our active lives" (Palmer, 1990, p. 6).

Developing a personal approach to leadership that joins one person with others in an effort to accomplish a shared goal is difficult. It requires being intentional and thoughtful. Working to become smarter means examining our own assumptions and realizing that others might see things differently. Gaining new insight means learning to identify and understand paradigms.

Understanding Paradigms

In every aspect of our lives, change is more rapid, confusing, and unpredictable than ever before. You buy and learn one word processing program only to find a new version released three months later. Daily newspapers bring awareness of complex local issues and the nightly news flashes images of conflict at home and abroad. The conventional ways of thinking about and organizing our shared experiences do not seem helpful anymore. Instead of individual determinism, competition, and predictable structures, we seem to need quickly responding systems, collaboration, and a new awareness of shared values that honor our diversity. We need new ways of looking at today's problems and new strategies for their solutions.

These different perspectives might be called different worldviews, frames, or paradigms. Paradigms are patterns and ways of looking at things in order to make sense of them. Some paradigms are clear and help us function well. For example, you have fairly clear paradigms about going to class the first day, attending a religious service, going to the airport, or attending the first meeting of an organization you wish to join. Consider going to that first class. You may sit in a preferred spot, expect to greet the person sitting beside you, get a syllabus, learn what text to buy, perhaps even get out a bit early. That paradigm might be shattered if you arrived to find no chairs or a professor who said, "I have not yet organized this class. What do you want to learn?" It is hard then to figure out what will happen; the rules no longer work; your established paradigms do not help fill in the gaps. Indeed, you might judge this class to be more exciting or more terrifying because it is unpredictable. In some paradigms, things are not immediately clear, as in those Magic Eye© puzzles that look like a splash of color until you get your eyes focused just right; then the image jumps off the page.

There are widely divergent paradigms for what it means to be a good leader. For some, a good leader paradigm signals a verbal, self-confident person clearly in charge and directing followers. Some would see a good leader as someone who delegates and involves others in the group's decisions and actions. Still others think beyond "good leader" to consider "good leadership." Some imagine a good leadership paradigm as a group of colleagues sharing in leadership, with each contributing to the group outcome and no one dominating others. Deliberately thinking about leadership paradigms may help identify what was previously unclear or even unseen and what now might be very obvious.

"Leadership to me when I was younger was my family priest. I used to see leadership as someone who was well liked, but now I see leadership as more of a person who treats people well and helps them out."— Andrew McGovern is a student at Hocking College and a member of the Fire and Horse Clubs.

As times change, standard approaches to a topic may no longer be effective. An awareness of needing new ways to approach problems may signal a paradigm shift. There have been times in our country's recent history when the predominant paradigm held that women were not capable of understanding issues sufficiently to vote, when education should only be a privilege of the elite, when corporations could do anything to enhance their profits, and when smokers could light up anywhere they pleased. A paradigm shift means a shift in the previously held patterns or views. A paradigm shift in paying your bills means instead of writing checks, you pay your bills through direct electronic banking deductions from your account. When your grandfather says, "We had no TV when I was a boy, and all our social life revolved around the church," he is observing a paradigm shift brought on by technology and transportation.

There have been numerous shifts in how people acquire information over time. Think of the changes from the early, sage-like scholars imparting wisdom to small groups of students sitting at their feet, to the volume-filled libraries we could borrow from, to the electronic retrieval systems that allow us to acquire information using a computer. Instead of going to the library to borrow a book, many of us download articles from a Web site. How reasonable is it in these changing times to use an old paradigm of measuring the quality of universities by the number of volumes in their libraries when any student can access thousands of volumes through inter-library loan?

A paradigm shift, however, does not necessarily mean abandoning one view for another. The new paradigm or view often emerges "alongside the old. It is appearing inside and around the old paradigm . . . building on it, amplifying it and extending it . . . not replacing it" (Nicoll, 1984, p. 5). We encourage you to examine the conventional paradigm of command-and-control as a method of leadership and seek to identify other paradigms that may be emerging through your own experiences as well as from reading this book.

If old patterns or paradigms no longer work well or if new knowledge highlights new dangers, those who see things differently and hold new paradigms begin to employ new approaches and paradigm shifts emerge. As we all begin to seek new ways to make sense out of the frequent confusion in our shared times, together we can find new solutions to our problems and more effective ways of relating through leadership.

Examining the Paradigms

Leadership has long been presented as an elusive, complex phenomenon. Over eleven thousand books and articles have been written about leaders and leadership, seeking to identify traits, characteristics, situations, and behaviors that signal leadership effectiveness (Bass, 1990). We will present an overview of several of these approaches in the next chapter so you can see how these paradigms have emerged. This amazing number of publications provides insight, but perhaps leadership is best described as using your personal philosophy of how to work effectively with others toward meaningful change.

Most of the existing research in leadership studies is centered on the individual leader rather than the process of leadership. Most approaches examine what a leader does to followers or with followers to accomplish some purpose. Comparatively little emphasis has been focused on followers or group members themselves. The conventional way of looking at people in groups (whether work groups or friendship groups) is first to identify a leader (or leaders) and then describe their followers. However, "understanding the relational nature of leadership and followership opens up richer forms of involvement and rewards in groups, organizations, and society at large" (Hollander, 1993, p. 43).

Much attention has been focused on the leader's behaviors to get followers to do what the leader wants. This kind of leader usually holds a positional role like chairperson, president, or supervisor. This emphasis on positional leaders promotes a passive approach to followers, often ignoring the role or effect followers have in the organization. This approach clearly does not adequately describe the leadership relationship among people in groups.

We must reconstruct our view of leadership to see that "leadership is not something a leader possesses so much as a process involving followership" (Hollander, 1993, p. 29). Again, we view leadership as *a relational process of people together attempting to accomplish change or make a difference to benefit the common good.*

Some leadership approaches, such as participative leadership, acknowledge that followers must be meaningfully involved in everything from setting goals to decision making. Followers must be active participants. Yet such approaches too often frame these strategies as if the leader is allowing the approach to be taken so that followers will feel better rather than sharing power because the organization will benefit from better decisions. This difference signals a paradigm shift from controlling follower behavior to empowering followers to be central to an organization's outcomes. Indeed, followers quickly see through and reject those leaders who ask for advice and input but rarely change their opinions. Followers usually embrace positional leaders who turn issues over to the group for discussion and decision.

"I believe that everyone needs to be a follower many times in life. Followers are essentially the drive behind most groups. It is the power of all that accomplishes much, but one person can change the direction of that power. Often followers have the clearest sight of all involved."—Laura A. Bennett is founder of Residents Against Substance Abuse at the University of Kansas and a member of the Friends of the Johnson County Libraries.

The Search for a New Conceptualization of Followers

A new pattern of how people work best together is emerging because of rapid information growth, complex interconnected world conditions, and the ethics of including each person's context. We need to reconceptualize how we view followers and the nature of the relationships in groups. It seems woefully inadequate to call group members by the term *followers*, implying they are following someone or something, unable to think for themselves, or remaining indifferent to the group's goals, when actually they are creating and shaping the context themselves.

Leadership scholars have been searching for a new term to more adequately describe followers and this process. Followers have been called members, employees, associates, or subordinates. Kouzes and Posner (1993) suggest calling them the constituents. "A constituent is someone who has an active part in the process of running an organization and who authorizes another to act on his or her behalf. A constituent confers authority on the leader, not the other way around" (p. xix). Although the concept is usually found in describing how political leaders are authorized by their constituents from their voting districts, it is useful in other situations as well. Imagine the senior class council discussing changes the provost's office is planning in the commencement ceremony; the president of the senior class will likely be empowered by her constituents and expected to carry the wishes of the council to the provost for consideration. The president would be speaking on behalf of others, not just carrying a personal opinion forward.

Crum (1987) likes the term *co-creator*, elevating the empowered, collaborative, transformational role of group members. "When we choose co-creation, we end separation, the root cause of conflict. . . . They know through responsible participation that they can empower each other and ultimately their institutions and society, thereby creating a life that is meaningful and satisfying for everyone" (p. 175). Positional leaders who see group members as co-creators will take important decisions to the group and ask, What do *we* want to do about this?

Rost (1991) implores us to see that we have moved from an industrial worldview to a postindustrial era. In the industrial view, people are merely resources like steel or other raw materials, whereas in the postindustrial view, people are essential because they bring information and wisdom and the capacity to adapt. He believes that the traditional meaning of the word *follower* is too embedded in all of our minds to adequately shift to a new meaning. Rost now encourages the use of the term *collaborator* for the role of people in this new way of working together. He notes, "I now use the word *followers* when I write about leadership in the industrial paradigm. I use the word *collaborators* when I write about leadership in the postindustrial paradigm. . . . no amount of reconstruction is going to salvage the word [follower]" (Rost, 1993, p. 109).

In this book, we use the term *participant* to refer to people involved in groups in this new paradigm. Participants are involved in the leadership process, actively sharing leadership with other group members. Participants include the informal or formal positional leader in a group as well as all active group members who seek to be involved in group change. Participants are active, engaged, and intentional. They participate.

A Word About Leaders

The word *leader* is used in this book in two primary ways. One use of the term refers to a person in a leadership position who has been elected, selected, or hired to assume responsibility for a group working toward change; the leader has defined responsibilities for decision making and action. Such a positional leader usually has a title of some kind like supervisor, general, team captain, chairperson, or vice president. Clearly, being in such a position does not mean that the person knows how to lead, is a good leader, or is looked to as a leader by others. We all know committee chairs, supervisors, or organization officers who did not seem to know what they were doing, let alone know how to lead anyone or anything toward change. We will say so when we use *leader* to mean a positional leader.

The other use—and the one we generally use—is entirely different. It refers to any person who actively engages with others to accomplish change. Whether as the positional leader or participant-collaborator-group member, a person can be a leader by taking initiative and making a difference in moving the group forward toward change. You can be that kind of leader.

Purposes of Leadership

Leadership should attempt to accomplish something or change something. Leadership is purposeful and intentional. On a more profound level, leadership should be practiced in such a way as to be socially responsible. This kind of social responsibility is involved both in the outcomes or content of the group's purpose, as well as in the group's process.

We are concerned about leadership that advances the welfare and quality of life for all. The outcomes of this leadership approach on a broad scale, on your campus or in your town, would contribute to the public good. On a small scale like in a club, this leadership would seek to incorporate the common good. The concept of common good does not mean the majority view but does mean shared purposes and common vision. This commitment to the public good or common good is a valuing of the role of social responsibility.

Social responsibility is a personal commitment to the well-being of people, our shared world, and the public good. It is "a way of being in the world that is deeply connected to others and the environment" (Berman & La Farge, 1993, p. 7). Being socially responsible also means you are willing to confront unfair and unjust treatment of others wherever it may appear—in classes, at work, or in your organizations. It means functioning within your organizations in ways that value relationships and act with honor and integrity toward your responsibilities and each other.

Somehow, too many people have developed into observers instead of activists in their daily lives. They act as if they are spectators instead of citizens and active participants. Instead of complaining or doing nothing, we need to become engaged in the processes of improving our shared experience whether at work, in clubs, in class, on a residence hall floor, or in any of our other communities. This is our civic responsibility.

Civic Responsibility

Civic responsibility is not as narrow as what ninth graders learn about in government class. Civic responsibility is the sense of personal responsibility individuals should feel to uphold their obligations as part of any community. Certainly, civic responsibility may mean voting in campus, local, state, or national elections. Yet civic responsibility means far more. It means noticing that key campus parking lot lights are broken and stopping by an office to report them instead of merely thinking, "Sure hope someone doesn't get assaulted in the dark." Civic responsibility means attending your academic department's brown-bag lunch seminar to support your friends who planned the event and to be part of this learning community. Civic responsibility means saying, "If I am a member of this community, I have a responsibility to work with others to keep it functioning and even make it better."

Making a Difference

Following the decade of the 1970s in which some political leaders seemed less than honest, a few religious leaders shattered their vows, and sports figures admitted to drug abuse and other offensive and illegal behaviors, it was no wonder that college students identified very few personal heroes. By the early 1990s, over 75 percent of the eighteen- to twenty-two-year-old students, however, said they could name people they admired—people who made a difference (Levine, 1993). These admired people were local heroes: parents, the neighbor who started a local recycling movement, a minister, or the people who drove hundreds of miles to stuff sandbags to reinforce the levees in the Midwest floods, or to rebuild houses after a hurricane in southern Florida. These were not major world leaders or rich corporate executives. These real heroes were average people who, together with others, made a difference in their communities, sometimes overcoming seemingly insurmountable odds to do so.

Steven Covey (1991), author of the popular *Principle-Centered Leadership*, encourages people to say, "I am not a product of my culture, my conditioning, and the conditions of my life; rather, I am a product of my value system, attitudes, and behaviors—and those things I control" (p. 257). This responsibility operates from a philosophy of being proactive instead of reactive. Instead of complaining about what "they" are not doing, this civic awareness acknowledges what "we" must do together. Clearly, oppressive structures such as racism and sexism can keep people from realizing their potential, but all of us can be more active agents in our own lives than we perhaps are.

Leadership Viewed from Different Frames

Leadership cannot be touched, smelled, or tasted but can be understood by how it is seen, heard, thought, and felt. Leadership is, therefore, a socially constructed phenomenon, and it is very real. To understand social construction, think of the *fact* of being one of two sexes—a woman or a man; however, the concepts of masculine or feminine are socially constructed. Many phenomena are given meaning by how they are constructed. Seeing, hearing, thinking, and feeling are all perceptual processes. People interpret their perceptions and draw meaning from them.

Many disciplines provide their own framework for viewing social constructions like leadership. Leadership is explored in many majors, including anthropology, history, sociology, psychology, political science, education, and business, as well as through literature or the arts. Leadership comes in various forms and relates to different disciplines and majors in different ways. When we think of leadership, we often think of political science—the study of systems of governance at local, state, and national levels in countries around the world. But leadership is also evident in other majors.

Consider how leadership might be constructed in your major. What paradigm might professionals in your field assume as a shared view? Anthropologists might study indigenous groups and try to discover how leaders are selected and the qualities that are believed to be most important by the members of their culture. Sociologists might study grassroots movements of people who embrace certain causes and how leadership develops in such groups. Psychologists might study the characteristics of leaders and followers and try to further the understanding of why they act in certain ways. Speech and speech communications majors often study how the messages leaders convey influence or inspire others to act. Organizational communicators are often concerned with how communication works in large, complex organizations and how various interpersonal communications can help or hinder such leadership processes. Education majors study leaders and leadership at all levels—from leadership in the classroom to being a district superintendent to running a college or university. Business majors study leadership in many different forms, including leading work teams and providing a vision for large businesses. Fine arts majors often learn the challenges of leadership firsthand through being a first chair in an orchestra or directing a school play, and science majors experience leadership in research teams and various application projects. And the list goes on.

Each field of study may emphasize different elements of leadership, yet each field has an interest in how people can work more effectively together toward some outcome. "Leadership is like beauty: it's hard to define, but you know it when you see it" (Bennis, 1989, p. 1). Every major can benefit from a better understanding of the nature of leadership. Think about your own major. How can knowing more about leadership make you more successful in your future career or other endeavors?

Leadership Requires Openness to Learning

The story is told of philosopher-author Gertrude Stein lying on her deathbed. Her longtime partner, Alice B. Toklas, leaned over in despair at the impending passing of her companion and asked, "Gertrude, what is the answer?" Gertrude thoughtfully looked up at Alice and replied, "What is the question?" Leaders and participants ask questions, inviting others into the dialogue, and are open to diverse ideas. The question mark becomes a tool of leadership because participants need to ask questions, listen, and learn. In his classic *Rules for Radicals*, Saul Alinsky (1971) writes, "The question mark is an inverted plow, breaking up the hard soil of old belief and preparing for the new growth" (p. 11). Asking questions invites the group to examine its purpose and practices instead of thoughtlessly continuing old practices.

Learning from Others

Conventional leaders, who may think they have all the answers and that their passive followers should merely obey, will be the dinosaurs of rapidly changing times. These times call for

leaders who know how to let go of the past in the face
of uncertainty because they have done it before and have

succeeded. It is a paradox. Effective leaders will be the ones whose experience has shown them that they cannot rely on their experience . . . they will use the expertise they have gained through experience to tap the experience and creative energies of others. (Potter & Fiedler, 1993, p. 68)

Leadership today shows that there is great wisdom and energy in the group. Everyone in the group has a great deal to learn from each other.

Personal Responsibility for Learning

The conventional view of leadership assumes that leaders do the planning and motivating and that they carry a major share of responsibility for accomplishing anything with their group. We do not believe this is true. All of us are responsible for ourselves and for helping others. The whole group of participants, including positional leaders, need to make sure the environment is open to learning, making mistakes, and sharing knowledge. Any behaviors or circumstances that block learning in organizations are likely to block empowerment and inclusion as well.

Self-development, with the goal of becoming more effective leaders and participants, is a primary goal of most colleges and universities. Leadership skills are life skills that can be applied to personal relationships, as well as to work and organizational responsibilities. By redirecting your own life in the context of family, values, and dreams, you can become a productive colleague with others. As we said in the Preface, we believe in this approach to leadership because all of us can learn about ourselves, about others, and about change. We stay vital and renewed through learning.

"As a leader, you are able to make a difference.
   Involvement has changed my life. The experiences,
   skills, and knowledge you learn from being involved

can't be taught in any college course. Involvement,
I feel, makes me more marketable in the 'real world'
than someone who just went to class."—Jeff L.
McElroy, who majors in communications, is a student
member of the board of regents at Western Illinois
University.

Jeff's message is a meaningful one. Certainly, learning occurs inside the classroom but is very real in the world of experience. Involvement on and off campus provides the laboratory for enriching this learning.

Watkins and Marsick (1993) present a useful model that applies to learning (see Figure 1.1). The model also applies to the learning that occurs in the teams and groups. This model presents three components to learning: *focus,* or knowing about the learning opportunities; *capability,* including the resources and skills to learn; and *will,* or the motivation to engage in learning. You begin your exploration of yourself in the leadership equation when you examine your own goals, roles, and capabilities. Stop for a minute and think about something you are trying to accomplish. What is your focus? What do you need to accomplish this goal? What is your motivation or will to persist? On an even more complex level, we believe that the most effective organizations and communities are learning environments in which learning is on-going, constant, pervasive, and valued.

Relational Leadership

This book will explore the evolution of leadership thinking and some of the many theories that help make meaning out of the varied and complex approaches to leadership. Yet, studying leadership does not magically make you a better leader or participant. As learners about leadership in the context of today's challenges and opportunities, we propose that you focus on core, basic principles of leadership that can guide your effectiveness. To reiterate: we define

FIGURE 1.1   The Learning Model

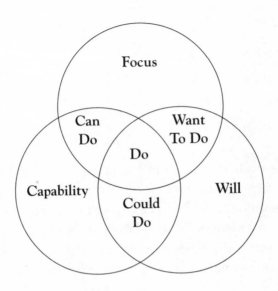

Source: From *Sculpting the learning organization* (p. 37), by K. E. Watkins and W. J. Marsick, 1993, San Francisco: Jossey-Bass. Copyright 1993 by Peter Smith, The Leadership Alliance Inc. Reprinted with permission of The Leadership Alliance Inc., Holland Landing, Ontario, Canada.

leadership as *a relational process of people together attempting to accomplish change or make a difference to benefit the common good.*

There is not one right way to lead. Leadership should not be studied as a recipe or a checklist. Perhaps most important is to develop a philosophy of leadership to guide actions. This philosophy would value being ethical and inclusive. It would acknowledge the diverse talents of group members and trust the process to bring good thinking to the socially responsible changes group members agree they want to work toward.

Relationships are the key to leadership effectiveness. Because leadership is inherently relational, it is perhaps redundant to use the term *relational leadership.* There is, however, strength in the affirmation of repetition. As leaders and participants in all our communities, we should be and expect others to be

- Inclusive
- Empowering
- Purposeful
- Ethical
- Process-oriented

These aspects of relational leadership then become foundational to working smarter. How we relate and work together in all of our communities (families, classes, organizations, work sites, and neighborhoods) matters. We need to examine our role as a member of these communities whether they are made up of five people in your family or fifty people on your residence hall floor.

The Real World

Does this approach to leadership seem ideal and unrealistic or real and possible? Why don't we see these leadership practices widely embraced and used by all around us? This confusion between a preferred and an actual state is called cognitive dissonance (Festinger, 1962). When the president of your university speaks eloquently at opening convocation about the campus being an ethical, learning environment open to change, yet your experience is that campus administrators resist trying anything new and even seem fearful of change, you likely feel dissonance. When the president of a student organization says, "We want to have all your feedback on this plan before we decide" and then proceeds to represent the plan so defensively that all comments are quickly silenced and you would not dare raise a question, there is dissonance.

Conversely, think of the times you have been treated with serious purpose, included, and aware that your contributions matter—perhaps in your study group, your favorite class, your office, or your committee planning a project like a clothing drive for a homeless shelter. These are the places where you matter because you find congruence in the principles you value and the values the group practices.

Even when things are not what they ought to be, each of us can practice a personal philosophy of being the kind of person, leader, or participant we value. This brings a sense of personal congruence. Educators have been challenged to see that "it is not nearly enough to teach students how the world *is*. We must also encourage them to think about how it *ought* to be. Without some hope for a better world, it is all too easy to think only of oneself and all too easy to leave the responsibilities of citizenship to others" (Harriger & Ford, 1989, p. 27; emphasis in the original). Clearly, community is not someone else's responsibility. It is a commitment from each participant. Likewise, leadership is not someone else's responsibility. It is a shared responsibility among participants. In short, as a participant, leadership is *your responsibility*.

Chapter Summary

In this chapter, we have asked you to explore aspects of your unique characteristics and experiences that you bring to leadership. Rapidly changing, complex times indicate a need to work together in different ways than those promoted by conventional or industrial approaches to leadership. The chapter introduced the value that leadership must be for socially responsible purposes. An overview of leadership with an emphasis on followers as active participants in the leadership process was presented in this chapter. This relational approach to leadership is inclusive, empowering, committed to common purpose, ethical, and process-oriented. Relational leadership is best practiced in learning organizations.

What's Next?

The next chapter presents an overview of how leadership has been understood over time. It discusses how the complexity of today's times demands a more relational way of solving shared problems.

Chapter Activities

1. Which of the six foundational principles used to develop this book do you most closely agree with and why? Which is most difficult to endorse and why? Which is the most difficult to practice and why? Which is the easiest to practice and why?

2. Create words that substitute for the term *follower* that would have an empowering connotation to others. How do you, or would you, react to being called a follower?

3. In response to the question, What is the purpose of leadership? Reflect and answer that question for yourself. What is your leadership purpose?

4. What community are you associated with or do you know about that is the most involving, ethical, empowering, and inclusive? How do people in this group empower others, make decisions, elicit feedback, and share power and authority? How does this community introduce and implement change?

5. How can knowing more about leadership make you more successful in your future career or other endeavors?

6. Using The Learning Model, stop for a minute and think about something you are trying to accomplish. What is your focus? How are you able to accomplish this goal? What is your motivation or will to persist?

Additional Readings

Gardner, J. W. (1990). *On leadership*. New York: Free Press.

Kelley, R. E. (1992). *The power of followership: How to create leaders people want to follow and followers who lead themselves*. New York: Doubleday/Currency.

2

The Changing Nature of Leadership

Leadership often is perceived as a prized, coveted phenomenon in our society. It is mentioned daily in newspapers, classrooms, student organization meetings, news broadcasts, and dinner conversations. The leaders who are revered by some people are admonished by others. As prominent leadership scholar James MacGregor Burns (1978) remarked more than twenty years ago, "Leadership is one of the most observed and least understood phenomena on earth" (p. 2). That is still true today.

For decades, hundreds of leadership scholars have attempted to define the term, postulate theories, conduct research, and write about the topic; others believe that all you need is common sense to understand and practice leadership. As noted in Chapter One, the social construction of leadership makes it difficult to arrive at a single definition of the term *leadership* because "leadership means different things to different people" (Yukl, 1994, p. 2).

The meaning of leadership varies from one country to another. Leadership in a collectivistic society like Japan's looks different from leadership in an individualistic country such as Germany because of cultural norms, cultural values, and the use of power (Hofstede, 1980). Scholars have remarked that "there are almost as many definitions of leadership as there are people who have attempted to describe the concept" (Stogdill, 1974, p. 259). Still others believe that "leadership is not a mysterious activity" (Gardner, 1990, p. xv) and that the tasks of leadership can be identified. What is your understanding of leadership?

Aside from the struggles and difficulties of studying leadership, society is crying out for capable and willing leaders to step up and make a difference in our communities and in our world. John W. Gardner (1965/1993), former Cabinet member and founder and former chair of Common Cause, entitled his 1965 essay, "The Antileadership Vaccine." Thus, he made the point that people are less willing to take on the challenges of leadership because of the growing distrust society has shown toward leaders. Leading, whether through a formal position or without a formal title, can be a rewarding and self-fulfilling experience. It can also be a frustrating, exhausting, and difficult process.

Despite the sharp criticisms of leadership studies, many advancements have been made in the field to increase our knowledge of and appreciation for the complexities of leadership (Heilbrunn, 1994). We know more about leadership today than our ancestors did at the turn of the century. Through research and analysis, many myths of leadership have been dispelled. Colleges and universities are developing academic majors, centers, and schools devoted to the study and practice of leadership. Our understanding of leadership is sharpened by recent research on the interactions between leaders and followers, the concept of change, self-leading teams, individual expressions of leadership, and shared leadership. Distinctions have been made between studying specific leaders such as Malcolm X, former president Ronald Reagan, or former British prime minister Margaret Thatcher and studying the *process* of leadership.

An extremely important consideration in our understanding of leadership is the context in which it is practiced. Leadership for what purpose? is a central question in our effort to dissect and understand leadership processes. The kind of leadership necessary to move social movements forward is very different from the type of leadership required in a military setting, especially on the battlefield.

Chapter Overview

In this chapter, we explore how the definitions and theories of leadership have changed over the years; we introduce some myths and truths about leadership, along with various metaphors of leadership. We also present some new perspectives about leadership that are now emerging out of recent scientific advances.

Myths About Leadership

The myths about leadership date back to the turn of the century when leadership was first formally studied by psychologists and sociologists. In ancient Greece, only men with potbellies were thought to be great leaders; in Native American tribes, only men who could ride a horse for twelve hours a day were considered to be leaders; and in Celtic lands, birds were thought to confer leadership powers. The myths of leadership include

- Leaders are born, not made.
- Leadership is hierarchical, and you need to hold a formal position (have status and power) to be considered a leader.
- You have to have charisma to be an effective leader.
- There is one standard way of leading.
- It is impossible to be a manager and a leader at the same time.
- You only need to have common sense to learn how to be an effective leader.

Truths About Leadership

The truths about leadership we propose are based on our collective research and years of study and teaching, and on our own experiences as leaders. We propose the following:

1. *Leaders are made, not born*. Many people have the capacity to lead an organization, community, family, profession, and, most important, themselves. Some individuals will not describe themselves as leaders based on traditional notions of formal leadership when, in fact, they do make a difference in their organization through their commitment, values, and action toward change. Leaders are not born with innate characteristics or skills predisposing them to be leaders (Gardner, 1990). A person's environment can influence the development of leadership skills and interests (Hughes, Ginnett, & Curphy, 1993).

2. *In today's fluid organizations, leadership occurs at all levels.* Progressive organizations are striving to flatten their hierarchies to empower people throughout the organization and to participate in the leadership process. Manz and Sims's (1989) self-managing teams concept is an example of people at the "worker-level" being responsible for high-level decision making and behavioral control over an organization's process and outcomes. People find meaning in their organizational life and work through shared experiences and a feeling of being empowered to make a contribution or difference.

3. *Having a charismatic personality is not a prerequisite for leadership.* A charismatic leader is one who has "profound and unusual effects on followers" (Yukl, 1994, p. 318). Charismatic leaders are often described as visionaries who have a strong desire for power; leaders have been called impression managers who have a keen ability to motivate others and set an example for others to follow (Yukl, 1994). However, many effective and accomplished leaders are not described as charismatic. For every positive example of a charismatic leader, we can find a negative charismatic. For example, Martin Luther King Jr. is described positively as a charismatic leader who organized a nation to fight for civil rights for all its citizens, whereas Adolph Hitler is viewed negatively as an example of a charismatic leader who influenced a nation to senselessly and unmercifully kill millions of people because of their race, religion,

sexual orientation, or disability. A more recent example of a negative charismatic is Marshall Applewhite, the religious leader of the cult Heaven's Gate, who induced thirty-eight people to commit suicide in the belief that an extraterrestrial spaceship would emerge from the Hale-Bopp comet to take them to a better existence.

4. *There is not one identifiable right way to lead an organization or group.* On an individual level, a person's leadership approach or style might be influenced by his or her sex, cultural identity, or personal value system. On an organizational level, the context of the setting might determine the type of leadership required to be effective. Leading volunteer civilian organizations calls for a very different leadership approach than does leading a for-profit organization.

5. *Some leaders and scholars believe it is important to make a distinction between the processes of management and leadership* (Bennis & Nanus, 1985; Gardner, 1990). Gardner (1990) goes to great lengths to describe the differences between the functions of managers and leaders. He defines a manager as "the individual so labeled [who] holds a directive post in an organization, presiding over the processes by which the organization functions, allocating resources prudently, and making the best possible use of people" (p. 3). The manager is closely bound to an organization or institution, whereas a leader may not have an organization at all. Florence Nightingale is an example of such a leader. Yet others find the exercise of determining the differences between leadership and management to have little utility and use the terms interchangeably (Yukl, 1994).

Another proposition is that managers are preoccupied with doing things the right way, whereas leaders are focused on doing the right thing (Zaleznik, 1977). There are distinctions between management and leadership, and there is also overlap in the functions associated with both processes (Gardner, 1990). It behooves leaders who also perform managerial tasks such as resource allocation and organizing systems to be effective managers and to perform those functions well. It is possible, and in some cases desirable, for a person to be an effective leader while being an effective manager.

The functions of both leadership and management, if they can be distinguished, are necessary in organizations.

6. *Leadership is a discipline that is teachable* (Gardner, 1990). Any participant with a desire to lead or to assume leadership responsibilities can be taught certain skills and processes. Leadership is not just common sense. Catherine the Great, John F. Kennedy, Sitting Bull, and Harriet Tubman did not rise to greatness serendipitously. They had a mission or purpose, and they all experienced life events that shaped their values and sharpened their skills. Learning about leadership and developing as a leader is a lifelong process involving preparation, experience, trial-and-error, self-examination, and a willingness to learn from mistakes and successes. Your own leadership development might start early in elementary school as the lead in your sixth-grade play, or it may begin later in your career when you become an elected official or community activist at the age of fifty.

Definitions of Leadership

The study of leadership has produced hundreds of definitions of the term spanning several decades and dating back to the early 1900s (Rost, 1991). Although the term *leader* can be traced in the English language to about 1300, the word *leadership* emerged in the 1800s and was used in the context of political influence (Greenwood, 1993; Stogdill, 1974). Less than a dozen formal definitions of leadership existed from 1900 to 1929. In the 1980s, we witnessed a keen interest in the task of defining leadership, with 110 definitions of leadership by scholars from a wide range of academic fields (Rost, 1991). According to Rost (1991), at least 221 definitions of the term can be found in books and other scholarly publications, and at least 366 publications on leadership do not include a formal definition of the term.

An early definition offered by Mumford (1906–1907) defined leadership as "the preeminence of one or a few individuals in a group in the process of control of societal phenomena" (in Bass, 1981, p. 7). Mumford's definition portrays the leader as controller of events and infers control over people. Early definitions such as Mumford's typically describe leadership as one person controlling others or inducing them to follow his or her command.

Contemporary definitions describe leadership as a relational process based on mutual goals toward some action or change. Another common aspect of most current definitions is that there is a level of interaction between leaders and followers who are working together to accomplish a goal or some type of action, and the interaction often is based on some type of influence. For example, Gardner (1990) defines leadership as "the process of persuasion or example by which an individual (or leadership team) induces a group to pursue objectives held by the leader or shared by the leader and his or her followers" (p. 1). Rost (1993) defines leadership as "an influence relationship among leaders and their collaborators who intend real changes that reflect their mutual purposes" (p. 99). Leadership scholar and author of *Finding Your Voice: Learning to Lead . . . Anywhere You Want to Make a Difference*, Larraine Matusak (1996) states that the leadership process entails "initiating and guiding and working with a group to accomplish change" (p. 5). And again, we want to emphasize that leadership, as defined in the Relational Leadership Model (to be discussed in the next chapter), is *a relational process of people together attempting to accomplish change or make a difference to benefit the common good.*

What does all of this mean, and why does it matter? Our understanding of how leadership works in contemporary organizations is influenced by an integrated framework of leadership definitions and theories that have emerged over time. Various academic fields such as anthropology, psychology, history, sociology, the arts, and philosophy add to the rich interdisciplinary nature of how leadership is studied and practiced. We know more about leadership as we approach a new millennium than we knew at the turn of the nineteenth century when only one scholarly definition of leadership could be found. Today, we know there is not one correct definition of leadership. This causes us to return to the question, What is the purpose of leadership?, in deciding which definition best fits a given context or situation.

Metaphorical Definitions of Leadership

Leadership also has been defined in interesting ways with the use of metaphors, that is, as "figure[s] of speech in which a word or phrase literally denoting one kind of object or idea is used in place of another to suggest a likeness or analogy between them: figurative language. . ." (*Webster's Ninth New Collegiate Dictionary*, 1986, p. 532). Cohen and March (1974) and Weick (1979) provide comprehensive examples of how leadership and organizations can be described and understood through metaphors. Cohen and March (1974) use eight metaphors to describe how one might perceive university governance and the functions of presidential leadership: the competitive market metaphor, administrative metaphor, collective bargaining metaphor, democratic metaphor, consensus metaphor, anarchy metaphor, independent judiciary metaphor, and the plebiscitary autocracy metaphor. Metaphorical examples provide us with a clearer or more visual understanding of a concept, process, or phenomena.

A common contemporary metaphor likens leadership to an orchestra or symphony. Think for a moment of the role and tasks of a symphony conductor and the musicians. The conductor is responsible for bringing out the artistic talents and gifts of each symphony member, while the musicians work together to blend and harmonize the music.

Peter Vaill (1991) uses the metaphor of managing as a performing art to describe artistry associated with management and leadership. Vaill encourages leaders to look at "action as a performing art" (p. 117), which allows examination of both the parts and the whole, as well as the interrelationships between the two. Form matters in art. Vaill illustrates how form or the quality process (p. 118) is inherent in management and leadership, using the example of whether the ends justify the means in weighing the importance of process and outcome.

Max De Pree (1989) also illustrates leadership as an art and parallels the leadership process, not as a science or a set list of tasks but rather as a "belief, a condition of the heart" (p. 148). De Pree's use of the art metaphor describes leadership as something intangible, a set of values, convictions, intimacy with one's work and passion. He goes on to say, "the visible signs of artful leadership are expressed, ultimately, in its practice" (p. 148). De Pree (1992) also uses the metaphor of a jazz musician to illustrate the leadership process:

> Jazz-band leaders must choose the music, find the right musicians, and perform—in public. But the effect of the performance depends on so many things—the environment, the volunteers playing in the band, the need for everybody to perform as individuals and as a group, the absolute dependence of the leader on the members of the band, the need of the leader for the followers to play well. What a summary of an organization! (De Pree, 1992, pp. 8–9)

De Pree's leadership jazz metaphor is powerful in illustrating inclusiveness, valuing individuality, showing the importance of the public good, and empowering people to realize their gifts and talents. The leadership jazz metaphor describes the emerging new model of leadership in today's organizations and communities.

Rost (1993) uses the metaphor of leadership as an episodic affair. "Any time people do leadership, they are involved in a process that is bounded by time, subject matter, specific leaders and collaborators engaged in the process, place, and context . . . it is an episode in people's lives" (p. 103). Leadership then is time-specific, place-specific, and context-specific; individuals experience leadership in episodic moments. For example, leadership does not occur routinely in people's lives during every moment they are working or volunteering in the community. People "do leadership episodically—ten minutes here, a half hour there, fifteen minutes now and two hours later" (p. 103).

We even have a metaphor—the "Fosbury Flop"—to describe the current paradigm shift in leadership (McFarland, Senn, & Childress, 1993):

In high jumping years ago, from high school track meets to the Olympics, the men and women who won always used the traditional scissors kick. Then Dick Fosbury showed up and invented a whole new way to jump over the bar, which came to be called the "Fosbury Flop." Very soon, if you couldn't convert your old belief in the scissors kick to a new belief in this more effective "Fosbury Flop," then you could no longer compete in the event. (p. 184)

And so it is with leadership in an ever-changing world in which we live. Our technology is changing, our demographics are changing, the concept of a neighborhood has changed, our religions are changing, how we learn is changing, and our governments are being reinvented. Maybe the first test of leading a dynamic and contemporary organization should be whether or not we can do the Fosbury Leadership Flop.

Generations of Leadership Theories

Next, we will explore the evolution of leadership theories and provide you with a glimpse of several major theories. This will give you a conceptual understanding of leadership theory. There is a wealth of information on leadership theories—so much that this chapter could be the basis of a book on leadership theory. At the chapter's end, you will find a list of sources that will give you a more in-depth description and analysis of leadership theories.

It cannot be overstated that leadership is a complex and elusive phenomenon. It can be bewildering to wade through the swampy waters of incomplete leadership theories and often-inconclusive research. The multidisciplinary nature of leadership adds to its contextual richness and reinforces the metaphor of leadership as an art form.

A metaphor can also be used to describe the state of leadership theory and research: leadership as an atom (Van Fleet & Yukl,

1989, p. 65). In earlier studies of the atom, it was proposed that the atom was "thought to be the simplest, single indivisible particle of matter" (Van Fleet & Yukl, 1989, p. 65). Just like the earlier scientific assumptions about the atom, leadership nearly a century ago was viewed as a simple, predictable, and uncomplicated construct. When leadership was placed under the microscope of social and behavioral scientists, it was discovered, as was the case with the atom, that leadership has many properties and many forms (Van Fleet & Yukl, 1989). "Where we once thought of leadership as a relatively simple construct, we now recognize that it is among the more complex social phenomena" (Van Fleet & Yukl, p. 66). Despite its criticisms and noted shortcomings, the field of leadership studies has been characterized as having a "robust (and respectable) intellectual history" (Heilbrunn, 1994, p. 66).

There are many ways to categorize the generations of leadership theories that have evolved over time. For the purposes of this chapter, leadership theory will be summarized using the following classification schema: *great man approaches, trait approaches, behavior approaches, situational contingency, influence,* and *reciprocal leadership approaches.* We will describe key leadership theories that have influenced scholars' and practitioners' understanding of leadership. These generations of leadership theories are presented in Exhibit 2.1.

Great Man Approaches

Great man theories preceded trait approaches. Darwinistic thinking dominated the first theories in the eighteenth century, under the assumption that leadership is based on hereditary properties (Bass, 1981). The great man folklore is based on brothers of reigning kings who had natural abilities of power and influence. It was believed that the intermarriage of the fittest would produce an aristocratic class superior to the lower class (Bass, 1981). Great women such as Joan of Arc and Catherine the Great were ignored as examples of leaders who were born with innate or natural gifts.

EXHIBIT 2.1 Summary of Leadership Approaches

Approach	Time Period	Major Assumptions	Major Criticisms
Great Man	mid 1800s–early 1900s	• leadership development is based on Darwinistic principles • leaders are born, not made • leaders have natural abilities of power and influence	• scientific research has not proved that leadership is based on hereditary factors • leadership was believed to exist only in a few elite individuals
Trait	1907–1947	• a leader has superior or endowed qualities • certain individuals possess a natural ability to lead • leaders have traits which differentiate them from followers	• the situation is not considered in this approach • many traits are too obscure or abstract to measure and observe • studies have not adequately linked traits with leadership effectiveness • most trait studies omit leadership behaviors and followers' motivation as mediating variables
Behavioral	1950s–1960s	• there is one best way to lead • leaders who express high concern for both people and production or consideration and structure will be effective	• situational variables and group processes ignored; studies failed to identify the situations where specific types of leadership behaviors are relevant

EXHIBIT 2.1 Continued

Approach	Time Period	Major Assumptions	Major Criticisms
Situational/ Contingency	1950s–early 1980s	• leaders act differently depending on the situation • the situation determines who will emerge as a leader • different leadership behaviors are required for different situations	• most contingency theories are ambiguous, making it difficult to formulate specific, testable propositions • theories lack accurate measures
Influence	mid 1920–1977	• leadership is an influence or social exchange process	• more research needed on effect charisma has on the leader-follower interaction
Reciprocal	1978–present	• leadership is a relational process • leadership is a shared process • emphasis on followership	• lack of research • further clarification needed on similarities and differences between charismatic and transforming leadership • processes of collaboration, change, and empowerment are difficult to achieve and measure

Trait Approach

In the early 1920s, great man theories gave way to trait theories of leadership. Trait approaches marked the emergence of the second generation of leadership theories. It was assumed that leaders had particular traits or characteristics such as intelligence, height, and self-confidence that differentiated them from nonleaders and thus made them successful (Bass, 1981; Bass, 1990; Yukl, 1994).

Trait studies produced varying lists of personal traits that would guarantee leadership success to an individual who possessed these extraordinary qualities. The research questions based on trait theory were, What traits distinguish leaders from other people? and What is the extent of those differences? (Bass, 1990, p. 38). Ralph Stogdill provided evidence that disputed trait theories with the premise that "persons who are leaders in one situation may not necessarily be leaders in other situations" (Greenwood, 1993, p. 7). In summary, research failed to produce a list of traits to ensure which characteristics leaders must possess to be effective; this paved the way for the behavioral approach of leadership research (Rost, 1993). What a leader *does* became more interesting than what a leader *is*.

Behavior Approach

"The one best way" approach to leading is a phrase commonly used to describe behavioral leadership theories that promote the notion that there is one best way to lead (Greenwood, 1993; Phillips, 1995; Van Fleet & Yukl, 1989). The behavior approach includes the analysis of "what managers actually do on the job" (Yukl, 1994, p. 12), which is related to the content of managerial activities, roles, functions, and responsibilities. Effective and ineffective leaders also were compared in behavior studies to find out how the behaviors of effective leaders differed from those of ineffective leaders (Yukl, 1994). Historically, the field of psychology largely influenced studies on the behavior approach to further knowledge of leadership in the 1950s and 1960s (Hughes, Ginnett, & Curphy, 1993).

The Ohio State studies and the University of Michigan studies are known as the seminal research projects on behavioral leadership theories (Yukl, 1994). Results from the Ohio State studies produced two dimensions of managerial behavior toward subordinates: *consideration* and *initiating structure*. *Consideration* was described as "the degree to which a leader acts in a friendly and supportive manner, shows concern for subordinates, and looks out for their welfare" (Yukl, 1994, p. 54) and *initiating structure* as "the degree to which a leader defines and structures his or her own role and the roles of subordinates toward attainment of the group's formal goals" (p. 54). It is possible for an individual to be high on consideration and low on initiating structure because the two dimensions are independent of one another. An individual also could be high on both consideration and initiating structure. Blake and Mouton proposed a two-factor approach: *concern for people* and *concern for production*. They developed the Managerial Grid Model in 1964 (Greenwood, 1993; Yukl, 1994). Research using their model concluded that effective managers show high concern for people and production.

The Michigan studies on leadership behavior included the "identification of relationships among leader behavior, group processes, and measures of group performance" (Yukl, 1994, p. 59). Three types of behaviors were identified that provided a distinction between effective and ineffective managers: task-oriented behaviors, relationship-oriented behaviors, and participative leadership. These studies suggested that leaders focus on high performance standards. Like the Ohio State studies, the Michigan studies showed that effective leader behaviors vary with the situation. To date, there is little research on leader behaviors that shows which specific behaviors are appropriate for specific situations (Yukl, 1994). A criticism of the behavior approach is that it offers simple explanations to complex questions (Yukl, 1994). The majority of research on leader behaviors has ignored situational variables and group processes. The results have been inconclusive and inconsistent, which opened the doors for situational contingency approaches.

Situational Contingency Approaches

Situational contingency approaches propose that leaders should vary their approach or their behaviors based on the context or situation. The situation determines who will emerge as the leader—the leader being "the product of the situation" (Bass, 1990, p. 38). The major research question is, "How [do] the effects of leadership vary from situation to situation?" (Yukl, 1994, p. 285). Contingency theories incorporate situational moderator variables to explain leadership effectiveness (Yukl, 1994). Situational theories emphasize that leadership behavior cannot be explained in a vacuum; elements of the situation must be included (Bass, 1990).

The Least Preferred Co-Worker (LPC Model) and the Path Goal Theory are two major situational contingency theories. The LPC Model was developed by Fiedler in the mid-1960s and "describes how the situation moderates the relationship between leader traits and effectiveness" (Yukl, 1994). This contingency theory of leadership focuses on the importance of the situation in explaining leader effectiveness. The path-goal theory originated in 1957 by Georgopoulos and others but is well known for its later applications by Robert House in the early 1970s (Van Fleet & Yukl, 1989). Van Fleet and Yukl (1989) note:

> If a group member perceives high productivity to be an easy 'path' to attain personal goals, then he or she will tend to be a high producer. On the other hand, if personal goals are obtainable in other ways, then the group member will not likely be a high producer. The task of the group leader is, then, to increase the personal rewards to subordinates for performance in order to make the paths to their goals clearer and easier. (p. 71)

Personal characteristics of group members and the work environment are the two contingency variables associated with path-goal theory. Skills, needs, and motives define personal characteristics of group members, whereas task structure, formal authority, system of organization, and the work group as a whole define the work environment (Van Fleet & Yukl, 1989). The effect of leader behavior is contingent on elements of the situation, which are task and subordinate characteristics (Yukl, 1994). These variables influence others' "preferences for a particular pattern of leadership behavior, thereby influencing the impact of the leader on subordinate satisfaction" (Yukl, 1994, p. 286).

"When I was younger, I thought leadership meant that you had to be a leader and everyone has to follow you. I have found that as a leader, I have to be a good listener, a good facilitator, and include programs that are initiated by other group members."—Yue Zhang is president of the International Activities Committee of the Union Board at North Carolina State University.

Influence Theories

In 1924 and 1947, Max Weber used the term *charisma* in a managerial context "to describe a form of influence based not on traditional power or formal authority but rather on follower perceptions that the leader is endowed with exceptional qualities" (Yukl, 1994, p. 317). Interest in charismatic leadership initially grew out of political, social, and religious movements in situations where a leader would emerge out of a crisis or exhibit extraordinary vision to solve a problem (Bass, 1990; Yukl, 1994). It was not formalized until 1977 when Robert House proposed a formal theory of charismatic leadership that could be explained by a set of testable variables (Yukl, 1994).

Charisma is often attributed to leaders by their followers and is based on the perceptions of followers and the attributions of the leader, the context of the situation, and the needs of individuals and the group. There are several theories of charismatic leadership, including House's theory of charismatic leadership, attribution theory of charisma, a self-concept theory of charismatic leadership, and psychoanalytic and social contagion explanations of charisma (Yukl, 1994). These theories vary based on the variables associated with the influence processes and how charismatic leadership behavior is defined.

House's theory of charismatic leadership is used for its noted comprehensiveness and proposed set of testable propositions. House's theory "identifies how charismatic leaders behave, how they differ from other people, and the conditions in which they are most likely to flourish" (Yukl, 1994, p. 318).

Conditions that facilitate charismatic leadership include times of crisis and times when followers are willing to challenge the status quo (Hughes, Ginnett, & Curphy, 1993). Charismatic leadership has received mixed reviews as a standard of practice in leadership situations. Too much deference to an individual leader by followers can create a dangerous scenario whereby the leader misuses the power or delivers a vision with an empty dream (Yukl, 1994). Just as there are positive charismatics, society has been blemished by negative charismatics who were powerful and influential enough to lead others to their deaths or lead organizations to their destruction.

Reciprocal Leadership Theories

Since the late 1970s, a grouping of leadership theories emerged that focused on the relational and reciprocal nature of the leader-follower interaction. These theories emphasized the mutual goals and motivations of both followers and leaders, and elevated the importance and role of followers in the leadership process. In other words, leadership was not just something that a leader does to followers. Leadership is a process that meaningfully engages leaders and participants, values the contributions of participants, shares power and authority between leaders and participants, and views leadership as an inclusive activity. Participants are empowered to provide leadership and make significant contributions to achieving the vision of the organization. In some cases, the participants are transformed into leaders. The leadership process encompasses the essential role of all people, including participants. We call theories describing this process *reciprocal leadership theories*.

Several theories could be included in the reciprocal leadership theory category. We focus on what we consider to be the major theories in this chapter because they most closely relate to the Relational Leadership Model, which will be presented in the next chapter. The major theories are *transforming leadership, servant leadership,* and *followership*.

Transforming Leadership Theory. A major reciprocal leadership theory—*transforming leadership*— was formulated by James Mac-Gregor Burns in 1978. Burns (1978) defines transforming leadership as "a process where leaders and followers raise one another to higher levels of morality and motivation" (p. 20). Transforming leadership can result "in a relationship of mutual stimulation and elevation that converts followers into leaders and may convert leaders into moral agents" (Burns, 1978, p. 4). Leaders appeal to followers' "higher ideals and moral values such as liberty, justice, equality, peace, and humanitarianism, not to lesser emotions such as fear, greed, jealousy, or hatred" (Yukl, 1994, p. 351).

Transforming leadership is based on the assumption that leadership is "inseparable from followers' needs and goals" (Burns, 1978, p. 19) and the "essence of the leader-follower relation is the interaction of persons with different levels of motivations and of power potential, including skill, in pursuit of a common or at least joint purpose" (Burns, 1978, p. 19). Power is used to realize common goals and purposes and not for purposes of exploitation or manipulation. A unique aspect of transforming leadership theory is its moral component.

The end goal of transforming leadership is that both leaders and followers raise each other to higher ethical aspirations and conduct. Burns believed that transforming leadership could be practiced at all levels of an organization and by both leaders and followers.

Examples of frequently mentioned transformational leaders include Gandhi, John F. Kennedy, Mother Teresa, Martin Luther King Jr., Abraham Lincoln, and Franklin D. Roosevelt (Bass, 1990; Burns, 1978). It is transforming leaders whom most people identify when they think about positive examples of leaders or role models (Bass, 1990).

Transforming leadership was contrasted with transactional leadership by Burns (1978) to demonstrate that the leader-follower interaction has two dimensions: *transforming leadership* and *transactional leadership*. Burns (1978) defines transactional leadership as the process whereby "one person takes the initiative in making contact with others for the purpose of an exchange of valued things" (p. 19). It is possible for a leader to engage in both transforming and transactional leadership. Transactional leadership appeals to the self-interests of followers, whereas transforming leadership appeals to higher ideals and moral values of both leaders and followers (Burns, 1978; Yukl, 1994).

For example, Gandhi, as a transforming leader, "elevated the hopes and demands of millions of Indians whose life and personality were enhanced in the process" (Burns, 1978, p. 20). Transactional leadership is exercised when a political candidate asks for votes in exchange for a promise to build more schools. Exhibit 2.2 lists the fundamental values associated with transforming and transactional leadership (Burns, 1978; Yukl, 1994):

EXHIBIT 2.2 Transforming and Transactional Leadership

Transforming Leadership	*Transactional Leadership*
(Based on higher or end values)	(Exchange or model values)
order	honesty
equality	fairness
liberty	responsibility
freedom	due process
justice	courage

Servant-Leadership. Servant-leadership theory begins by viewing the leader first as a servant—a person who first wants to serve others. The servant, through focusing on the primary needs of others and the organization, then transforms himself or herself into a leader (Greenleaf, 1977). A servant-leader is someone who joins a club, a community, or a social movement with the sole goal of serving others to make a difference. The individual does not engage in these activities in order to lead the group or enhance a résumé. Mother Teresa was commonly characterized as a servant-leader (Rogers, 1996). There are many examples of servant-leaders in local communities—people who dedicate themselves to building communities so they become better places for others. These servant-leaders can be residents, local business people, community activists, and politicians.

Servant-leaders view institutions "in which CEOs, staffs, directors, and trustees all play significant roles in holding their institutions in trust for the greater good of society" (Spears, 1995, pp. 6–7), which is the reciprocal nature of this leadership process. Peter Block (1993) refers to this concept as stewardship. In the servant-leadership process, both leaders and participants are stewards of the organization who dedicate themselves to taking care of the needs of others and the organization's needs and to uplifting the mission and values of the enterprise.

The biggest difference between a servant-leader and a person who wants to lead an organization is the servant-leader's motive of putting the needs of others before his or her own needs. A person who joins the student government association because she wants to provide better academic services and advising based on the desires of the student community is an example of a servant-leader. Someone who gets involved with student government because she wants to run for office and maybe someday even be president is simply an example of someone with leadership aspirations. The end goal of servant-leadership is for those who are served to grow, to become more knowledgeable and empowered, to gain interdependence or independence, and to become servant-leaders themselves.

Followership. Followers in many ways have been viewed in the leadership literature as sheep in need of a leader to tell them what to do, how to do it, and when to do it. The latest thinking on followership has been provided by Robert E. Kelley, a professor in the Graduate School of Industrial Administration at Carnegie Mellon University. Kelley redefines followership and leadership. He does not subscribe to the industrial model of leaders, in which leaders are superior to followers (Kelley, 1992), but defines the roles of leaders and followers as having equally important but different activities. Followership is a role people assume in the leadership process.

Kelley (1988, p. 144) outlines five followership patterns along the dimensions of *independent, critical thinking and dependent, uncritical thinking, alienated followers, sheep, yes people, survivors,* and *effective followers.* Effective followers share these qualities. They

- Manage themselves well
- Are committed to the organization and to a purpose, principle, or person outside themselves
- Build their competence and focus their efforts for maximum impact
- Are courageous, honest, and credible

The reciprocal nature of leadership and followership is that followers see themselves as "coadventurers" (Kelley, 1988) with leaders. Organizational successes are due to both effective followership and effective leadership. Effective followers need to be empowered, honored for their contributions, and valued for the satisfaction and pride that they take in their roles of helping the organization achieve its goals and vision.

Two examples of followership in action come from opposite ends of the organizational continuum. New members of an organization can have an incredible impact by demonstrating their commitment through the aspects of followership just mentioned. This is also true of past officers of an organization. If they are able to stay connected to the organization, their positive impact can be extremely helpful to the current leaders.

"I think there is a certain time to lead and a certain
time to follow. I am used to leading and not used to
following. Knowing when to lead and when to follow
is important. What I have learned in being a leader
is that it is good to let others lead."—Jamion Berry is
the founder of Brothers United (an African American
Fraternity) and majors in preengineering and
chemistry at Kenyon College.

Emerging Leadership Paradigms. Rost (1991) describes the leadership theories in the twentieth century using the Industrial Paradigm Model. Leadership theory in the twentieth century mirrored the industrial era in that the theories were "structural-functionalist, management-oriented, personalistic in focusing only on the leader, goal-achievement dominated, self-interested and individualistic in outlook, male-oriented, utilitarian and materialistic in ethical perspective, and rationalistic, technocratic, linear, quantitative, and scientific in language and methodology" (Rost, 1991, p. 27).

In summary, the theories that emerged from the early 1900s to the early 1970s are grounded in the industrial paradigm. For this reason, Rost (1993) calls for a "total transformation of our concept of leadership" (p. 98). The reciprocal leadership theories allowed us to experience a paradigm shift from the industrial paradigm to the postindustrial paradigm of leadership. We believe that a more integrated understanding of contemporary leadership theory is necessary—one that relies on new ways of thinking about leadership. In the following sections, we will examine various aspects of this new, postindustrial paradigm.

Leadership Maps for a Rapidly Changing World

Much of what is taught in school has prepared people to live and lead in a neat, controllable world. But recent discoveries have indicated that the world is a lot more messy than it once was believed to be. This may be an orderly world but the order is often obscured. It is a world in which control is not possible, especially if other people are involved—a world filled with chaos but one in which chaos is viewed as something to be embraced rather than feared. To successfully navigate in this world, new maps are needed—maps describing the leadership that is needed in an era of rapid change. As Stacey (1992) notes, "An old map is useless when the terrain is new" (p. 4), and the world is certainly a different place than it was fifty, forty, thirty, or even twenty years ago. Exhibit 2.3 highlights some of the differences between the industrial and postindustrial perspectives of how the world operates.

Chaos, as we are using the term, has been defined as "order without predictability" (Cartwright, 1991, p. 44). As Stacey (1992) notes, "Chaotic behavior has two important characteristics. . . . it is inherently unpredictable, while at another level it displays a 'hidden' pattern" (p. 62). This view of a world as turbulent, ever-changing, risky, and always challenging is echoed and expanded in some recent work describing the quantum or chaotic world. When you hear the word *chaos*, what do you imagine? Do words like *unorganized, untidy, wild, scary, anarchy, messy,* and *unproductive* come to mind? If you can let go of your need to have the world be completely rational and orderly, you may recognize this list of adjectives as a set of descriptors for how the world *really* operates. This notion of the world as yin and yang, rational and nonrational, orderly and messy is at the heart of how this real world is described.

Another way of conceptualizing the concept of chaos is to ask yourself two questions. First ask, How is my life (or organization) like a machine? The words you might use to describe your life (or organization) using a machine metaphor apply to the rational, orderly side of life. For example, as with machines, certain operating

EXHIBIT 2.3 Moving from the Industrial to the Postindustrial
Paradigm

Industrial Perspectives	Postindustrial Perspectives
Stability	Change/Risk
Discussion	Dialogue
Structure	Order
Balance	Disequilibrium/Confusion
Certainty	Uncertainty
Controlled	Chaotic
Permanent	Temporary
March in step	Dance in rhythm
Talk	Listen
Local or global	Local and global
Known	Unknown/Unseen
Facts	Force fields of information
Share information	Create knowledge
Hierarchy	Web
Safe	Dangerous
Problems are "out there" (theirs)	Problems are "in here" (ours)
Proven pasts/products	Creative solutions/futures
Money and bottom line	Values and vision
Policies and procedures	Opportunities and purposes
Restructuring	Recommitting
Divisions of the University	Communities of learning
Teaching	Learning
Covering the subject	Uncovering the subject
Hearing	Thinking
Explaining	Exploring
Protecting	Connecting
Providers	Partners
Individual	Integrity/Collaboration
Contract	Trust
Skill development	Personal development
Programs	Outcomes
Learning in the classroom	Learning everywhere
Receiving	Reflecting

EXHIBIT 2.3 Continued

Industrial Perspectives	Postindustrial Perspectives
Driving by dollars	Sailing with soul
Set limits	Set expectations
Critical analysis	Critical thinking

Source: Adapted from Curt Kochner (in McMahon, T., Kochner, C., Clemetsen, B., & Bolger, A.) (1995). *Moving beyond TQM to Learning Organizations: New perspectives to transform the academy.* Paper presented at the annual meeting of the American College Personnel Association, Boston, MA, March 18–22. Reprinted with permission.

procedures must be followed to make organizations work in a bureaucracy. When using organizational or institutional funds or reserving meeting rooms, certain procedures must be followed. These procedures are predictable and do not vary from month to month. Not following these procedures will cause problems for the organization.

Now ask, How is my life (or organization) like a weather system? The nonrational, unpredictable, uncontrollable side of life will be included in the words you will use. For example, like the weather, organizational crises are usually unexpected. They can occur without warning, and their emergence cannot be predicted precisely. Yet the organization must be prepared to deal with these storms. Both of these qualities are in operation at all times in the universe. To embrace only one perspective is to deny the other part of life. A former student government leader described the differences between these two perspectives in this manner: "The (rational/controllable) world is how I wish things were. The other (chaos) world is how I know things are."

The chaotic world is a quantum world—a world of wholes, not parts. It is a connected world in which relationships are everything.

It is a world filled with "strange attractors of meaning" (Wheatley, 1992, p. 122) and force fields that help shape the behaviors of individuals and organizations. It is a world in which multiple realities exist and where it is difficult to identify exactly what caused something to occur. It is a world in which living things invariably organize themselves based largely on the feedback they gather from the environment around them. Finally, it is a world that cannot be controlled (Wheatley, 1992). This chaotic world has much to offer as we think about the changing nature of leadership. This section will explore the key elements to framing the world as more chaotic, or more like a weather system than a machine.

Wholes and Parts

Since the 1600s, the world has embraced the theories of Sir Isaac Newton. These Newtonian principles include the idea that you can understand something by breaking it down into its various parts. By studying these parts, it was believed, you could construct an understanding of the whole. The quantum approach, however, notes that the only way to understand something is to study it as an entity— as a whole.

Leadership in this quantum world is challenging. Its perspective must be broad, all-encompassing. It must see the big picture, something that is often difficult to do. It must focus on the complicated interactions between and among all the participants and the environment. The big picture can change rapidly, but it is often the slow, subtle changes that are the most difficult to observe. Learning to see these changes and to act accordingly are important aspects of leadership.

An example of this perspective occurs in the slide shows many organizations develop for end-of-the-year meetings. These shows usually capture humorous and emotional moments in the life of the organization but do not really provide a complete picture of the organization. The slide show (the "parts") is only complete when it becomes representative of more than the image on the screen. For example, a slide of a major event that your group sponsored may show a successful event with people involved and getting along together. If you had helped plan the event, you may know the real story—that planning the event was a dreadful experience, with people seldom getting along, yet it somehow all came together at the end. You smile when you see the slide because the image reminds you of all the behind-the-scenes challenges you faced. A videotape version of this event (the "whole") would provide a much more complete picture of what really happened for all who were not directly involved. To understand an organization, it is not enough to study the individuals who make up the group. You must also understand the complex interactions between and among members, as well as the culture that exists within the organizational environment.

Relationships and Connections

The quantum world is an inclusive world in which relationships and connections with people like yourself and people who are not like yourself are nurtured and encouraged. These connections are so important that Margaret Wheatley (1992) wrote, "None of us exists independent of our relationships with others" (p. 34). This collection of relationships and connections has been conceptualized as a "web" (Allen, 1990b; Helgesen, 1990, 1995). We suggest that this web, where movement anywhere in the system has a rippling effect throughout the whole system, can be as valuable a metaphor for organizations as the hierarchical pyramid.

Another way to realize the importance of connections is to consider the concept of *andness*. Andness occurs when you make a connection with something or someone—you are literally "and-ing" with it or them. Unless you "and" with something or someone, no exchange occurs, nothing is produced, no new energy is created. Think about it this way. We all know that $1 + 1 = 2$. But think about this in human terms. Think about your very best friend or co-worker. When you two get together, you accomplish amazing things, much more than any two people you know. In this case, a synergy exists, and $1 + 1 = 5$ or 10 or even 100. Now consider working on a project with someone with whom you cannot "and" or connect. In this case, the two of you are like two skewed lines in space, never to intersect, $1 + 1 = 0$ (Meadows, 1982). If you can successfully "and" with the concepts of chaos theory, you will see countless examples of it in action every day.

Leadership in this relationship-filled world cultivates and nourishes the formation of relationships both in and outside of the organization. When the bonds among participants in the group are tightened, the group becomes stronger. However, these same strong bonds may make the group less inviting to potential new participants. A very real in-group versus out-group dynamic can emerge that will eventually harm the entire organization. This can present a challenging dilemma for any leader.

Another area of challenge for leaders is to keep connected to the environment in which the organization is situated. For many, this will be the campus, but it might also be the local community or as large as the state, nation, or world.

Being closely connected to the outside environment is important because it keeps the organization from being jerked around by outside events. An example of such an event might be a new campus policy relating to student organizations. If you are part of the group that developed the policy, you have had some input into its formation and have kept the organization informed in an on-going manner. The new policy, while possibly not universally embraced, has not come as a complete surprise, and you know the reasons behind its development. This is a very different dynamic from being sent the policy in the campus mail and told that your organization must now follow the new guidelines. Building relationships in and outside of your organization can be stimulating and enjoyable. Although it is time consuming, it is an absolutely necessary aspect of leadership.

Strange Attractors of Meaning

As was noted earlier, order is sometimes hard to see in the world, but it is described by a concept called *strange attractors of meaning*. Attractors are like giant magnets, exerting a strong influence on the people and things around them. This is the common purpose that all participants in the organization embrace. For individuals, strange attractors include the values, principles, and people they hold most dear—in essence, their reasons for living. In an organization, the primary strange attractor is the organization's mission, its vision, its reason for existence.

This creates an interesting paradox. In the quantum world, control is not possible. Because everyone has free will, people generally cannot control other people, no matter how hard they try. Yet people *can* be strongly influenced by ideas and information so that their behaviors will be in accordance with the values and goals of an organization. The key is for these values and goals to be strongly felt and held dear by the members. Think about the mission statements of student government, Habitat for Humanity, and fraternities and sororities. These organizations were originally formed to provide a voice for people and to help others. They are powerful words, and when these words are put into actions, great things can occur.

"The world is much smaller than in my parents' age. The onset of telecommunications, the Internet, and other breakthroughs have led us to a more 'global community.' This has made us reexamine our core beliefs."—Jason Scott, majoring in chemical engineering at Auburn University, is a member of Circle K International.

We believe that leadership must be inclusive, empowering, purposeful, ethical, and process-oriented. Helping the group create and continually incorporate such a compelling vision into its organizational life is a challenge for any leader. Most newly elected officers want to begin doing things immediately. The very idea of taking some time to thoughtfully reflect on why the organization exists and to determine what values and ideals it needs to reflect can seem like a complete waste of time. Yet, we guarantee that time spent reflecting will be time well spent.

Force Fields and Information

Visualize walking into a library. What do you hear, see, smell, feel? You probably do not hear much—maybe people talking quietly. You can see people studying and librarians working. You can possibly smell the books once you get into the stacks. A feeling of tranquility is everywhere, unless it is during midterms or finals, when you will be able to actually feel the stress. Now visualize walking into a student union or the campus center. What do you hear, see, smell, feel? You probably hear many different sounds, most of them loud. You see activity everywhere, unless it is late at night or very early in the morning. Smells of various kinds of food may be evident. Certainly a feeling of energy, of busyness is in the air. The different sounds, sights, smells, and feelings that you get when you enter these two types of environments are the result of different invisible "fields" that exist in each one.

These fields are created through the dissemination of information. For example, information is evident throughout the buildings and is driven by the purpose of the building. For the library this purpose is to provide a center for reading, studying, accessing information, and checking out books. The union or campus center provides a center for involvement in various activities, dining, and meeting. These two very different purposes are reinforced by the signage, policies, and staffing patterns that operate in the building. As Wheatley (1992) notes,

Something strange has happened to space in the quantum world. No longer is there a lonely void. Space everywhere is now thought to be filled with fields, invisible, non-material structures that are the basic substance of the universe. We cannot see these fields, but we do observe their effects. They have become a useful construct for explaining action-at-a-distance, for helping us understand why change occurs without the direct exertion of material "shoving" across space. (p. 48)

In an organization, force fields compare to the organizational culture or climate that is produced by countless bits of information generated by the participants, structure, and purpose of the group. An interesting example of this force field phenomenon involves the reputation of an organization. What do you think other students on your campus would say about your organization? Would it be generally positive or negative? What information did they gather to come to this conclusion, and how did they gather it? Think about how one good or bad article in the campus newspaper can cause a complete change in how others feel about your organization. One of the responsibilities of leadership is to create and disseminate information in such a way that others will form a positive opinion of the community, group, or organization.

Another example of this concept would involve how a group uses information to create a welcoming atmosphere for visitors. Having current participants wear name tags at meetings makes it a lot easier to identify visitors and for visitors to associate participants' names with their faces. Having a one-page information sheet that describes the group—its mission, its meeting times and places, its officers and participants—can provide a wonderful orientation to the group, why it exists, how it operates, and who are some of the key participants.

A Nonlinear World

This world of chaos is a nonlinear world. That means it is often difficult to determine the cause of something; the effects are often masked or hidden or are off in the distance somewhere. Rather than A leading to B proceeding to C, A may go to Q then back to D then to C. For example, you try a certain approach to address an important issue that is facing your organization. It works up to a point but then ceases to be effective, so you shift to a different approach. This new method does not work at all, so you have to try a third way, which may be moderately successful. This is how the world really works; it is full of starts and stops, advances and retreats, wrong turns and right turns, and lots of pauses.

This nonlinearity can be frustrating if you are looking for specific reasons why something occurred. Conversely, it can be very freeing because you can look for "multiple partial solutions" to the issues or concerns facing your organization, or for several causes that all may have similar effects. If you think about the big issues facing your organization—or the world for that matter—you can see that they will not be solved with one approach, with one specific action. Rather, they will be partially solved or addressed through a number and variety of different approaches or actions. This is a different way to look at problem solving than the traditional cause-and-effect approach. If you can use this perspective, problems begin to seem a bit less overwhelming and much more approachable.

An obvious question is, Do multiple partial solutions solve problems completely or only partially? The underlying assumption behind this question is that all problems have complete solutions. Most problems facing communities, groups, and organizations are difficult and have no simple answer. If there is an answer that seems obvious, it will have been tried some time in the past and may or may not have succeeded. Because of the complex nature of these problems, partial solutions may be all you can expect to develop. But you will be surprised at how much several partial solutions can accomplish.

Imagine the scenario of your campus having three armed robberies in various parking lots over a three-week period. No one solution will resolve this problem. Multiple partial solutions are essential. The physical plant might improve parking lot lighting.

Campus police could search out suspects. Professors of evening classes could encourage students to walk in pairs. The campus newspaper and various electronic lists may regularly update the community on safety news to keep them vigilant. New student orientation might include safety sessions—and you can imagine other partial solutions.

Another example of this would be when an organization is faced with a dwindling number of participants. The leaders of the organization may recognize the severity of the situation and share these thoughts and feelings with the participants in the hope that it will motivate them to recruit more actively. Each participant may be required to bring over a certain number of possible recruits. If this fails, the group's officers may make more recruitment-related activities mandatory and possibly assign higher and higher fines for not participating. There is no one best approach to an organizational issue like this. The organization will probably be more successful if it tries a number of different approaches simultaneously rather than searching for the single action that will solve the problem.

Self-Organizing Groups

The quantum world is filled with self-organizing systems, that is, collections of living things whose behaviors are being constantly shaped by the surrounding environment and by the actions of those around them. This may sound nebulous, but think about how a peer group shapes the behaviors of its participants or the profound impact that a culture has on its society. Try not to underestimate the influence that participants in an organization have on each other, even if they are not designated leaders of the group. Groups of people *will* organize themselves (Wheatley & Kellner-Rogers, 1996). As a participant, you need to work hard to see that the principles that shape this organizing are the ones that support the organization's mission.

The actions of the participants in your organization are obviously very important. Sometimes these actions are of great benefit to the group, and at other times they are not helpful at all. When the behaviors of some participants become detrimental to the group, leaders often search for ways to control these inappropriate actions. Certainly, there are times when this controlling function may be one of the roles that the leader serves, but there is another way to look at this situation. If we embrace the idea that people's behaviors are shaped by the surrounding environment and by the actions of the people around them, we need to carefully consider what actions we want to reinforce. By reinforcing these positive behaviors strongly and effectively from the very beginning of the life of the organization, sometimes the inappropriate behaviors can be minimized.

Consider the example of a fraternity or sorority. In this group, older participants have a profound influence on the younger participants. The stated mission of the organization will undoubtedly be antihazing, yet the younger participants may find the older participants still holding on to the outdated traditions that equate brotherhood or sisterhood with physical or psychological harm that is administered in the guise of creating loyalty. In this case, the chapter organizes itself around the principles of hazing and not around the principles stated in its mission.

Feedback Loops

Feedback loops occur when aspects of the environment send information back to an individual or system that has initiated some behavior. It is the reaction that results from some action. These loops are like positive or negative reinforcement that is repeated over and over again. This type of feedback can cause actions or behaviors to be repeated, often on a larger scale or with greater frequency. It can also cause actions or behaviors to be extinguished (to cease).

Examples of the concept of feedback loops abound in organizations. Consider what happens when people come to an organization's meeting for the first time, feel welcomed, and are even contacted after the meeting and thanked for attending. They feel positive about the organization and are apt to come to another meeting. It is important to carefully consider what kinds of behaviors you want to reinforce within your organizations and be sure to reward (or reinforce) them. Conversely, consider what kinds of actions can harm your organization and move quickly to extinguish these behaviors. For example, there may be a certain way that you and your organization's participants want your meetings to be run. Within these parameters, some behaviors will be considered appropriate, and others the organization will consider to be inappropriate. Leaders (and participants) of the organization need to move quickly and appropriately to extinguish the inappropriate behaviors from the very beginning. Hoping that things will get better later on seldom makes them improve.

The Importance of Initial Conditions

An associated concept has to do with the importance of initial conditions. Two objects may be initially positioned very close together, yet after their movements are amplified over and over again by feedback loops, they may be far apart after a relatively short period of time. A concrete example of such a phenomenon would be how important it is for new resident assistants (RAs) in the residence halls to begin working with students to form a community from the very beginning of the year. If the RA waits too long, the opportunity will be missed because students will have already established their daily patterns of behavior. What is considered to be acceptable behavior on the floor or wing will have been established, almost by default. This also points to the great importance of first committee or group meetings, first meetings with advisers, first days of class or on the job. As a shampoo commercial succinctly put it, "You'll never have another chance to make a first impression."

Multiple Perspectives

This world of wholes, connections, strange attractors, and force fields is also a world of many perspectives—a world in which the existence of multiple truths and realities is both acknowledged and used. Consider music, books, movies, or television shows. Ask your friends to tell you what their favorite CDs, books, movies, and television shows are right now. You will probably get a number of different answers. Some love industrial rock music, others prefer classical, still others enjoy rhythm and blues. Some people love slapstick comedy; others hate it. Some people even enjoy *The Three Stooges*. Each of these preferences is right for somebody, not necessarily for everybody. If you are trying to solve a problem, the tendency can be to look for a single answer to it. But because people have such different perspectives, a better idea is to look for different *partial* solutions. You will be more likely to come up with some possible answers and can begin solving the problem. To use a baseball example, several singles are a lot easier to hit than a home run.

But What Does All This Mean?

Imagine this conversation between two students walking out of a leadership class.

JOHN: Man, that chaos stuff was weird. I didn't get it at all. I mean, imagine saying stuff like control is not possible. I always thought that was what leadership was all about—the leader knows what's going on and makes plans accordingly—the leader has to be in charge. The last part of that chapter made it seem like everything was up for grabs. I can't be a leader in a world like that! It's too crazy.

KAREN: Tell me more.

JOHN: Well, it was sort of "out there" like something out of the "X-Files" or something. It didn't have anything to do with me or my life and it certainly didn't have anything to do with leadership.

KAREN: Maybe it does. Remember last year when we were working on that campus beautification project? We expected about a dozen people to help us, and we ended up having close to fifty show up!

JOHN: Yeah, and we'd promised anyone pizza if they'd come and help.

KAREN: All our plans went out the window. We didn't have enough tools, and we certainly hadn't planned on it raining. Then the pizza place didn't have our food ready when we went to pick it up even though we'd called them to confirm our order. That was some silly day but I can't remember feeling more energized. [Karen smiles as she tells the story.]

JOHN: Yeah, it sure was a great day, and things *did* work out, even though all our planning didn't seem to amount to anything. We rolled with it pretty good, didn't we? [John's starting to smile.]

KAREN: Yeah, it was tough but we did it. Who knows. Maybe we *are* cut out to be leaders in this chaotic world. One of things I learned that day is that I didn't really enjoy uncertainty. I hated not being sure about what was going to happen next. I mean I've always been a planner, and I'm way organized all the time so I just figured that would get me through any situation. In fact, I've even tried out a couple of these chaos ideas and they seem to be working. At least I'm getting some results, and I'm not as stressed out as I was when I was trying to control every part of my life. I still do lots of planning, but I know I have to be pretty flexible.

JOHN: Well, chaos isn't how I want the world to be, but maybe it's the way the world really is. [John pauses.] Maybe we are cut out for leadership after all. I guess we'll have to be!

Chapter Summary

The studies on leadership theory are often described with what we call the "but" phenomenon. There are numerous theories on leadership, "but" we still know very little about if and how leaders make a difference and their effectiveness on the organization; leadership has been studied as a scientific discipline for several decades, "but" we still have made little progress; there are numerous research studies on leadership, "but" the results are often inconclusive and ambiguous.

Scholars, practitioners, and students of leadership just within this decade are making progress in reformulating their ideas and research questions to fit the changing nature of our organizations and our world. Yukl (1994) calls for researchers and scholars to greatly improve the quality of leadership research and theory. Perhaps researchers need to experience a Fosbury Flop in their formulation of leadership theory and research design.

Leaders and leadership researchers need to work collaboratively to forge new knowledge and discoveries about leadership processes in contemporary organizations. Scholars and researchers cannot work in isolation of individuals who practice leadership "out in the field" at all levels of an organization or in a community. As we continue to search for answers and knowledge about leadership, we see the glass as half full rather than half empty.

In this section, we also explored a new world—the quantum world—and noted how it is different from the linear, rational world that has been traditionally used as a model for how the world works. Leadership in this new world requires embracing rapid change and constant learning. These are exciting, challenging, turbulent times in which to be alive. They call for new and different ways of conceptualizing and leading in organizations and the world.

What's Next?

The next chapter presents a leadership model that emphasizes the role of relationships. This Relational Leadership Model highlights the importance of being inclusive, empowering, purposeful, ethical, and process-oriented.

Chapter Activities

1. Describe your personal best leadership experience—an experience in which you were most effective. What theory or metaphor best describes your leadership approach and why?

2. What motivates you to take on leadership responsibilities or roles and why? Why do you lead?

3. For each of the leadership theory categories (trait, behavioral, and so on), provide examples of specific leaders and participants whose leadership can be described based upon that approach. Give examples of people who practice these theories.

4. Using Rost's postindustrial leadership definition and paradigm, describe how an organization, office, or community in which you belong would look like if this type of leadership was practiced. What would be the same? What would be different?

5. If the glass is half full of our understanding of leadership theory and concepts, what do you think we need to learn to further our knowledge of how leadership works in contemporary organizations?

6. Think about your life. What provides the order in your chaotic world? Is it values? Relationships? Family? Your faith? Now think about your organization. What provides the order or structure within this group? Does your organization's strange attractor provide an order that is thought to be positive or negative? Does it need to be changed? If so, how can you do this?

7. Think about the last time you did something in your organization that others would describe as being "outside the lines." What was it? Why did others think it was "way out"? Was it successful? Why or why not?

Additional Readings

Kellert, S. (1993). *In the wake of chaos*. Chicago: University of Chicago.

Matusak, L. R. (1996). *Finding your voice: Learning to lead . . . anywhere you want to make a difference*. San Francisco: Jossey-Bass.

Rost, J. C. (1993). Leadership development in the new millennium. *The Journal of Leadership Studies, 1*(1), 92–110.

Senge, P. (1990). *The fifth discipline: The art and practice of the learning organization*. New York: Currency/Doubleday.

Spears, L. C. (1995). *Reflections on leadership. How Robert K. Greenleaf's theory of servant-leadership influenced today's top management thinkers*. New York: Wiley.

Wheatley, M. (1992). *Leadership and the new science: Learning about organization from an orderly universe*. San Francisco: Jossey-Bass.

3

A New Way of Understanding Leadership

In the previous chapter, we reviewed how theorists' view of leadership has changed from the belief that leaders are simply born, to the idea that the best way to learn about leadership is to study the behaviors or practices of people who are viewed as leaders. Theorizing has evolved even further into an understanding of leadership as a complex process. Indeed, leadership is a transforming process that raises all participants to the level of leadership; all participants can become effective leaders. Today's understanding of wholeness in a chaotic world leads to a flexible understanding of leadership in which individuals and openness to change are valued.

Leadership can best be understood as philosophy. At its core, understanding philosophy means understanding values. "Affect, motives, attitudes, beliefs, values, ethics, morals, will, commitment, preferences, norms, expectations, responsibilities—such are the concerns of leadership philosophy proper. Their study is paramount because the very nature of leadership is that of practical philosophy, philosophy-in-action" (Hodgkinson, 1983, p. 202). It is critical that we each develop our own personal philosophy—one we hope will include the elements of the model presented in this chapter.

Chapter Overview

This chapter presents a relational model of leadership to consider in building your own personal philosophy. Each of the elements of the model is presented in detail to give you more information about each component.

Relational Leadership

Leadership has to do with relationships, the role of which cannot be overstated. Leadership is inherently a relational, communal process. "Leadership is *always* dependent on the context, but the context is established by the *relationships* we value" (Wheatley, 1992, p. 144). Although a person could exert leadership of ideas through persuasive writings or making speeches, most leadership happens in an interactive relational context. We emphasize once again: we view leadership as *a relational process of people together attempting to accomplish change or make a difference to benefit the common good.*

Chapter Two presented an overview of how leadership theories and models have changed over time. These changing frameworks are reflected in the descriptive terms that have been affixed to the word *leadership.* Examples include situational leadership, visionary leadership, servant-leadership, transforming leadership, and principle-centered leadership. We have used the term *relational leadership* as a reminder that relationships are the focal point of the leadership process.

Relational leadership involves a focus on five primary components. This approach to leadership is *inclusive* of people and diverse points of view, *empowers* those involved, is *purposeful* and builds commitment toward common purposes, is *ethical,* and recognizes that all four of those elements are accomplished by being *process-oriented.*

The model provides a frame of reference or an approach to leadership in contemporary organizations. With these foundational philosophies and commitments, an individual can make a meaningful contribution in any organization. This model is not a leadership theory in itself, and it does not address the change outcomes for which leadership is intended. It is a framework connecting five key elements that can serve as a responsive approach to leadership. Figure 3.1 will give you a visual image of the elements of the model.

The components of relational leadership are complex concepts. Think about your own level of comfort or knowledge about each component as you read the related dimensions of each element. Exhibit 3.1 identifies some important knowledge, attitudes, and skills that are embedded in each element. These reflect the knowledge, attitudes, and skills that would be helpful in understanding relational leadership. Brief applications of the core elements to the knowing-being-doing model conclude each section. For example, in order to practice inclusiveness, you must

Know yourself and others (knowledge).

Be open to difference and value all perspectives (attitudes).

Practice listening skills, building coalitions, and effective civil discourse (skills).

FIGURE 3.1 Relational Leadership Model

EXHIBIT 3.1 Relational Leadership Model

Leadership Component	Knowing (Knowledge/ Understanding of...)	Being (Belief that...)	Doing (Skills in...)
Inclusive— of people and diverse points of view.	self and others citizenship frames and multiple realities world views organizational cultures	differences in people are valuable fairness and equality are important in the treatment of all people everyone can make a difference need to conceptualize groups and organizations as web-like in structure	developing talent listening building coalitions framing/re-framing engaging in civil discourse
Empowering— of others who are involved.	power empowerment impact of power on policies and procedures self esteem	everyone has something to offer concern for the growth and development of others is necessary and important contributions of others are to be solicited and valued power, information, and decision making are to be shared willingly	gate-keeping sharing information learning at individual and team levels encouraging or affirming others building capacity of others promoting self-leadership practicing renewal

EXHIBIT 3.1 Continued

Leadership Component	Knowing (Knowledge/ Understanding of . . .)	Being (Belief that . . .)	Doing (Skills in . . .)
Purposeful—means having an individual commitment to a goal or activity. It is also the individual ability to collaborate and find common ground with others to establish a common purpose, a vision for a group, or work toward the public.	change process and models role of mission/vision	an attitude that is hopeful, positive, and optimistic helps everyone individuals, groups, and organizations can improve individuals, groups, and organizations can make a difference	identifying goals envisioning making meaning thinking creatively involving others in vision-building process
Ethical—driven by values and standards and leadership which is "good" or moral in nature.	development of values influence of systems on justice and care models of valuing of self and others ethical decision making	socially responsible behavior is to be encouraged in all people character development happens through participation in groups and organizations high standards of behavior for each person helps everyone actions which benefit others are preferred over actions which are pursued for self gain	behaving congruently trusting others and being trustworthy being reliable and responsible acting courageously identifying issues as needing an ethical decision confronting inappropriate behavior in others

EXHIBIT 3.1 Continued

Leadership Component	Knowing (Knowledge/Understanding of. . .)	Being (Belief that. . .)	Doing (Skills in. . .)
Process-Oriented—how the group goes about being a group, remaining a group, and accomplishing the group's purposes.	community group process relational aspect of leadership systems perspective	process is as important as outcome effort of a high quality is to be encouraged good things happen when people trust the process	collaboration reflecting making meaning challenging engaging in civil confrontation learning giving and receiving feedback

Relational Leadership Is Inclusive

Being inclusive means understanding, valuing, and actively engaging diversity in views, approaches, styles, and aspects of individuality such as sex or culture that add multiple perspectives to a group's activity. As a foundation for valuing inclusion, you will have a chance to explore your own attitudes and attributes in Chapter Four and examine those of others in Chapter Five.

You saw in the last chapter that although many things seem unpredictable and even unconnected, there is unity in nature; seemingly unrelated parts influence each other as well as the whole. By applying these concepts to the leadership world, we learn to understand that the group or organization represents unity or wholeness built from and influenced greatly by the smallest subunits of that system. "As we move away from viewing the organization as a complex of parts and deal with it as a unity, then problems met in leadership can make more sense and solutions become obvious" (Fairholm, 1994, p. 59).

Individuals are important because they concurrently represent and influence the whole. The purpose, vision, and values of the whole come to life as each individual member describes and applies them. The goal is not to overcome the variations and differences among participants—indeed, those variations bring creativity and energy—but to build shared purpose. "Leading others to lead themselves is the key to tapping the intelligence, the spirit, the creativity, the commitment, and most of all, the tremendous, unique potential of each individual" (Manz & Sims, 1989, p. 225).

"Being inclusive is difficult because you must step out of your comfort zone in order to expand your organization or vision. Inclusive means sharing ideas or beliefs rather than selling or telling."—Lindsey Yellid is a member of Kappa Alpha Theta Sorority at the University of Michigan.

Being inclusive means developing the strengths and talent of group members so they can contribute to the group's goals. "Leaders enhance the learning of others, helping them to develop their own initiative, strengthening them in the use of their own judgment, and enabling them to grow and to become better contributors to the organization. These leaders, by virtue of their learning, then become leaders and mentors to others" (McGill & Slocum, 1993, p. 11).

It is not sufficient just to be a participative leader involving group members in the work of the organization. Organizations have to go further and recognize that in many cases the organizational culture has to change to effectively involve people who have different backgrounds and different views, and who may not embrace the dominant cultural norms.

The group might be so accustomed to voting on every decision that they have alienated members who find this uncomfortable. Those members might like to use a consensus model of decision making to make sure the views of all are included in each significant decision. For example, the Student Union film committee might have traditionally provided films that interest only one segment of the campus. They would need to examine that practice and involve others with different interests in order to diversify programming. Organizational practices, such as always meeting at 9 P.M., may exclude the involvement of people such as adult learners and those who cannot be on campus at that time because of family or work obligations; or commuting may be a problem. When the group realizes, for example, that no commuter students, or students of color, or men are involved in their activities, that should be a signal that something is wrong. Other ways of communicating and consulting with people should be found, as should other ways of including diverse interests in group decision making.

Involving Those External to the Group

Being inclusive means identifying the shareholders and stakeholders external to the group who have some responsibility (a share) or interest (a stake) in the change that is being planned. It would be exclusive, not inclusive, for a group to assume that they should or could accomplish a major change alone. One organization like the Latino Student Union might seek to change a campus practice about how scholarship programs are advertised to new Latino students. Being inclusive means the Latino Student Union should also consider which other campus groups or offices might be stakeholders in resolving this issue because they have a shared interest or could be affected by the consequences of any action (Bryson & Crosby, 1992). The Latino Student Union might then reach out to form coalitions or some involvement with such groups as the Council of Black Fraternity and Sorority Chapters, the Black Student Union, the Multicultural Affairs Committee of the Student Government Association, and other related student organizations like the Honors Program. In addition, the Latino Student Union should identify the shareholders in resolving the issue—the Financial Aid Office, the Dean of Students' office, and the Office of Minority Affairs. These offices would each want to get the word out about their programs to students and need not be thought of as negative or antagonistic to the changes. They might in fact appreciate help in resolving problems they may have in the current process.

Stakeholders may not all hold the same view of a problem, and they may not all seek the same solutions. Bryson and Crosby (1992) clarify how a stakeholder's position on an issue (ranging from high support to high opposition) is influenced by the importance with which they view the issue (ranging from least important to most important). This makes stakeholders' responses more understandable (see Figure 3.2). As they work toward being more inclusive, relational leaders will want to assess possible stakeholder reactions in determining their approaches.

Even if stakeholders disagree on an issue, they should be involved. Involvement helps stakeholders gain new views on issues and may build support among various stakeholders toward an intended change. Building support and forming coalitions are related skills for relational leaders.

FIGURE 3.2 Responses of Stakeholders to Shared Issues and Goals

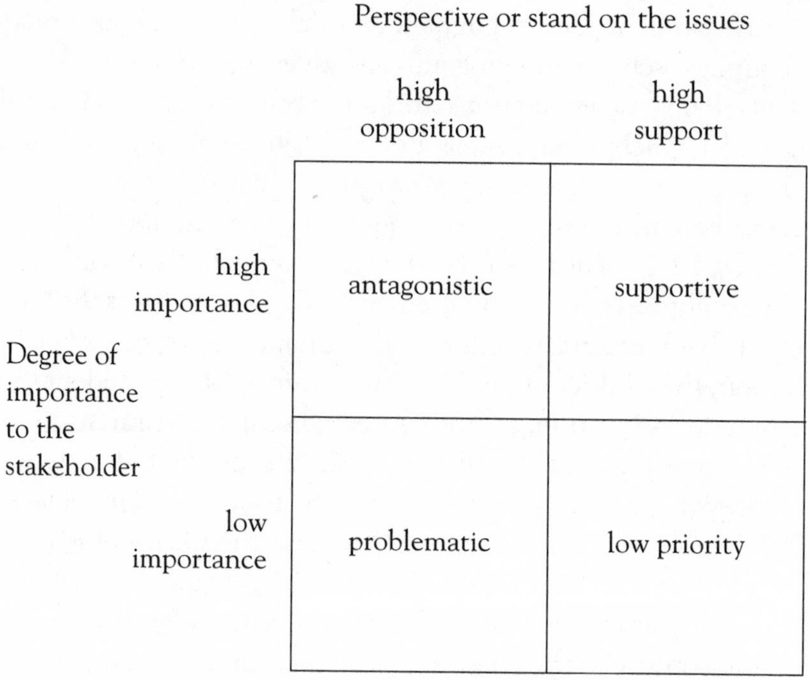

Perspective or stand on the issues

	high opposition	high support
high importance	antagonistic	supportive
low importance	problematic	low priority

Degree of importance to the stakeholder

Source: Bryson & Crosby, 1992, p. 268 (based on Nutt & Backoff, 1992, p. 191). Copyright 1992 by Jossey-Bass. Adapted with permission from Jossey-Bass, Inc., Publishers.

Knowing-Being-Doing

Being inclusive means knowing yourself and understanding others. Exhibit 3.1 highlights aspects of being inclusive to illustrate how you might explore this component. It means understanding how different groups or individuals might approach issues from different perspectives or frames. It means maintaining the attitudes that respect differences and valuing equity and involvement. It means thinking of the networks and webs of connection instead of seeing issues and problems as isolated and discrete. It means having the skills to develop the talent of members so they can be readily involved. It means listening with empathy and communicating with civility.

Relational Leadership Is Empowering

"Thriving on change demands the empowerment of every person in the organization—no ifs, ands, or buts" (Peters, 1989, p. xiv). Empowerment has two dimensions: (1) the sense of self that claims ownership, claims a place in the process, and expects to be involved and (2) a set of environmental conditions (in the group or organization) that promote the full involvement of participants by reducing the barriers that block the development of individual talent and involvement. So, empowerment is claimed ("I have a legitimate right to be here and say what I feel and think") as well as shared with others ("You should be involved in this; you have a right to be here too; tell us what you think and feel"). Being empowering means mitigating aspects of the environmental climate that can block meaningful involvement for others. Empowering environments are learning climates that expect successes and know they can learn from failures or mistakes.

The root word in the concept of empowerment is *power*. Understanding power dynamics is essential in moving toward a philosophical commitment to empowerment. Where possible, positional leaders must be willing to share their power or authority, and participants must be willing to assume more responsibility for group outcomes. Power has traditionally been viewed on a zero-sum basis. Conventional approaches assumed that if one person in an organization is very powerful, then someone else has less power. Instead, different types of power exist concurrently among people in any kind of relationship. Power dynamics range from power "over" (autocratic approaches) to power "with" (collaborative approaches) or power "alongside" (collegial approaches). Some approaches to leadership would go further and describe power "from," referring to the authority and power afforded to a leader from a group of participants. Effective positional leaders know that their power and ability to be effective comes from the members of their group—their participants (Kouzes & Posner, 1987).

Sources of Power

How a person uses power and reacts to the power of others must be examined in relational leadership. In their classic work, French and Raven (1959) identify five primary sources of power that individuals bring to their relationships with others. These bases of social power are *expert power, referent power, legitimate power, coercive power,* and *reward power.*

Expert power is the power of information or knowledge. Expertise may come through professional development and formal education (such as that received by engineers or dentists), from possessing specific information (like remembering the results of a recent survey or knowing the rules in the student handbook), or from extended experience (like being the mother of three children or being a seasoned baseball player). We trust experts and give them power over us, based on their assumed higher level of knowledge or experience.

Referent power refers to the nature and strength of a relationship between two or more people. Think of the wise senior who is so highly regarded that her words carry great weight in the group discussion.

Legitimate power is due to the formal role a person holds, usually because he or she has the responsibility and authority to exert some degree of power. Those in authority generally know that their legitimate power is fragile.

Coercive power influences individuals or groups through imposing or threatening punitive sanctions or removing rewards or benefits. Coercion accomplishes behavior change but usually at great cost to the relationships among those involved. Because leadership is an influence relationship, it is essential that this influence be "noncoercive" (Rost, 1993, p. 105).

Conversely, reward power influences behavior through the ability to deliver positive outcomes and desired resources. Rewards may be extrinsic rewards like raises, plaques, or special privileges. They may also be intrinsic rewards for intangibles like praise or support.

You may intentionally use some source of power. For example, you might prepare very well before a meeting so you will be an expert on some topic. Conversely, others may attribute some source of power to you without your knowing what is happening, as, for example, when someone fears your disapproval because you have referent power. To empower ourselves and others, it is essential to understand power.

Understanding Power

In many cases, we give power away. We do it when we do not trust our own opinion if it contradicts that of an expert. We assume the expert knows more. Yet when the doctor too readily concludes that you just need bed rest and you know something hurts, you should insist that your doctor explore other alternatives. When the person with legitimate power announces a plan or an approach, we give power away if we do not say, "We would like to talk about that first because we might have some additional ideas that would be helpful." We may also have power attributed to us that is undeserved. When the group assumes that because you are an English major, you would be best at writing the group's report, they may be in error.

Power is not finite and indeed can be shared and amplified. Some think that power should be framed differently and seen with a similar frame as love: the more you give away, the more you get. If the leadership paradigm of your colleagues is very conventional, they may see sharing power as indecisive or an avoidance of responsibility. Others may abuse the power shared with them, but those in legitimate authority roles who share their power usually find that they build stronger groups. Groups who claim empowerment can have a major impact on an organization.

Self-Empowerment

Empowerment is claiming the power you should have from any position in the organization. Self-empowerment then is the recognition that you have a legitimate right to be heard and the self-confidence to be part of a solution or the change process. "The E-word by itself, is a non sequitur unless it's used with *self-discovery* . . . it provides *a means of empowering yourself as you explore your natural, educational, and professional attributes in sizing up your leadership prospects*" (Haas & Tamarkin, 1992, p. 35). Murrell (1985, pp. 36–37) presents six methods through which you might become empowered:

1. Educating (sharing information and knowledge)
2. Leading (inspiring, rewarding, directing)
3. Structuring (creating structural factors such as arranging your day, bringing people to the table, changing policies or processes so that the change lives beyond the people who created it)
4. Providing (making sure others have resources to get their job done)
5. Mentoring (having close personal relationships)
6. Actualizing (taking it on—being empowered—claiming it)

Valuing the empowerment of all members creates a larger group of participants or citizens who generally take more ownership of group tasks and processes and who feel committed to the outcomes of the change.

Mattering and Marginality

Empowerment places you at the center of what is happening rather than at the edges where you might feel inconsequential. This may be understood best by examining the concepts of mattering and marginality. Schlossberg (1989b) has extended and applied the work of sociologist Morris Rosenberg on mattering to her own work in studying adults in transition. "Mattering is a motive: the feeling that others depend on us, are interested in us, are concerned with our fate, . . . [which] . . . exercises a powerful influence on our actions" (Rosenberg & McCullough, 1981, p. 165, as cited in Schlossberg, 1989b, p. 8). In new situations, in new roles, or with new people, we may feel marginal, as if we did not matter unless the group welcomes us and seeks our meaningful involvement. In contrast, mattering is the feeling that we are significant to others and to the process. Think of the anxiety and perhaps marginalization of potential new members coming to their first meeting of the Campus Environmental Coalition—or any group. They could scarcely be noticed, become isolated, and perhaps ignored, or they could be welcomed, involved, and engaged.

Empowering Environments

Groups, organizations, or environments can promote mattering or can keep people on the periphery. We need environments that promote the development of the human spirit on a local scale, thus creating a "fundamental shift of mind, in which individuals come to see themselves as capable of creating the world they truly want rather than merely reacting to circumstances beyond their control" (Kiefer & Senge, 1984, p. 68).

Empowerment is likely to happen in organizational environments where people recognize that things can always be better than they are now. These organizations expect to learn and seek new solutions. Empowering organizations seek to eliminate fear or humiliation and operate on trust and inclusivity. If you do not feel empowered in a particular group, you might assess the dynamics in the organization to see if they are encouraging or controlling. There may be an in-group and an out-group, and those in the out-group are excluded from access to information and opportunities to shape decisions (Kohn, 1992). If the organizational dynamics are basically supportive, however, perhaps you need to enhance your self-empowerment by building competencies, networks, or attributes to let you make a meaningful contribution.

Empowerment and delegation are not the same thing. A leader cannot give tasks to participants to do, no matter how important those assignments may be, and assume that participants will subsequently feel empowered. Indeed, if the leader retains a great deal of power or control when delegating, participants may feel manipulated, unprepared, resentful, or victimized. Conversely, if a positional leader has clearly acted congruently in sharing authority and responsibility with the group and has its trust, then sharing tasks can be empowering and can enhance community. Empowerment is achieved by enabling the involvement of group members.

Knowing-Being-Doing

Being self-empowered and supporting conditions that empower others requires an understanding of the basic concepts of power and influence. Being self-empowered requires self-knowledge and self-esteem. Empowering others requires a commitment that each individual has something to offer. Encouraging others to become empowered means knowing how to share information, bringing people into the group process, and promoting individual and team learning.

Relational Leadership Is Purposeful

Being purposeful means having a commitment to a goal or activity. It is also the ability to collaborate and to find common ground with others to establish a common purpose or a vision for a group. It is the ability to work toward the public good. Creating a common purpose can mean working hard toward resolving differences among participants, finding a common direction, and building a shared vision. Even if a participant does not have a vision, that person knows enough to ask others, "Remind me what we are working toward. What do we all hope will happen?" Trusting the process, several in the group will chime in with their ideas, and someone will have the talent to express those words in terms of the vision and common purpose that will bring nods of agreement from nearly every person present. It is important that all group members be able to articulate that purpose and use it as a driving force. That is an essential element in relational leadership.

The conventional paradigm of leadership often asserts that the positional leader must have a clear vision. Research, however, has shown two primary types of vision activity: *personalized vision* and *socialized vision* (Howell, 1988). Personalized vision refers to a person, usually the person with legitimate authority, announcing a dream or plan and imposing it on others. Participants seem to have little choice and must adopt this vision, which results in varying degrees of personal ownership or commitment. Some business literature would have us think that true transformational leadership would emulate Lee Iacocca, who, with singular personalized vision, transformed a whole enterprise—the Chrysler Corporation. Even if this is handled well by the person with legitimate power to do so, it does not ensure commitment. If that person has high referent power as well, then members of the group might be more willing to adopt that vision as their own.

"It is no longer what we do, but how we do it,
who we affect, and letting both mind and heart
guide the way . . . every leader is a follower of a higher
purpose."—John I. May is an economics and art major
at St. John's University in Collegeville, Minnesota.
He is active in a volunteer organization and is a
teaching assistant for economics classes.

Socialized vision is building a vision from among group members, recognizing that people support what they help create. Sharing vision does not mean that each person must create and possess a vision but that each person must be involved in the process of building a vision with others. Think about your personality preferences. Do you think creatively and see possibilities in everything, or are you shaking your head right now thinking "No way!" Do you have ideas about your future and a vision of how things might be? Such a vision is a picture of "a realistic, credible, attractive future" for yourself or your organization (Nanus, 1992, p. 8). After hearing a presentation on empowering leadership and the importance of shared vision, one of our colleagues approached the presenter. She said, "I just am not creative or cannot articulate a vision. I am practical and realistic. I feel capable but am more of a maintainer than a builder. I can keep things going more than I am able to think them up in the first place." The first piece of advice that organization consultant Burt Nanus (1992) shares with those trying to avoid failures in organizational vision is, "Don't do it alone" (p. 167).

Being purposeful with a group vision helps you set priorities and make decisions congruent with that dream. "Vision animates, inspirits, and transforms purpose into action" (Bennis & Goldsmith, 1994, p. 101). This action component to vision is described well by the engraving in an eighteenth-century church in Sussex, England:

> A vision without a task is but a dream,
> a task without a vision is drudgery,
> a vision and a task
> is the hope of the world.

> (From *Transcultural Leadership*, p. 106, by G. F. Simons, C. Vásquez and P. R. Harris. Copyright © 1993 by Gulf Publishing Co., Houston, Texas. Used with permission. All rights reserved.)

Your individual, purposeful commitment to the shared vision of a terrific group project means you will make sure to do your part, share resources, and support your teammates because you expect the same of them. Vision guides action. "It's not what a vision is, it's what a vision does" (Kazuo Inamori, as cited in Senge, 1990, p. 207). A vision of a homecoming weekend reaching the broadest possible group of alumni guides all the committee's choices about that event.

A vision inspires energy and purpose. General Norman Schwarzkopf observed, "I have found that in order to be a leader, you are almost serving a cause" (Wren, 1994, p. 4). Purposeful participants have emotionally identified with a purpose and a dream. "There is no more powerful engine driving an organization toward excellence and long-range success than an attractive, worthwhile, and achievable vision of the future, widely shared" (Nanus, 1992, p. 3).

Working for Change

One common purpose that pulls people together is working toward change. Rost (1991) proposes that leadership is happening when the group *intends* to accomplish change, not just when they do accomplish change. Having the intention of improving a situation, accomplishing a task, or implementing a common purpose is part of the change process. Change may not happen for many reasons, but the core fact that the group intended to make a difference is central. John Parr (1994), president of the National Civic League, writes, "Positive change can occur when people with different perspectives are organized into groups in which everyone is regarded as a peer. There must be a high level of involvement, a clear purpose, adequate resources, and the power to decide and implement" (p. xiii).

Some situations are profoundly hard to change. It is hard to move away from the status quo—the way things are. Change theory proposes that change often begins when something unfreezes a situation. The cycle is often presented as unfreezing → changing → refreezing. This "unfreezing" may be caused by a trigger event such as a carjacking from a remote campus parking lot, a student protest, or small attendance at a group's expensive activity. People pay attention to the problem with a focus they did not have prior to the incident. Unfreezing may also occur when external policies change—when a new law is enacted, for example. Unfreezing makes it possible to address an issue or policy that has not commanded the attention of those who need to address it. The change process is then engaged, and the issue is addressed. Even after a change is implemented, it would be an error in these times even to consider any issue "refrozen." Instead, it is best to consider the outcome to be "slush," so that no solution is seen as final but permeable and open to be readdressed easily. It may be best to consider solutions as automatically open for review, regularly evaluated, and flexible. The classic change model (Lewin, 1958) describing the change process as moving from the present state through a transition state to a desired state still works, but we encourage a caution that the desired state should now be viewed as less rigid or resistant to further change.

Change can be thought of as moving some situation away from the status quo to a different place. To understand why that movement is hard, examine the driving forces pushing for change and the resisting forces keeping change from happening to preserve the status quo. Clearly, not all change is appropriate or supportable. When it is, the driving forces working toward change should be enhanced and the restraining forces minimized. This "force-field analysis" is a useful method for identifying aspects of the situation that could enhance change (Lippitt, 1969, p. 157).

We are constantly faced with the dynamic tension of how things are and how we think they ought to be. This "is-ought" dichotomy asks us to face reality but work toward true transformative change, real change—to move toward the more hopeful vision. This "creative tension" brings energy to the change effort (Senge, 1990, p. 150). Connecting personal hopes and commitments to a group vision is a creative process. This process can be time consuming. As we describe more fully in Chapter Seven, when a group is newly formed, building a group vision can be energetic and hopeful if the group quickly comes to agreement and commitment, or it can be anxious and cautious if the group shows little agreement. When joining an ongoing group in which a vision has already been established, new participants have to determine whether they can connect to that vision or feel they can help shape the continued evolution of the group's vision over time.

The focus of each change may take different change agents—people who are able to facilitate the change happening. Consider the following categories of change agents:

- Those who influence personal change: parents for their families, counselors for the troubled, individuals for friends in need

- Those who influence organizational change: executives, managers, and union leaders for work settings; administrators and teachers for educational systems; clergy for religious institutions; administrators, doctors, and nurses for health-care systems; students for the campus culture; consultants for their clients

- Those who influence large-scale social change: politicians for the general public; civil servants for government; political action groups for special interests; researchers for the scientific community; opinion leaders for the media (Conner, 1993, p. 9)

As a shareholder or a stage holder in numerous arenas, purposeful participants can be change agents that do help accomplish shared goals.

Knowing-Being-Doing

Being purposeful requires having an attitude of hope, an ability to make a commitment; it builds on a sense of personal and group empowerment. Robert F. Kennedy saw the empowerment and hope that come from having common purpose and vision. He was fond of quoting playwright Bernard Shaw (who said that some people "see things . . . [as they are] and . . . say 'Why?' But I dream things that never were; and I say, 'Why not?'"). Sharing vision requires insight into one's own actions, the skills to listen to find common purpose, the ability to develop strategies needed to set purposeful goals, and the open mind to imagine possible outcomes.

Relational Leadership Is Ethical

A seven-year-old goes into the grocery store with his father. Upon arriving home, the father discovers that little Johnny has a pocketful of candy that was not a part of the purchase. Horrified at Johnny's stealing, the father demands that Johnny return the candy to the store, confess to the store manager, apologize for his behavior, and promise never to steal from any store again. For some of us, an incident like this was our first real lesson in what is good and bad, what is virtuous and immoral. Early in our lives, in lessons such as this one, we were taught to value honesty over dishonesty, kindness over cruelty, and doing the right thing over breaking the law.

Ethical and Moral Leadership

The Relational Leadership Model emphasizes ethical and moral leadership, meaning leadership that is driven by values and standards and leadership that is good—moral—in nature. The language we use to examine ethical, moral leadership is of utmost importance. Some have a tendency to use the terms *ethics* and *morals* interchangeably (Henderson, 1992; Walton, 1988). Others differentiate between them, yet draw a strong relationship between ethics and morals (Shea, 1988). Shaw and Barry (1989) define ethics as "the social rules that govern and limit our conduct, especially the ultimate rules concerning right and wrong" (pp. 2–3).

The derivative of *ethics* is *ethos*, from the Greek words "character" and "sentiment of the community" (Toffler, 1986, p. 10). Other definitions of ethics include "the principles of conduct governing an individual or a profession" and "standards of behavior" (Shea, 1988, p. 17). Being ethical means "conforming to the standards of a given profession or group. Any group can set its own ethical standards and then live by them or not" (Toffler, 1986, p. 10). Ethical standards, whether they are established by an individual or an organization, help guide a person's decisions and actions. For the purposes of this model, ethics will be defined as "rules or standards that govern behaviors" (Toffler, 1986, p. 10).

Stephen Covey, author of the best-selling book *The Seven Habits of Highly Effective People* (1990), uses the metaphor of "leadership by compass" to illustrate principle-centered leadership (p. 19). Principles, like values, ethics, standards, and morals, "provide 'true north' direction to our lives when navigating the 'streams' of our environments" (p. 19).

Professions often establish codes of ethics or standards. Lawyers must adhere to the American Bar Association's code of ethics for attorneys, and the American Medical Association promotes a code of ethics for physicians. Every McDonald's restaurant prominently displays a code of standards that pledges excellence in its food and service. Upon closer examination, these organizations are promoting standards by which they expect professionals and employees to live.

Moral means "relating to principles of right and wrong" (Toffler, 1986, p. 10) or "arising from one's conscience or a sense of good and evil; pertaining to the discernment of good and evil; instructive of what is good or evil (bad)" (Shea, 1988, p. 17). Morals are commonly thought to be influenced by religion or personal beliefs. Moral leadership is concerned with "good" leadership, that is, leadership with good means and good ends.

Our philosophy of leadership is values-driven. We repeat: leadership is *a relational process of people together attempting to accomplish change or make a difference to benefit the common good*. Such leaders and followers act out of a sense of shared values—the desire to cause real change and a commitment to mutual purposes. The actions of leaders and participants emanate from a set of values, which we hope are congruent and shared. Values are "freely chosen personal beliefs" (Lewis, 1990, p. 9) or the "guiding principles in our lives with respect to the personal and social ends we desire" (Kouzes & Posner, 1993, p. 60). Simply stated, values are our personal beliefs.

Although there is much disagreement in the leadership literature over definitions and theory, and about whether leadership is values-neutral or values-driven, it is safe to say that most people expect leaders to do the right thing. According to a 1988 Gallup poll of twelve hundred workers and managers, 89 percent of the respondents "believed it was important for leaders to be upright, honest, and ethical in their dealings" (Hughes, Ginnett, & Curphy, 1993, p. 170). Unfortunately, only 41 percent of those surveyed believed that their supervisor exhibited these qualities (Hughes, Ginnett, & Curphy, 1993). When fifteen hundred executives from twenty countries were asked what the requirements were for an ideal chief corporate officer, personal ethics rose to the top of the list (Kidder, 1993 [Roper poll]). A Gallup poll showed an increase from 47 percent in 1981 to 60 percent in 1989 in the number of people who believed that a strict moral code is necessary (Kidder, 1993).

As leaders and citizens, our challenge today is to close the gap between our expectations of ethical leadership and the reality of frequent breaches of ethical conduct by our leaders. We need bold, courageous leadership—leadership that is by word and deed ethical and moral. It is encouraging that a growing number of people express their abhorrence of the breaches of ethical conduct by national and local leaders and that a vast majority of the populace believe that ethics play a critical role in leadership.

John Gardner (1990) thoughtfully makes the connection between shared values and a moral commitment to do the right thing. He reflects:

In any functioning society everything—leadership and everything else—takes place within a set of shared beliefs concerning the standards of acceptable behavior that must govern individual members. One of the tasks of leadership—at all levels—is to revitalize those shared beliefs and values, and to draw on them as sources of motivation for the exertions required of the group. Leaders can help to keep the values fresh. They can combat the hypocrisy that proclaims values at the same time that it violates them. They can help us understand our history and our present dilemmas. They have a role in creating the state of mind that is the society. Leaders must conceive and articulate goals in ways that lift people out of their petty preoccupations and unite them toward higher ends. (p. 191)

Gardner implies that leadership "toward higher ends" is ethical in nature and includes positive, constructive ends rather than results or outcomes that are destructive, harmful, or immoral.

To underscore the importance of the relationship between leadership and ethics, we join with those scholars who propose that ethics is the central core of leadership. Without a commitment to doing the right thing or a sound code of ethical standards, leadership cannot emerge. Although some argue that the phrase "ethical leadership" is redundant because leadership cannot be experienced without an element of ethics, we feel that leadership that lacks ethical behavior and actions is anything but leadership. Indeed, you may be thinking right now that Hitler was a leader but just did not lead in a worthy cause. We agree with other scholars, however, that Hitler's actions were not leadership. They were dictatorship (Burns, 1978).

Burns (1978) elevates the importance of values and ethics in the leadership process through his theory of transforming leadership. He notes that "the ultimate test of moral leadership is its capacity to transcend the claims of multiplicity of everyday wants and needs and expectations, to respond to the higher levels of moral development, and to relate leadership behavior—its roles, choices, style, commitments—to a set of reasoned, relatively explicit, conscious values" (p. 46). Aligned with Burns's bold thinking to cast leadership in a moral foundation is the recent shift in societal views from leadership as values-neutral to leadership as values-driven (Beck & Murphy, 1994; Bok, 1982, 1990; Kouzes & Posner, 1987; Piper, Gentile, & Parks, 1993). Moral or ethical leadership is driven by knowing what is virtuous and what is good.

Leading by Example

As an exercise, a leader and a participant must ponder soul-searching questions such as, What do I stand for? How far am I willing to go to advance the common good or to do the right thing? Based on their research on leaders, Kouzes and Posner (1987) propose five practices of exemplary leadership. One of these practices is "Modeling the Way" or practicing what one preaches. Leaders "show others by their own example that they live by the values that they profess" (p. 187). What one stands for "provides a prism through which all behavior is ultimately viewed" (p. 192).

Leading by example is a powerful way to influence the values and ethics of an organization. This means aligning your own values with the worthy values of the organization. Exemplary leadership includes a congruency between values and actions. The cliché attributed to Ralph Waldo Emerson—What you do speaks so loudly that I cannot hear what you say—implies an even greater emphasis on the importance of values being congruent with actions. Jimmy Carter is the first contemporary president said to have gone on to do better things after the presidency. Indeed, his work in diplomacy and for such community services as Habitat for Humanity attests to his congruence. It is one thing to profess values and quite another to act on them.

Terry (1993) provides a cautionary note that action without authenticity erodes what can be considered ethical or moral leadership. Terry defines authenticity as "genuineness and a refusal to engage in self deception" (p. 128). Being true to oneself as a leader is a prerequisite for ethical and moral leadership.

The task of leading by example is not an easy one. Most, if not all, leaders begin with the goal of wanting to do the right thing. Some leaders get derailed by peer pressure or the temptation to trade leading for the common good with leading for personal gain or the uncommon good. What sustains ethical and moral leadership is a stubborn commitment to high standards, which include honesty and trustworthiness, authenticity, organizational values, and doing the right thing. It takes courage and chutzpah to stand among your peers and advocate a decision that is right yet unpopular. Imagine the tremendous courage of a fraternity chapter member or ROTC junior officer who says, "No, I do not think we can make our pledges drink until they pass out and then drop them off naked in the woods. It is not only dangerous but it is not how I want to bring them into our brotherhood. I won't be a part of it, and I hope you will not either. I will help plan activities that are fun and more worthwhile, but we cannot do this."

"To handle ethical dilemmas, the single most important quality to remember is to be honest with yourself and others. Tell the parties involved honestly and openly how you feel about the particular issue. Help them understand delicately your position, but stand strong in the dilemma. One other important aspect is listening and not jumping to conclusions."— Andrea Jean Grate, from Alfred University, is director of student orientation and is planning a career in student affairs.

Although it appears that we are stating the obvious by stressing the importance of leading by example and with integrity, regrettably there are numerous accounts of local and national leaders who have been caught embezzling, putting humans at risk for the sake of profit, and hiding the truth. Richard M. Nixon began his presidency with good intentions and then succumbed to political corruption. Leading with integrity is not a neat and tidy process, yet it probably is the driving force that allows leaders to continue in their capacities. We will return to the topic of ethical leadership in Chapter Nine with a closer examination of ethical decision making, ethical theories, and creating and sustaining ethical environments in groups and organizations.

Knowing-Being-Doing

Being ethical means being grounded in beliefs, values, and principles. It means being worthy of trust and full of character. Being ethical means confronting unethical practices and being congruent with one's own principles. Being ethical lets you go to bed at night and know you did the right thing, even if it did not accomplish your final goal—but you did not sacrifice your integrity.

Relational Leadership Is Process-Oriented

Process refers to how the group goes about being a group, remaining a group, and accomplishing a group's purposes. It refers to the recruitment and involvement of members, how the group makes decisions, and how the group handles the tasks related to its mission and vision. Every group has a process, and every process can be described. Processes must be intentional and not incidental.

When asked how her view of the universe as orderly in its chaos has influenced her work with organizations, Wheatley (1992) observes "the time I formerly spent on detailed planning and analysis I now use to look at the structures that might facilitate relationships, I have come to expect that something useful occurs if I link up people, units or tasks, even though I cannot determine precise outcomes" (p. 43–44). These are the processes of connecting people with each other and connecting people with ideas and visions. When they design and implement ethical, inclusive, empowering processes, groups can trust the processes to take them through difficult times, resolve ambiguous tasks, and be assured that together they will be better than they might be individually.

Too often, processes devalue the people involved by being highly controlled, valuing winning at all costs, excluding or shutting out those who have an interest in change, or expecting everyone to think and act alike. Attending to the process means being thoughtful and conscious of how the group is going about its business so participants might say, "Wait a minute. If we do it this way, we'll be ignoring the needs of a big group of students and that is not our intent."

Several key processes are essential to relational leadership. These processes include collaboration, reflection, feedback, civil confrontation, community building, and a level of profound understanding called meaning making. We will discuss several of these here and in subsequent chapters. Being process-oriented means that participants and the group as a whole are conscious of their process. They are reflective, challenging, collaborative, and caring. Being process-oriented means being aware of the dynamics among people in groups. Many groups jump right into the task or goal and lose a focus on the process. When participants focus on the process of group life or community life, they are forced to ask, Why do we do things this way? How could we be more effective? Participants ensure that they keep working and learning together.

Cooperation and Collaboration

Competition seems embedded in many of our American structures. The adversarial legal system, sports teams, the game of bridge, and the competitive free market economy all illustrate the way competition permeates our shared life. It is hard to imagine a different paradigm. Even while avoiding trying to beat others and not needing to always be number one, many people feel a strong need to compete with themselves. Perhaps they need to better that last exam grade or beat the last Tetris score.

In the early 1980s, researchers at the University of Minnesota reviewed 122 studies conducted over a fifty-year period on the role of competitive, cooperative, or individual goal orientations in achievement. Researchers concluded that "cooperation is superior to competition in promoting achievement and productivity" (Johnson, Maruyama, Johnson, Nelson, & Skon, 1981, p. 56). They further distinguished the strong benefits of cooperation (not competition) in the internal functioning of the group from the incentives when competing with other external groups (Johnson et al., 1981). Working cooperatively with other participants is a desirable process.

Studies consistently show that members of various kinds of groups prefer positional leaders and colleagues who establish cooperative or collaborative relationships with them instead of competitive relationships (Kanter, 1989; Spence, 1983; Tjosvold & Tjosvold, 1991). Even a group member who enjoys competition in athletics is not likely to enjoy working in a setting such as a sports team, committee, study group, or job site where others are competitive and try to beat each other or use competitive practices like withholding information or degrading others' contributions. Indeed, "the simplest way to understand why competition generally does not promote excellence is to realize that *trying to do well and trying to beat others are two different things*" (Kohn, 1992, p. 55). A person's best work is done under conditions of support and cooperation, not under fear, anxiety, or coercion.

The concepts of cooperation and collaboration are different. "Collaboration is more than simply sharing knowledge and information (communication) and more than a relationship that helps each party achieve its own goals (cooperation and coordination). The purpose of collaboration is to create a shared vision and joint strategies to address concerns that go beyond the purview of any particular party" (Chrislip & Larson, 1994, p. 5). Wood and Gray (1991) assert that "collaboration occurs when a group of autonomous stakeholders of a problem engage in an interactive process, using shared rules, norms, and structures, to act or decide on issues related to that domain" (p. 146). In November 1994, IBM and Apple announced their first joint project to create a power chip that will be the basis of computer development for both companies. This collaboration serves both companies better than their previous competitive models. Both cooperation and collaboration are helpful processes: cooperation helps the other person or group achieve their own goals, whereas collaboration joins with another person or group in setting and accomplishing mutual, shared goals. The "collaborative premise" is a belief that "if you bring the appropriate people together in constructive ways with good information, they will create authentic visions and strategies for addressing the shared concerns of the organization or community" (Chrislip & Larson, 1994, p. 14). It would be cooperation for the Habitat for Humanity group to send their membership recruitment flyer out with the Food Cooperative flyer to save postage. It would be collaboration for those two groups and several others with a common environmental purpose to design a new flyer to attract new members to these shared causes.

For the group to be effective, all members must be prepared to do their part. Chapter Two presented how music provides a good metaphor for this kind of teamwork. Musicians must be individually skilled and committed and yet know that they are part of a collective—a team. Further, imagine a performance of jazz music with improvisational dance. Both dancers and musicians find wonderful rhythms and sounds, simultaneously interpreted, shaping each other's work. The collaboration, respect, and commitment to their common purposes as dancers and musicians are obvious. Yet, those artists did not just walk into a studio and create movement. The dancers knew their bodies, and the musicians knew their instruments. They knew how and why and when to react. Their self-awareness of their own strengths, limits, talents, and abilities created the collaboration in their joint effort. In a parallel manner, think of a terrific class project in which individuals volunteer their knowledge and skills ("I can set up that computer program" or "I can call those businesses for donations"), and the division of labor starts to shape a strong project. Knowing yourself well and seeking to know the members of the group provide a group atmosphere conducive to collaboration.

Meaning Making

Leadership requires a process of truly understanding (that is, making meaning) throughout the shared experience of the group. Meaning has both cognitive (ideas and thoughts) and emotional (feelings) components, which "allows a person to know (in the sense of understand) some world version (a representation of the way things are and the way they ought to be) and that places the person in relation to this world view" (Drath & Palus, 1994, p. 4). Part of this meaning making involves the recognition that in our rapidly changing world, we are continually challenged to see that data become information, information becomes translated into knowledge, knowledge becomes wisdom, and wisdom becomes meaningful thought and action. Imagine this flow as

DATA → INFORMATION → KNOWLEDGE → WISDOM → THOUGHT AND ACTION

Meaning making is "the process of arranging our understanding of experience so that we can know what has happened and what is happening, and so that we can predict what will happen; it is constructing knowledge of ourselves and the world" (Drath & Palus, 1994, p. 2). Drath and Palus (1994) make it clear that two understandings of the word *meaning* guide our thinking about meaning and leadership. One use is when symbols, like words, stand for something. This process of naming and interpreting helps clarify meaning and is essential for the perspectives needed in reframing and seeing multiple realities. For example, one person might call a particular action lawlessness, and another might call it civil disobedience. What one person might call destructive partying, another might see as group bonding and celebration. Coming to agreement on the interpretations of symbolic words and events helps a group to make meaning. Senge (1990) refers to these as mental models.

The second use of the word *meaning* involves "people's values and relationships and commitments" (Drath & Palus, 1994, p. 7). People want to matter and to lead lives of meaning. When something is of value, one can make a commitment, find personal purpose, and risk personal involvement—it matters, it has meaning. In contrast, if something is meaningless or of no value, then it does not engage emotion and build commitment. However, we should be careful not to judge too quickly. Sometimes, important matters may seem to have no value. For example, a group of students expressing concern about getting to their cars in remote parking lots after late-night classes deserves a careful hearing. Those listening may be student government officers who live in nearby residence halls or

campus administrators who have parking spaces near their buildings. The relational empathy skill of trying to see things from
another's perspective will validate that meaning. (Refer to Chapter
Five for more on relational empathy.)

Understanding how we make meaning helps a group frame and
reframe the issues and problems they are seeking to resolve. The
framing process involves naming the problem and identifying the
nature of interventions or solutions that might be helpful. If a problem is framed as "The administration won't provide money for additional safety lighting," it leads to a set of discussions and strategies
focused on changing the administration. Reframing means finding
a new interpretation of the problem that might create a new view
that helps a group be more productive (Bryson & Crosby, 1992).
Reframing this same problem might bring a new awareness of coalitions, shareholders, and stakeholders if it were readdressed as "How
can we bring the talent of our campus to address the problem of a
dramatic rise in crimes against women?"

Reflection

Vaill (1989) proposes that the rapid pace of change and the need to
make meaning from ambiguous material requires individuals and
groups to practice reflection. Reflection is the process of pausing,
stepping back from the action, and asking, What is happening?
Why is this happening? What does this mean? What does this
mean for me? What can I learn from this? Lao Tzu (Heider, 1985)
encourages time for reflection:

> Endless drama in a group clouds consciousness. Too much
> noise overwhelms the senses. Continual input obscures gen-
> uine insight. Do not substitute sensationalism for learning.
> Allow regular time for silent reflection. Turn inward and
> digest what has happened. Let the senses rest and grow still.
> Teach people to let go of their superficial mental chatter and
> obsessions. Teach people to pay attention to the whole body's

reaction to a situation. When group members have time to reflect, they can see more clearly what is essential in themselves and others. (p. 23)

Reflection can be accomplished when a group intentionally discusses its process. If groups discuss their process at all, they usually reflect only on their failures. They try to find out what went wrong and how to avoid those errors again. To be true learning organizations, groups also need to reflect on their successes and bring to every participant's awareness a common understanding of answers to such questions as, Why did this go so well? What did we do together that made this happen? How can we make sure to work this well together again? Horwood (1989) observes that "Reflection is hard mental work. The word itself means 'bending back'. . . . The mental work of reflection includes deliberation. . . . rumination . . . pondering . . . and musing" (p. 5). Reflection is a key process in becoming a learning community.

In a study of successful leaders, Bennis (1989) observed that these effective leaders encouraged "reflective backtalk" (p. 194). They knew the importance of truth telling and encouraged their colleagues to reflect honestly what they think they saw or heard. "Reflection is vital—at every level, in every organization— . . . all [leaders] should practice the new three Rs: retreat, renewal, and return" (Bennis, 1989, p. 186). One form of group reflection is when the group processes (discusses) a shared experience. As a difficult meeting winds down, any participant (or perhaps the group's adviser) might say, "Let's take time now at the end of this meeting to process what we liked about how we handled the big decision tonight and what we think we should do differently next time." Reflection is also useful for keeping a group on track. A group might intentionally review its goals and mission in the middle of the year and discuss how their activities are supporting that mission or whether they should be redirected. Reflection is an essential component of a process to keep individuals and the whole group focused and intentional.

Knowing-Being-Doing

Being process-oriented means valuing process and understanding how the process influences the group's climate and outcomes. It means having a systems perspective that considers more than just one's own interests in the process. Participants must know something about how groups function (Chapter Six) and about how a sense of community is built (Chapter Eight). Being process-oriented in relational leadership means developing and promoting in others the skills of collaboration, reflection, meaning making, and civil confrontation.

What Would This Look Like?

You will acquire many leadership skills over time. It is easy to confuse some management tools like running meetings or planning agendas with real leadership. Using the principles of relational leadership, you can reframe typical skills like agenda planning so that they are more effective. The goals of the agenda for your group meeting will not be just to get through the topics to be presented or decided in the quickest time but will involve the most people, empower voices that might have been excluded before, make sure no one is railroaded and that fair decisions are made, involve others in building an agenda, and use collaborative practices.

Remember the times you have been to a meeting and the leader made all the announcements. A small group of two or three in-group members seemed to run the whole show, and you never said a word. We have all had that experience. You felt marginalized and might have wondered why you even bothered to attend. Think of a meeting where people disagreed hotly and then someone quickly moved to vote on an issue. A vote was taken with the resulting majority winning and a dissatisfied minority losing or feeling railroaded.

Imagine the differences in a meeting when the positional leader or convener says, "It is our custom to make sure everyone is involved and heard before we try to resolve issues. The executive committee has asked three of you to present the key issues on the first agenda item; we will then break into small groups for fifteen minutes to see what questions and issues emerge before we proceed and see what we want to do at that point. In your discussion, try to identify the principles that will be important for us to consider in the decision we eventually make." Even if you do not agree with this approach, you would feel more comfortable suggesting a different model because the tone of the meeting is one of involvement and participation.

Chapter Summary

Conditions in our rapidly changing world require that each of us become effective members of our groups and communities in order to work with others toward needed change and for common purpose. The way we relate to each other matters and is symbolic of our social responsibility. Taking the time needed to build a sense of community in a group acknowledges that relationships are central to effective leadership. Relational leadership is inclusive, empowering, ethical, process-oriented, and purposeful. Attention to those practices builds a strong organization with committed participants who know they matter.

What's Next?

After understanding the various ways leadership has been viewed and the current need for new models of leadership that value relational approaches, it is essential to understand people as participants in those relationships. Perhaps the most important person to understand is you. The next chapter encourages you to explore aspects about yourself that are important in leadership; following that is a chapter exploring aspects of others and how they may be different from yours.

Chapter Activities

1. Think of a leader you would consider to be a role model, someone who practices what he or she preaches and lives by high standards. What is it about the role model you identified that qualifies that person as an exemplary leader? What values does he or she profess, and what practices does he or she consistently live by? Think of local, national, or historical exemplars.

2. What do you stand for? As a leader, what legacy do you want to leave in your organization or community?

3. Describe your leadership compass. What principles or ethics guide your personal life and your leadership?

4. As you review the five elements of this relational leadership model, which are most comfortable for you? Which involve knowledge, skills, or attitudes that you have not yet learned or developed?

5. In their simplicity, models often omit concepts that could have been included. What concepts would you add to any of the five elements of this model, or what new elements do you think should be included?

6. Think of a typical leadership group or situation in a career related to your major (for example, teaching a class, running a staff meeting, working with a project team). How would this model be received in that setting? How would it most help you be effective in that setting?

Additional Readings

Bryson, J. M., & Crosby, B. C. (1992). *Leadership for the common good*. San Francisco: Jossey-Bass.

Chrislip, D. D., & Larson, C. E. (1994). *Collaborative leadership: How citizens and civic leaders can make a difference*. San Francisco: Jossey-Bass.

Drath, W. H., & Palus, C. J. (1994). *Making common sense: Leadership as meaning-making in a community of practice*. Greensboro, NC: Center for Creative Leadership.

Lappé, F. M., & Du Bois, P. M. (1994). *The quickening of America: Rebuilding our nation, remaking our lives*. San Francisco: Jossey-Bass.

A social change model of leadership development: Guidebook version III. (1996). Los Angeles: University of California Los Angeles Higher Education Research Institute.

PART TWO

Exploring Your Potential for Leadership

The Relational Leadership Model emphasizes the importance of relationships among participants in the process of purposeful change. Developing and maintaining healthy and honest relationships starts with a knowledge of self and an openness to appreciate and to respect others.

This section contains two chapters to enrich your self-awareness. These chapters help you explore yourself in relation to others as foundational components of developing a personal leadership philosophy. Lao Tzu (Heider, 1985) noted:

> The wise leader's ability does not rest on techniques or gimmicks or set exercises. The method of awareness-of-process applies to all people and all situations.
>
> The leader's personal state of consciousness creates a climate of openness. Center and ground give the leader stability, flexibility, and endurance.
>
> Because the leader sees clearly, the leader can shed light on others. (p. 53)

In the relational leadership model presented in the previous chapter, we encouraged you to be *inclusive, empowering, purposeful, ethical,* and *process-oriented.* Think again about what you need to know, or be, or do to participate effectively in relational leadership.

You might return to Exhibit 3.1 to assess yourself and these concepts again.

Ask yourself some thoughtful questions to explore your self-awareness, awareness of others, leadership, and this model:

Inclusive: How comfortable and effective are you including others? Do you understand your own motivations when you agree or disagree with others? When you interact with people different from you, are there differences you find easy to accommodate or difficult to understand?

Empowering: Do you know how to build on your own strengths and on the strengths of others? Do you find it easy or difficult to share authority and responsibility?

Purposeful: Do you have clear goals and an awareness of commitments that are important to you? Do you have to get your own way, or are you able to find common purpose with others? Do you know how change occurs?

Ethical: Do you find it easy to act with integrity and authenticity? Can you identify the values and principles that guide your actions? Are you trusting or distrustful of others?

Process-Oriented: Do you know what approaches you prefer for facilitating change and accomplishing goals? Do you prefer collaboration or competition? How effective are you at civil discussions, even when you strongly disagree with someone?

The most productive thing you could do to become more effective as a leader and as an active participant is to learn to see yourself clearly. This section will help you explore what you value, how you are developing character, how you learn best, and how aspects of yourself (like your gender, culture, and communication pattern) have been shaped. In learning to see these aspects of yourself, we hope you can be more sensitive to others.

4

Understanding Yourself

Imagine the times you have been sitting in class or a meeting and had thoughts like these:

He doesn't seem to have a clue that he comes across as so authoritarian; he doesn't seem to trust any of us to be competent, let alone committed!

She avoids taking on any tasks that would require her to stand up in front of the group and speak; her esteem seems so low.

She is so good at helping us all be part of the discussion; she is really terrific at integrating so many diverse views. I wish I could do that.

He is so creative; he can always think of five or six options that don't even come to my mind!

Why in the world do I always pick away at all the details of an idea and end up sounding so negative?

I am so proud that I didn't hesitate a minute to disagree when she made such a hurtful comment.

My sense of humor really helped the group get through the tense moment tonight and keep things in perspective.

Seeing your own strengths and weaknesses and those of others so clearly requires focused reflection. Being aware of how you prefer to think, to relate, to learn, and to find personal meaning is an important self-awareness skill. Being able to articulate what you believe and what you value helps you understand your own motivations and behaviors. Knowing your strengths and weaknesses helps you grow and relate to others with credibility.

Because leadership happens in the context of interpersonal relationships, self-understanding is essential to authenticity in those relationships. Perhaps the most basic life skill that translates to leadership effectiveness is honest, authentic self-awareness and the openness to grow, learn, and change.

Chapter Overview

This chapter challenges you to think of the things about yourself that shape your personal identity and fuel your motivations. It explores the role of self-awareness in leadership, including aspects of self-concept and self-esteem. It also explores how you form your values and the role of values in developing character. Your personality preferences for how you approach decisions and how you learn are also addressed. Along with studying leadership, you must study you.

Development of Self for Leadership

The *Star Wars* trilogy were movies with deeper meaning behind their adventuresome entertainment. In *The Return of the Jedi*, young Luke Skywalker seeks to learn the secrets of the famous Jedi Master, Yoda. Luke is initially incredulous that this small, green creature is The Master and further disappointed not to be given or taught Yoda's secrets. Yoda instead takes Luke on a journey into himself, teaching him to focus and trust his own internal power to literally move mountains. This inward journey provides the self-awareness of identifying abilities, strengths, and weaknesses. The journey develops a sense of trust in yourself to be congruent and to truly know the basis of your effectiveness.

The common observation of many acknowledged leaders is that no one can teach you about yourself except you (Bennis, 1989). Counselors, advisers, friends, or family can help with this process, but awareness ultimately requires you to study yourself. Bennis (1989, p. 56) observes four lessons from which to develop self-knowledge:

- You are your own best teacher.
- Accept responsibility. Blame no one.
- You can learn anything you want to learn.
- True understanding comes from reflection on your experience.

"Leadership means self-discovery, getting a better yield out of your attributes" (Haas & Tamarkin, 1992, p. 6). In your life so far, you have probably learned to set goals, motivate yourself to meet them, and feel personally responsible if you do not. It is hard for some people to translate the life skills of self-control and internal motivation into guides of action as members of a group. If you often sit in a meeting and think, "It's not my responsibility; I will just let the leaders do it. After all, it's their job," then you need to develop more self-leadership skills.

Your decision to be a person who can make a difference (evidenced by reading this book) is a statement about self-leadership. You know you cannot credit or blame external factors such as teachers, supervisors, parents, or positional leaders for your motivation. Sadly, there may be acts of discrimination or oppression that have held you back, but you are now looking ahead and asking, What can I do to matter and to make a difference in the things that are important to me?

Strengths and Weaknesses

Each person brings a different mix of strengths and weaknesses to any situation. The irony is that some of your strengths, if overemphasized, become your weaknesses, and things you consider weaknesses may actually be seen as strengths by others. You may be a strong critical thinker who can readily find flaws in logic. That can be a terrific strength in helping your group prepare and present its position on a topic, or it can be seen as negative and blocking if someone is presenting an idea to you and you just naturally begin to be critical instead of trying to connect and listen. The converse can be true as well: to be humble and quiet may mean your opinion is never heard and your voice is left out of decision making. But it can also mean you are a keen listener who is very tuned in to others' thoughts. Leadership self-awareness grows when you can identify your personal strengths and weaknesses in working with others toward change.

Clifton and Nelson (1992) suggest that you pay attention to the things you see others doing and to your inner mind saying, "Oh, I would love to try that." Sometimes it is hard to identify strengths. Clifton and Nelson recommend that you learn five characteristics of a strength and scan your life for them.

1. Listen to yourself when you have done something well, even if no one else noticed.

2. Identify the satisfaction you feel when you know something you did was terrific and gives you a feeling of well-being.

3. Know what things you find easy to learn quickly: putting together a model, talking to strangers, mastering a new Nintendo game, reading patiently to a small child.

4. Study your successes for clues of excellence, for "glimpses" (p. 50) of what can be excellent—for what things you do very well. Whether giving a speech or helping someone feel very special, by examining whatever your success has been, you will discover what you can do well.

5. Think about your patterns of excellence—when a song pours out, when you focus on every word of the lecture and understand its deep meaning, when you practice a skill (whether cooking, playing basketball, or public speaking), and you feel it improve each time you do it. Clues to your strengths are all

around you. Identifying and labeling them can affirm your confidence and esteem by acknowledging that you do bring reliable talents to situations and can contribute to the leadership of a cause.

All of us can learn to overcome our weaknesses. Some think that weaknesses "can be removed but they cannot be transformed into strengths. The goal, therefore, is to manage weaknesses so the strengths can be freed to develop and become so powerful they make the weaknesses irrelevant" (Clifton and Nelson, 1992, p. 73). A person can either manage weaknesses so that they do not repress other strengths or overcome them and turn them into strengths.

"The biggest way I handle my weaknesses is to recognize my weaknesses. I used to believe that I was the perfect leader. Once I realized that I have weaknesses, my leadership improved greatly. Since I recognize my weaknesses, I surround myself with people who can help me in these areas."—Bret Fox is pursuing a master's degree in electrical engineering at the University of Akron and is governor of the Ohio District of Circle K International.

By any account, Stephen J. Cannell is a successful writer, having written and produced such television shows as *The Rockford Files*, *Wiseguy*, and *Hunter*. He always seems to have a show on the air. He is imaginative, creative, and clever. He also has dyslexia. He will never be a quick reader or an accurate speller, but he manages those weaknesses and has found ways to prevent them from blocking his strengths (as told in Clifton & Nelson, 1992, p. 71). Helen Keller could neither see, hear, nor speak, but she learned to communicate remarkably well. Olympic athlete Jackie Joyner Kersey deals daily with asthma. Their weaknesses vary, but these gifted people have learned to manage weakness so that it does not hold back their strengths.

Some weaknesses, however, may be problematic because they cause you to function poorly. These need to be tackled directly. For example, you may not speak well in front of a group. You can, however, manage this weakness by learning ways to make a presentation that are more comfortable for you, like using overhead transparencies, handouts, or encouraging group interaction. The actor James Earl Jones had a debilitating childhood stutter, which he overcame so successfully that he became a remarkable orator. John F. Kennedy was at first a poor public speaker but through carefully crafting speeches and practicing with diligence, he became inspirational. One of our students observed that she thought herself to be a terrible speaker, but she enjoyed class discussions and had fun arguing her points. One of her classmates pointed out how related those skills are. What she perceived as a weakness was viewed differently by others. If it is very important to you, then you can learn to do anything better than you do it now.

Esteem and Confidence

John W. Gardner tells a story of sitting beside Martin Luther King Jr. at a seminar on education. The first presentation was a speech entitled, "First, Teach Them to Read." After observing this title, King whispered to Gardner, "First, teach them to believe in themselves" (Gardner, 1990, p. 10).

How you think and feel about yourself is the energy that fuels your motivation. Self-concept is how we objectively describe ourselves; usually, it is based on our roles and attributes. You might say, "I am a mother of a two-year-old and like to go with the flow, keeping all my options open" or "I am an older-than-typical student with above-average intelligence and high motivation" or "I am a creative person with musical abilities." Self-esteem is the subjective element of how you feel about yourself. For example, you might say, "I am a creative person with musical abilities but am unskilled socially and uncomfortable around those in authority. I feel proud of my musical and creative skills and feel disappointed in myself for not being more socially skilled." Self-awareness would lead to hav-ing an accurate self-concept. Honoring your strengths and address-ing your weaknesses are essential first steps toward higher self-esteem.

Esteem is enhanced if you can identify your strengths and weak-nesses and know that you are growing and progressing in the areas you want to improve. High self-esteem is a result of valuing your self-concept. Low self-esteem may mean you expect something bet-ter or different than you feel. You may have a 3.3 grade point aver-age as a biology major, have a group of supportive friends, and have just been elected vice president of your campus chapter of Amnesty International. You may feel proud and have high regard for those accomplishments. If, however, you are working for a 3.9 because you want to go to medical school, you might feel badly about your grades and have low esteem about your academic ability.

Self-confidence is the ability to know that you can rely on your strengths, competencies, and skills in the many contexts in which you find yourself. Some people consistently do well in whatever they do, but they are never sure they can do well and therefore have low self-confidence. Perhaps self-confident people have better memories and know that they have done well before and can do so again.

Accepting ourselves is perhaps one of the hardest life tasks. Realizing that you cannot change some things about yourself is a step toward higher self-esteem. For example, you will not become 6'2" if you are now 5'6"; you will not become another race, change your siblings, or get rid of your freckles. You can, however, learn new skills and add to your knowledge base.

If some aspects of yourself are negative influences on your self-esteem, you must differentiate between those you can actually do something about from those you just need to think about differ-ently, which can lead to a higher level of self-acceptance. Perceiv-ing things differently is called cognitive reframing—a different way of thinking. You may have felt bad when thinking of your person-ality as shy and quiet, but you might feel empowered to frame those same characteristics as thoughtful and reflective. Reflecting on her own youth, singer-actress Bette Midler said, "I didn't belong as a kid, and that always bothered me. If only I'd known that one day my differentness would be an asset, then my early life would have been much easier" (cited in *The Quotable Woman*, 1991, p. 39).

Understanding Yourself

What makes you the way you are? How much of your perception, values, temperament, personality, and motives come from the way you were raised, the influence of your surroundings, and your contextual environment? How much of the way you are is inborn or genetic?

Debates have raged for years over whether to attribute human behavior to nurture (socialization) or nature (heredity). Becoming aware of the influence of either nurture or nature in your own development is essential to understanding yourself. For example, you may be tall and may have learned that some people find you imposing; they assume you will be outgoing and aggressive, even though you are quiet and shy. Or you may be small but have learned that people react eventually to the quality of what you have to say. Some might even say, "You seem bigger than your height." You may have learned to be relational or thoughtful or funny or anxious.

Regardless of how you came to be the way you are, you can intentionally choose to develop desired traits or skills. You cannot change your height or some other genetic attribute, but you can address many of the things you have learned by bringing them into your awareness. Although you cannot always change the way others view you, because they bring their own biases and attributions, you can at least be authentic as you try to be the person you would like to be.

Discussing your self-awareness is a form of the psychological study of individuality. If you feel uncomfortable with the concept of individuality, it could be because describing human perception or behavior in categories or types makes you feel boxed in or stereotyped.

You may feel constrained or categorized. You may also feel uncomfortable because focusing on your own needs or on yourself is considered selfish or inappropriate in your family or culture. Instead, we hope you welcome the opportunity for personal insight by reviewing the ways scholars understand the ranges of human behavior. By knowing how others respond, you can assess how their response is like or unlike your own. For example, if you have had a death in your family or the loss of someone you love, you may find comfort in knowing that there are predictable stages in the grief process for many people and that your reactions are very normal (Kübler-Ross, 1970). Because you are unique, however, you may find your grief reaction to be more pronounced or less severe than Kübler-Ross's model suggests, based on such factors as how close you were to the person who died, the comfort you receive from your family, or your religious practices. Whatever the phenomena being presented in various theories about human behavior, you can then connect with what is most like you or least like you to better understand yourself and to see how others might be similar or different from you.

Factors That Shape Your Identity

Several central, salient characteristics have probably made you the person you are and the person you will become as you age. Consider how your ethnic, racial, or cultural background has made a difference and shaped the way you are. How do you believe or behave differently because you are a man or a woman? How has your sexual orientation influenced your attitudes and behaviors? How does your age influence your interests and views? Do you have specific abilities or disabilities that shape your perceptions or skills? How has your birth-order position in your family influenced your development? What significant roles do you have that bring responsibilities that shape your decisions—being a son or daughter, a volunteer, a parent, an office manager, a Sunday School teacher, or an athlete? How has your sense of spirituality shaped your worldview? How important is religion in guiding your thinking? Individuals may do things differently because they are male or female, old or young, Irish Catholic, Jewish, or Muslim. How has your family's socioeconomic status influenced your development and your views of leadership? Mapping your personal context must include many elements that contribute to your sense of identity.

We believe the capacity for leadership is within each of you. As we noted in Chapter Two, many observers of leadership agree that leaders are made not born and that everyone has a "leader within" (Haas & Tamarkin, 1992). Meaningful interaction and effective leadership processes can result if individuals are aware of their own motivations and understanding of the personal context of others. The leader-within-you may be willing to assume positional leadership roles or may be more comfortable with active participant roles. Either way, within you is the capacity to make a difference.

Values, Beliefs, Ethics, and Character

As difficult as it may be to determine how characteristics like your sex, ethnicity, or religion influence the way you think and act, it is even more complicated and important to identify the values and beliefs that lead to your ethical behaviors and build your character.

Values and Beliefs

Among the hardest things to articulate are the values that guide actions. If your actions and thoughts are a mystery to you, you may not have adequately examined your own value system. Beliefs shape values, which influence thoughts and actions. If you can articulate your values, then you are likely aware of the principles and beliefs that serve as your guides.

Contrasts in value systems are rarely as clear as when *Star Trek's* Mr. Spock dispassionately says to Bones, a surgeon on the U.S.S. Enterprise, "You are too emotional, doctor. That is not logical." Bones always explodes and shouts back, "Mr. Spock, how can you be half human and not have one ounce of feeling in you?" Each of us has preferences in how we construct our own value systems. You may prefer to be logical and scientific, or you may be emotional; you may prefer to be concrete, or you may just come to know what's important by using your intuition. Knowing that you have preferences in how you construct your value system should help you understand yourself and others better. No one process is preferred over others; your process reflects how you have come to construct meaning from your experience.

"Without ethics you are bound to lose your integrity, and who is willing to work with someone without integrity?"—Peter Tate is a biology and public health major at the University of Michigan and serves as president of the Black Greek Association.

The discussion of values should always raise the very good question, Whose values for what purpose? Some values, such as promise keeping and nonviolence, are so fundamental that they have been found to be norms in most civilized societies (Bok, 1990). In a study of diverse men and women committed to meaningful change, researchers asked each person, "If you could help create a global code of ethics, what would be on it? What moral values, in other words, would you bring to the table from your own culture and background?" (Kidder, 1994, p. 17). Their findings led to eight moral values likely to be exceptionally important in our shared global future: love, truthfulness, fairness, freedom, unity, tolerance, responsibility, and respect for life (pp. 18–19).

Values such as these are integral to the development of character. Understanding values becomes a central component to understanding others and to achieving a common purpose. Imagine this scene:

Shaking his head, Scott approaches his two friends, Khalil and Michael. "I just cannot believe it!" Scott laments. "I just heard that James vetoed the activity fee allocations to the student Hillel Association. I think he is biased and power hungry and I'm quitting student government. I just won't have anything to do with student government anymore, not with a president who does stuff like that!"

"Hey, just wait a minute, Scott," Michael implores. "I think James is exceptionally fair and reasonable, and I'd trust him with my life. Something else must be going on that we just don't understand. He must have a reason if he did this, and knowing him like we do, I bet it is a good reason. It also may not be coming down like you think."

"Yeh, I agree completely. I know him pretty well and he's OK. Let's go talk to him," Khalil adds.

James's character and reputation for integrity among those who know him are solid and defensible. When a person is known for a solid value system grounded in integrity and authenticity, others may disagree with a decision but cannot find fault with the character of the decision maker.

Character and Ethical Behavior

Integrity in relationships is central to the value systems needed among people working together toward change. Authenticity is rooted in action that is "both *true* and *real* in *ourselves* and in the *world*" (Terry, 1993, pp. 111–112). Whether framed as integrity, authenticity, or credibility, the very core of your character is central to sincerely linking with others in the spirit of community to work toward change. When asked what leadership qualities he looked for in leaders in the U.S. Army, Desert Storm's General Norman Schwarzkopf said, "Probably far more important to me than competence was character . . . integrity . . . ethics . . . and morality. . . . I looked for people who . . . were willing to serve a cause and were what I would call *selfless* leaders rather than *self-serving* leaders" (Wren, 1994, p. 2).

A person of character promotes ethical decision making and expects ethical behavior from others. The Josephson Institute of Ethics proposes six pillars of character that are "enduring and indispensable" to ethical leadership practices (Jones & Lucas, 1994, p. 4). These pillars are trustworthiness, respect, responsibility, fairness, caring, and citizenship.

"I take great precaution when handling any ethical dilemmas because I feel once you fail to practice in an ethical manner, it is very difficult, if not impossible, to regain the people's trust. Turning to my adviser or other administrators for advice when dealing with dilemmas that I am either unsure of or inexperienced with has proven most helpful to me."—Zachary Hampton is a business administration, health care planning, and management major at Alfred University. He is president of the student senate.

Trustworthiness is far more than truth telling. Being worthy of trust means being honest, demonstrating integrity, keeping promises, and being loyal. It means being known for standing up for your own convictions. *Respect* means that you treat others seriously, not that you admire or agree with all their views or behaviors. Being respectful is a commitment to treating others in ways that do not demean or take advantage of them. *Responsibility* means accepting accountability for your own actions and being conscious of the moral and ethical implications of deciding not to act. Being responsible means being accountable, pursuing excellence, and exercising self-restraint. *Fairness* is working toward a just and equitable outcome. Being fair means being open-minded, willing to listen, and confronting your own biases that might influence your decisions. *Caring* means your awareness of being concerned for each person's well-being and your attention to not being hurtful. Care requires empathy and kindness. *Citizenship* is the civic virtue of knowing that as a member of a community, you have responsibilities to do your part to contribute to the well-being of the group. *Citizenship* means you are willing to abide by laws and obligations.

A Person of Character:

- Is trustworthy (is honest, has integrity, keeps promises, is loyal)
- Treats people with respect (is courteous, nonviolent, nonprejudiced, accepting)
- Is responsible (is accountable, pursues excellence, shows self-restraint)
- Is fair (just, equitable, open, reasonable, unbiased)
- Is caring (kind, compassionate, empathetic, unselfish)
- Is a good citizen (is law-abiding, does his or her share, performs community service, protects the environment)

After a concert on campus one Friday night, two students were counting the ticket sales receipts. The money in the cash drawer was $120 short for the number of tickets sold. Baffled at the difference, the students turned in the accounts the next day and presented the problem to the Student Activities Office. That afternoon, a third student came into the office carrying an envelope containing $120. The money had apparently come in during a ticket sales rush and was set aside instead of being locked in the cash drawer.

The office accountant clerk asked her, "Why didn't you just keep the money? No one would have known."

The student's quick, indignant reply was, "But I would have known, and I don't do things like that!"

That student's consciousness of her own value system and commitment to integrity was so embedded that she could not imagine behaving any differently. The trust and respect she earned in her relationships led to an assessment of her character that was above reproach. "Leadership . . . requires a special kind of dedication, a special kind of belief. I think that you must have defined for yourself a set of moral and ethical values in which you chose to make your decisions in life as you move along. Then you must be true to yourself" (Schwarzkopf, as cited in Wren, 1994, p. 5). Vaill's analogy (1989) that our values become our rudders in times of permanent white water rings true.

"Leadership is a respect which must be earned anew each day. Leadership without respect is like fool's gold—it looks good, but upon closer inspection it becomes worthless."—Christopher Williams is a political science and speech communication major at Texas A&M, who plans to be a lawyer. He is president of the Memorial Student Union.

Personal Style Preferences

Understanding how you express your values through your preferred interactions or decision making helps you understand yourself and serves as a bridge to exploring diversity within groups. You may see yourself as a caring person committed to being fair and just, yet are puzzled as to why some people perceive you as judgmental or rigid. Understanding your personality preferences helps explain how you function in the world and how you are perceived by others.

Psychological Type

How humans adapt to the world around them is different for everybody because of personality preferences. The study of personality consumes the content of many psychology courses, books, and specialized journals. You are so accustomed to the way you view things, get things done, interact, and make decisions that you perhaps cannot imagine doing them differently. It is essential to realize that you have the capacity to broaden your approaches, but the first step is to identify them.

Carl Jung (1923) identified four core functions of human adaptation that he called personality archetypes or temperament types. These four functions include how we relate to the world, perceive the world, make judgments, and make decisions. Jung's typology includes four pairs of adaptive orientations that are diametrically opposed to each other. These combinations describe where we get our energy (extravert-introvert), how we gather information from the world around us (sensing-intuiting), how we prefer to process that information (feeling-thinking), and ways we prefer to make decisions (judging-perceiving).

The first of these four core functions concerns our mode of relating to the world. There are differences between those who are oriented to the outer world (extraverts) and those who prefer their own inner world (introverts). Those who are extraverts (E) prefer the outer world of people and things. Extraverts do their best thinking out loud and in dialogue with others. Extraverts get energy from being around people; they are sociable. When given twenty minutes of free time before she has to leave her residence hall room, an extravert will go out into the floor lobby to see what's going on. People who are introverts (I) are more oriented to their inner world of feelings and ideas. Introverts prefer to think things through and reflect before forming or stating their opinions. They do their best work through internal reflection. Introverts gain energy by creating private space, even when in a crowd. Introverts may do very well in highly interactive settings but leave those settings drained of energy needing private time to renew. Given the same twenty-minute break, an introvert might write an entry in his journal or pull out the file on his upcoming meeting and review what will be covered. The use of these words is sometimes confusing because *extravert* does not mean outgoing, and *introvert* does not mean shy and withdrawn. The terms refer instead to a preferred orientation to the outer or inner world.

The second core function includes your preferences for perceiving the world around you—sensing or intuiting. Sensing people (S) rely on the five senses and prefer concrete facts and details. Sensing people are very practical and realistic, preferring the present or past to the abstractions of the future. Intuiting people (N) prefer the big picture and like to see things as a whole. They are innovative and use imagination to develop many possibilities. Intuitive people like to project into the future, living in anticipation of how things can be better, improved, and changed. Sensing people might say, "If it's not broken, don't fix it," whereas intuitives say, "There has to be a better way" (McCaulley, 1990, p. 407). The differences in these two preferences are the source of great misunderstandings and it "places the widest gulf between people" (Keirsey & Bates, 1984, p. 17). You may hear this gulf being expressed in a discussion when one person says, "Wait a minute. We need more information before we decide" or "What do the rules in the student handbook say?" The other person then might say, "We cannot know everything, and we are close enough to have an idea of what might work. Let's just give it a try and see what happens." Groups need both kinds of people—those grounded in reality and those who think of possibilities.

The third core function is the mode of judging—thinking or feeling. Those who prefer thinking (T) use logic and rationality— the head rules rather than the heart. Thinking approaches are rewarded in school systems through critical thinking, analysis, and reliance on the objective scientific method. Feeling-type people (F) prefer to make judgments that account for relationships and the importance of human values and beliefs, with an emphasis on personal friendships. Those who prefer feeling (Fs) may find those who prefer thinking (Ts) to be cold and too objective, whereas Ts may find Fs too emotional and unable to stand firm on a decision. This is the only scale that shows a sex pattern, with men making up

60 percent of the T preference group and women making up 60 percent of the F preference group. Misunderstandings that are on occasion attributed to sex differences may actually reflect personality differences.

The fourth core function involves how you prefer to make decisions—by judging or perceiving. Those with judging preferences (J) prefer order and emphasize resolving issues and making decisions to create order. People who use J preferences like tying up loose ends and seeking closure; they like clear beginnings, deadlines, and endings. Perceiving-type people (P) prefer to keep things open-ended by gathering as much information as possible and being flexible. People with P preferences handle ambiguity well, are known to go with the flow, and are comfortable leaving things open-ended or unresolved. Those with J preferences may seem close-minded or driven, and those with P preferences may seem unfocused and have a hard time getting anything done.

We each have developed preferences of how we most comfortably perceive and judge our worlds. These pairs (and the sixteen primary personality types that emerge) help us understand ourselves and others (Myers, 1980). Your four-letter composite profile is a combination then of E/I, S/N, T/F, and J/P. See Exhibit 4.1 for cue words that provide additional explanation of these preferences. Which set seems most like you?

We can and do use all eight of these processes but generally prefer a consistent pattern. If you are right-handed, you could write with your left hand if you had to, but you prefer your right hand. If you are an introvert, you can and do enjoy people and good conversation, but you must have time and space to think and reflect to do your best work. If you are an extravert, you certainly can listen and reflect, but you prefer the energy of interacting with others to build and refine your ideas because you like to "think out loud." Understanding the impact of our preferences and comfortably using our nonpreferred strategies is a skill to acquire. Indeed, the subtitle of *Developing Leaders* (Fitzgerald & Kirby, 1997) is *Integrating Reality and Vision, Mind and Heart*.

EXHIBIT 4.1 Type Indicator Cue Words

Extravert (E)	versus	Introvert (I)
(75% of population)		(25% of population)
Sociability		Territoriality
Interaction		Concentration
External		Internal
Breadth		Depth
Extensive		Intensive
Multiplicity of relationships		Limited relationships
Expenditure of energies		Conservation of energies
Interest in external events		Interest in internal reaction

Sensing (S)	versus	Intuition (N)
(75% of population)		(25% of population)
Experience		Hunches
Past		Future
Realistic		Speculative
Perspiration		Inspiration
Actual		Possible
Down-to-earth		Head-in-clouds
Utility		Fantasy
Fact		Fiction
Practicality		Ingenuity
Sensible		Imaginative

Thinking (T)	versus	Feeling (F)
(50% of population)		(50% of population)
Objective		Subjective
Principles		Values
Policy		Social values
Laws		Extenuating circumstances
Criterion		Intimacy
Firmness		Persuasion
Impersonal		Personal
Justice		Humane

EXHIBIT 4.1 Continued

Thinking (T)	versus	Feeling (F)
Categories		Harmony
Standards		Good or bad
Critique		Appreciate
Analysis		Sympathy
Allocation		Devotion

Judging (J)	versus	Perceiving (P)
(50% of population)		(50% of population)
Settled		Pending
Decided		Gather more data
Fixed		Flexible
Plan ahead		Adapt as you go
Run one's life		Let life happen
Closure		Open options
Decision-making		Treasure hunting
Planned		Open ended
Completed		Emergent
Decisive		Tentative
Wrap it up		Something will turn up
Urgency		There's plenty of time
Deadline!		What deadline?
Get show on the road		Let's wait and see. . .

Source: Keirsey & Bates, 1978, pp. 25–26. Copyright 1978 by Prometheus Nemesis Book Co. Adapted with permission.

Perhaps the best-known method of assessing Jungian personality types is the Myers-Briggs Type Indicator (MBTI). Your college counseling center will likely have this instrument. You might also like to complete the Keirsey Temperament Sorter, which is based on the same principles from *Please Understand Me* (Keirsey & Bates, 1984). You may not need the instrument at all if you identified with the descriptions of each of the four core functions and could identify your preferences.

The MBTI is useful in understanding relationships in a leadership setting. Research using the MBTI indicates that 65 to 75 percent of the general population are extraverts (E) and that women are slightly higher than men in this preference. Introverts (I) predominate in fields of study such as science and among careers as university teaching. Those who prefer sensing (S) are three times more prevalent in the population than intuitives (N). "Groups at the intuitive end . . . are more likely to include educators, consultants, and student leaders" (McCaulley, 1990, p. 407). Approximately two-thirds of men prefer thinking (T), and two-thirds of women prefer feeling (F). However, women who prefer thinking approaches are in the majority among graduate students, engineering students, and business executives. Men with feeling preferences predominate in the arts, counseling, and some health fields. The general population contains about 55 percent judging types (J), but studies of leaders show this to range upward to 91 percent, clearly indicating the preferences among positional leaders to reach closure and get decisions made (McCaulley, 1990). Leaders come from all groupings of preferences, but clearly certain patterns of preferences may exist in some careers or fields that draw on those preferences as strengths. McCaulley asserts, "From the type perspective, one would not ask the question, 'What type is the best leader?' Rather, one would ask, 'How does each type show leadership?'" (p. 412).

This theory of psychological type has been widely used in leadership assessments to understand self, others, and the dynamics of relationships and leadership processes, but it is not without flaws. There is some indication that type is not stable, that you can change your pattern over time. The action-oriented extravert may become a more contemplative and reflective introvert later in her life. Scores on the MBTI may be related to the context you have in mind when you complete the instrument. Assessments like the MBTI are occasionally used inappropriately. It would be inappropriate in hiring decisions to assume that someone can be no different than her four-letter score, when actually she may be well-developed in using several preferences. The three of us have found the concept of personality preferences so helpful in understanding ourselves that we encourage you to consider this framework for your own self-exploration.

Becoming aware of your personality preferences helps move you further toward self-awareness. As awareness grows, you begin to see the need to build other skills and to have a wider range of responses in decision making and in your relations with others. A useful application occurs when you realize that the conflict you have with another may be because of a clash in preferences, which can lead to more understanding ways of relating. You will then find it comfortable to say, "Sorry, I know it seems like I am jumping the gun, but I just do my best thinking out loud," or "I know I am asking lots of detailed questions, but it helps me understand the bigger picture" or "These were interesting ideas presented today; I am just not yet ready to decide. I need to think about this overnight. Can we decide at our meeting tomorrow?"

Approaches to Learning

One of the elements of leadership is that it is focused on accomplishing something or changing something. How individuals understand the need for change and how effectively individuals and groups can adapt to change is a learning process. Human beings go through a continual process of adaptation to changing conditions whether those conditions are imposed or induced. You may even be faced right now with the need to adjust to new challenges at home, at work, in classes, or in some of your organizational roles. At its root, this process of adaptation is the learning process: learning new knowledge, new skills, or clarifying attitudes and values.

Because this book is grounded in the principle that you can learn to enhance your leadership skills and that effective organizations need to be learning communities, we want you to expand your own awareness of how you learn best. One of the key dimensions of the Relational Leadership Model is a process orientation. Learning together is one of those key processes.

We each have preferences in how we learn best. Just as you have a preference for extraversion or introversion, intuition or sensing, thinking or feeling, or judging or perceiving, you may also have a preference for either deductive or inductive ways of thinking. Being deductive means you like to see the big picture, know what the final outcome is likely to be—or what the whole is—and then you are comfortable looking at the parts and pieces. You like to see the forest before you examine all the trees. If you are inductive, you like to build up to the big picture or conclusion by assembling all the parts and evolving your conclusion. You prefer to see each tree before you stand back and see the forest. A deductive learner might be frustrated with an inductive learner and say, "Where in the world are you going with this argument? You are losing the forest in all the trees!" Understanding the difference in approach, that same deductive learner might say, "It would help me to know where this is going so I can fit your examples into the bigger picture."

There are learning applications of the Jungian types presented as personality preferences in the previous section. Use of the MBTI would bring a complex understanding of the combinations of your four codes (E/I, S/N, T/F, and P/J). For purposes of illustration, some simple applications follow.

If you are extraverted (E), you are likely to enjoy group learning tasks and projects, learn readily from group discussion, and like to think aloud as you respond to questions and comments in the group. Extraverts value experience and often "leap into academic tasks with little planning . . . they prefer trial-and-error process because it allows them to think while they are active" (Jensen, 1987, p. 183). If you are an introvert (I), you listen keenly and find you carry on a great dialogue in your head. You might prefer to keep a journal, and you probably do well with written assignments when there is time to reflect. When something important comes up, you prefer to think about it first and not jump to a hasty conclusion.

"Introverts do not always share what they know, [group members] may be slow to appreciate their talents and depth of knowledge" (Jensen, 1987, p. 194).

If you are a sensing (S) learner, you like details and facts and might prefer inductive thinking. You value the history and background of an issue to establish the context to learn about it. As practical people, sensing types do not value "learning for its own sake" (Jensen, 1987, p. 194) but do value usefulness and applicability. If you are an intuitive learner (N), you like the big picture and do not retain the small details well. You may be quick to jump to conclusions with little information. You like possibility-thinking, and you cast a wide net to gather a great deal of information from diverse sources. Academic learning depends heavily on communication with words and written symbols like formulas and diagrams. Learning from such abstractions requires the learner to make translations "from symbols into meaning by the listener's intuition, [and] the translation is naturally easier for intuitives than for sensing types. Intuitives use their favorite kind of perception, but sensing types have to use their less-liked, less-developed kind of perception, which takes more time and effort, especially when the words are abstract" (Myers, 1980, p. 147).

A thinking (T) learner is logical, analytical, and often a critical thinker. If you have a T preference, you find it comfortable to be objective about material and issues and may see ideas separate from personal values. A feeling learner (F) relates personally to the material. This subjective approach connects to one's personal values so that it may be hard not to take a criticism personally.

A perceiver (P) may have a hard time organizing material to learn it or present it. Material seems so interconnected that creating an organizing system is hard. A judger (J) organizes learning into categories, makes use of models and charts readily, and uses headers in writing papers. Exhibit 4.2 presents some learning implications of personality type indicators.

Think of the classes or organizations you know that are made up

EXHIBIT 4.2 Type and Learning Styles

Extraversion (E)	*Introversion (I)*
Es learn best in situations filled with movement, action, and talk. They prefer to learn theories or facts that connect with their experience, and they will usually come to a more thorough understanding of these theories or facts during group discussions or when working on cooperative projects. Es tend to leap into assignments with little "forethought," relying on trial-and-error rather than anticipation to solve problems.	Since Is may be more quiet and less active in the classroom, teachers may feel the need to press them into taking part in group discussions. Such pressure, however, will often only increase their withdrawal. Teachers need to respect their need to think in relative solitude, for that is how they think best. Is will be more willing to share their ideas when given advance notice. This will allow them time to think about how they will become active in the classroom.

Sensory Perception (S)	*Intuitive Perception (N)*
Ss learn best when they move from the concrete to the abstract in a step-by-step progression. They are thus at home with programmed, modular, or computer-assisted learning. They value knowledge that is practical and want to be precise in their own work. They tend to excel at memorizing facts.	Ns tend to leap to a conceptual understanding of material and may daydream or act-out during drill work or predominantly factual lectures. They value quick flashes of insight but are often careless about details. They tend to excel at imaginative tasks and theoretical topics.

continued

Exhibit 4.2 Continued

Thinking Judgment (T)	Feeling Judgment (F)
Ts are most motivated when provided with a logical rationale for each project and when teachers acknowledge and respect their competence. They prefer topics that help them to understand systems or cause-and-effect relationships. Their thought is syllogistic and analytic.	Fs are most motivated when given personal encouragement and when shown the human angle of a topic. Fs think to clarify their values and to establish networks of values. Even when their expressions seem syllogistic, they usually evolve from some personally held belief or value.

Judgment (J)	Perception (P)
Js tend to gauge their learning by the completion of tasks: reading "x"–amount of books, writing "x"–amount of papers, or making "x"–amount of reports. They thus prefer more structured learning environments that establish goals for them to meet.	Ps tend to view learning as a free-wheeling, flexible quest. They care less about deadlines and the completion of tasks. They prefer open and spontaneous learning environments and feel "imprisoned" in a highly structured classroom.

Source: Modified and reproduced by special permission of the publisher, Consulting Psychologists Press, Inc., Palo Alto, CA 94303. From *Applications of the Myers-Briggs Type Indicator in Higher Education*, p. 186, by Judith Provost & Scott Anchors, editors. Copyright 1987 by Consulting Psychologists Press. All rights reserved. Further reproduction is prohibited without the Publisher's written consent.

of one predominant type. Often a major will attract students who are more similar than different. If, however, you are mismatched in learning style, you may wonder why the group does not readily see the benefit of your suggestions, or perhaps it even rejects a process you propose. Groups that may be composed of one predominant *just like organizations* type of learning will find strength in including other approaches to enrich the outcome.

Highly diverse groups of learners need to acknowledge that people learn differently and offer options and choices that will appeal to the diversity within a group. For example, student government organizers who are planning a retreat during which goals and plans for the year are to be set might (1) send out materials ahead of time (appealing to the introverts and intuitors), (2) plan large-group presentations (appealing to the introverts and the thinkers), (3) plan small-group discussions (useful for the extraverts and feelers), and (4) plan case study applications. Also, they might work through how a possible goal might be put into an action plan with a related budget (useful to the sensors and judgers). If only one approach were used, it would relate less well to the entire group. It is clearly helpful to know your own preferred learning style and understand how others may prefer to learn differently.

Preferences in how we take in information, relate to others, make decisions, and learn are all essential areas of awareness in relational leadership. These applications of Jung's principles may help you explore your own personality and attitudes in new ways.

Chapter Summary

This chapter reviewed some important aspects of your self-awareness that become key to understanding yourself as a participant and as a leader. The chapter reviewed basic values that are essential in a person of character. Building on the psychological and educational approaches to leadership, we presented some models to assess your personality preferences and your learning preferences. We also explored ways to examine your strengths and weaknesses, with a goal of having a realistic self-concept with healthy self-esteem and self-confidence.

What's Next?

Understanding yourself and building your capacity for self-leadership is a foundational asset for effectively relating to others. Chapter Five will encourage you to explore yourself in the context of others. The chapter will further present how interpersonal relations can be enhanced by understanding differences and commonalties with others. This understanding is helpful in communicating and building empowering relationships with other participants.

Chapter Activities

1. Think about your sex, ethnicity, sexual orientation, special abilities or disabilities, age, socioeconomic status, religion, birth order, and any other possible influences that come to mind. How have these factors influenced your personality and learning preferences?

2. Write your own personal mission statement. What is your purpose in life? What values are important to you? What do you want to be? What attributes and capabilities are important to you?

3. Review Bennis's lessons for developing self-knowledge and provide examples from your own life. When were you your own best teacher? When did you accept responsibility for something that did not go well? When did you learn something you really wanted to learn? When did you learn something through the process of reflection?

4. Contact your college counseling center to complete the Myers-Briggs Type Indicator (MBTI). That will help you understand your personality preferences.

5. Many people use positive affirmations to enhance their self-esteem. While they will not make up for a lack of skill or ability, they can help you develop your confidence. An example might be, "I am going to do a good job speaking in front of

this group." Saying this phrase over and over to yourself, up to twenty times throughout the day, can help you believe in yourself. Develop two or three affirmations that you can use to strengthen your self-confidence.

6. Another technique is creative visualization. While this will not make up for a lack of skill or ability, it can help you develop your confidence. Identify something you have to do in the next couple of days that is causing you to worry. Now visualize yourself accomplishing this activity successfully. Repeat this visualization whenever you begin to worry about the upcoming event. After the event is over, consider whether or not using visualization helped you.

Additional Readings

Covey, S. (1989). *The seven habits of highly effective people*. New York: Simon & Schuster.

Keirsey, D., & Bates, M. (1984). *Please understand me: Character & temperament types* (4th ed.). Del Mar, CA: Prometheus Nemesis Books.

Kolb, D. (1983). *Experiential learning: Experience as the source of learning and development*. Englewood Cliffs, NJ: Prentice Hall.

Manz, C. C., & Sims, H. P., Jr. (1989). *Superleadership: Leading others to lead themselves*. New York: Prentice Hall.

5

Understanding Others

A central goal of understanding yourself is to develop a sense of awareness that can result in true community and common purpose with others. There are three central questions (Komives, 1994, p. 219) to ask yourself in any setting:

- How am I like no one else here?
- How am I like some others here?
- How am I like everyone here?

Each of us brings uniqueness and individuality to any situation. As we explored in Chapter Four, your skills, background, and preferences create a unique person—you. But you are not alone. To be truly inclusive and empowering, you must also understand others.

Chapter Overview

This chapter briefly explores some characteristics of gender, ethnicity, or culture that illustrate how differences need to be understood as you work toward leadership that is inclusive and empowering. The chapter also explores various leadership processes, including communication, conflict resolution, and decision making, that are influenced by diverse approaches. The chapter concludes with a discussion of communication skills such as empathy and assertiveness that are useful in working effectively with others in leadership.

Individuality and Commonality

In Chapter Four you explored your value system, your psychological preferences, and your preferred ways of learning. Others might be similar or very different from you. Even if others look the same, they may have different values, preferences, or approaches to learning. Some of these differences in ourselves and others come from our gender, ethnicity, or culture; some come from our environments.

In the grand scheme of living human species, we are more alike than we are different. Finding common human purpose is the focus on which to center our perceptions of difference. Poet Maya Angelou (1994) has remarkable insight into the commonalties of being human. In her poem "Human Family," she described all of our uniqueness as people that set us apart but concludes, "We are more alike, my friends, than we are unalike" (pp. 224–225).

In any group setting, you can look around and see others who look like you. You will see men or women, people with visible racial or ethnic characteristics, or people of different ages. Also, you might see people wearing symbolic attire like your own: a wedding ring, a sorority pin, a pink triangle, a Star of David, or tennis whites. You might also identify with others when they express ideas you agree with, share experiences you have had, or have goals you also hold, regardless of visible characteristics that might have initially made them seem unlike you. You may begin to find similarities of interests: being in the same major, living close together, thinking alike about a recent election, working out daily, or being affiliated with the same religion. Finding some people like you creates a feeling of association called subcommunities.

On a transcendent level, something binds you to everyone around you, no matter how different they may seem: you all want to learn the subject in a particular course; you all value the goals of the organization meeting you have attended like the PTA or a Bible study class; or you all want to work toward a common purpose like changing the university's policy on weekend library hours. The challenge of leadership is coming to common purpose from the vast differences that individuals bring to a situation. Finding the purpose, vision, and common commitments that create a "we" from a group of individuals is the challenge of community.

The English language may well be the only one that values the individual to such a degree that the letter "I" is capitalized when referring to the word for the first person singular. This emphasis on the individual is grounded in a predominantly Western tradition. Those with non-Western roots may find it easier to envision "we" because those cultural traditions emphasize the collective, the family, or group. To truly establish a sense of "we," the individual needs to let go of self enough to see the connections to others. Buber (1958) encouraged an exploration of "I-Thou"; leadership educators have encouraged "I → you → we" (National Leadership Symposium, 1990). This might best be expressed symbolically by showing that the focus on the individual (I) needs to be de-emphasized (i) to truly listen and engage with another (you) as equals, so that all can move forward to become a community (we) (see Figure 5.1).

One challenge, then, is to understand yourself well enough to know how you are seen by others and to modify your own behaviors and attitudes to encourage a spirit of openness and connection with others. The second challenge is to engage in the hard work of understanding others so that together you can form meaningful community and engage in coalitions for group change.

FIGURE 5.1   I, You, and We

$$\text{"I"} \Rightarrow \text{"i"}$$
$$\Updownarrow \Rightarrow \text{"we"}$$
$$\text{"you"}$$

Groups are made up of great diversity. Even if members are all of one sex or one race or one major, there are great differences in personality, learning preferences, and experiences. The pluralism of a group refers to the plethora of differences that need to be understood in order to accomplish shared purposes. Pluralistic leadership results when heterogeneous groups of people work together to accomplish change. Pluralistic leadership is enhanced when a person understands and has developed an appreciation for and possesses the skills needed to communicate across these borders and come to common understandings.

Understanding Gender Diversity

It is salient to ask yourself, How does my gender influence my attitudes and behaviors? How does my experience as a man or woman shape my worldview? Characteristics of gender differences are too numerous to develop fully, but it is important to realize that we all deal with both sex roles and gender roles. The two terms are often used interchangeably, but sex roles are those expectations resulting from biology, like pregnancy or growing facial hair, whereas gender roles are socially constructed expectations that get labeled masculine or feminine.

Gender roles may be limiting and inaccurate when assigned to individual men and women. For example, whereas only women can bear children, women are not the only sex to be nurturing of children. Historically, men's involvement in the development of children has been limited because that role has been considered feminine and nurturing. Likewise, women may be athletic, but it has been hard for women to engage in sports that require high physical contact, like football and rugby, because those sports are considered masculine. Women who are not nurturing or men who are not athletic may suffer from gender role discrimination by acting or being different from conventional paradigms. Those who hold a conventional leadership expectation that leaders should be decisive, in charge, competitive, and self-reliant may be holding a traditional masculine paradigm that excludes many women, as well as many men who are very capable but who do not lead from that perspective.

From the beginnings of our lives, our gender role perceptions are shaped by the many messages we receive from the environment. Even those parents who make sure the storybooks their children read do not promote gender role or sex role stereotypes and give dolls to their sons and trucks to their daughters soon realize that other socialization agents (like peers, toys, television, and conversations on the bus going to school every morning) reinforce traditional gender messages. Many boys learn to be tough, objective, and competitive, and many girls learn to be polite, caring, and supportive.

To understand how men and women have come to be like they are, we can learn from children's development. The way we play in childhood establishes patterns of how we work and communicate as adults. Boys often play outside in rough and tumble games, and extraverted leaders shout commands in competitive settings. Winning or losing becomes very important. Most games are played using teams. Even inside games like electronic games for Nintendo or the computer often have elaborate hierarchical systems with complex rules and procedures frequently preferred by boys. Girls, however, often play inside in calm settings with one another or a small group of friends. Their play stresses intimacy and values social relationships. Many of their preferred games have no winners or losers but every person gets a turn. Such games are jumping rope, playing hopscotch, or playing house (Tannen, 1990).

The social learning that happens with play and many other experiences leads females often to seek and value intimacy and relationships, whereas males often seek and value independence. "Intimacy is key in a world of connection where individuals negotiate complex networks of friendship, minimize differences, try to reach consensus, and value the appearance of superiority which would highlight differences. In a world of status, independence is key, because a primary means of establishing status is to tell others what to do, and taking orders is a marker of low status" (Tannen, 1990,

p. 26). Think of how rare it is in entertainment to find people who play roles that are different from conventional gender roles. Two examples are Sigourney Weaver as a space warrior in *Aliens* and Robin Williams as a desperate, loving father in *Mrs. Doubtfire*.

Childhood play experiences also contribute to the development of the thinking or feeling orientation described in the Jungian preference types in Chapter Four. Remember that there is great variation among men and among women, but these patterns do raise our awareness and understanding of differences.

Men and women tend to hold different attributions for their successes and failures. Many women tend to credit their successes to external factors like luck and being in the right place at the right time. They might say, "Oh I don't deserve the credit. So many people helped." They credit their failures to internal factors like not being prepared or not having the right skills or not having enough time. Many men, in contrast, tend to credit successes to internal factors like being prepared and capable; they attribute their failures to external factors like fate, others not doing their part, or bad luck.

However, "psychological and physiological data on sex-linked traits suggest that the degree of overlap between the sexes is as important, or more important, than the average differences between them" (Lipman-Blumen, 1984, p. 4). Both men and women are capable of making good decisions, leading effectively, being responsible group members, and communicating with clarity, but they may go about doing those things differently than the other sex would. The fact that we persist in observing differences speaks to the power relationships that continue to exist in which men's ways, views, and artifacts have had higher status. Because men have traditionally held many visible leadership positions, the conventional paradigm of leadership was often reflected as having these same male characteristics.

Expectations that limit people's range of roles and suppress their individuality will likely inhibit their effectiveness in their communities. Sex or gender, however, is only one identity perspective we bring to a situation. We have other salient identities that are based on attributes such as our culture, ethnicity, age, or sexual orientation.

Understanding Cultural Diversity

Culture encompasses everything about how a group of people think, feel, and behave. It is their pattern of knowledge. It is a "body of common understandings" (Brown, 1963, p. 3). Culture is "the sum total of ways of living; including values, beliefs, esthetic standards, linguistic expression, patterns of thinking, behavioral norms, and styles of communication which a group of people has developed to assure its survival in a particular physical and human environment. Culture, and the people who are part of it, interact, so that culture is not static" (Hoopes & Pusch, 1979, p. 3). We may be so embedded in our culture that it is hard to see it clearly.

Culture is, therefore, a broad term that could be applied to an office or a campus, to aging, or to a group of people who share common race or ethnicity. Many cultures coexist simultaneously in any group. Effective leaders need to develop an appreciation for multiculturalism to build inclusiveness, collaboration, and common purposes. A prerequisite to developing a greater sense of multiculturalism is the conscious awareness of culturally informed assumptions (Helms, 1992; Pederson, 1988).

In the 1980s and 1990s, culture has often been described in terms of race and ethnicity. We encourage you to be cautious about the construct of race. Race is a "somewhat suspect concept used to identify large groups of the human species who share a more or less distinctive combination of hereditary physical characteristics" (Hoopes & Pusch, 1979, p. 3). Humans are far more complex than the one variable of race might indicate. What has been identified as a race (for example, Latino) may actually reflect several races (for example, black or white) and many countries of origin. In addition, individuals may be biracial or multiracial and might grow up in the dominant or minority culture.

Within a race there can be a variety of nationalities or ethnicities (for example, Irish, Jamaican, Cambodian, French, or Italian). An ethnic group is made up of people identified by racial, national, or cultural characteristics. Membership in the group is usually determined by birth, and the group is usually an interdependent subunit of a larger culture (Hoopes & Pusch, 1979, p. 3).

Historically, the dominant culture—the culture in the powerful majority—has not had to examine its beliefs and practices. The majority norms often became the standards used to judge others who are not in the majority. In the last decade, America's attention to racial and ethnic diversity has led to new awareness of what it means to be white and of European origin in the American culture. Peggy McIntosh (1989) coined the phrase the "invisible knapsack" to describe the concept of "white privilege." Even well-meaning people in the majority culture often take for granted the benefits of white privilege, which include shopping without being followed, being able to buy or rent housing of one's choice, and easily finding toys and pictures that look like one's self (Talbot, 1996). In a general sense, it is useful to think of the privileges afforded any of us by virtue of personal characteristics that place us in a powerful "majority" (for example, being male, heterosexual, able-bodied, educated, financially comfortable) and examine closely how unconsciously affirming the privileges associated with those characteristics may actually cause or influence the oppression of others, even though oppression is unintended. We must also examine how the characteristics of that privilege may be attached to our expectations of what it means to be a leader and not to value, or even recognize, leadership that may take on different characteristics.

Your Cultural Heritage

We encourage you to read about your cultural heritage to see how you may have acquired the values and beliefs of your culture or ethnicity and in what ways you have diverged from them. Read also about a group that is different from your own. You might study the white or European American cultures, African American or black culture, Asian American, Latino or Hispanic or Chicano cultures, Native American traditions, and the international students who come from other countries. Learn more about aging and adult development, religious diversity, and regional differences. In any case, it will be useful to be aware of the assumptions that a person coming into a group might have that would influence that person's behavior. It may be most useful to start with yourself.

"I hit the ground running and began to pace myself off of people in front of me. I slowly began to acculturate by observing the mainstream. I still maintained my individuality and core of my thinking, but altered some outward manifestations as my thinking changed. I continued to allow myself to grow intellectually, spiritually, physically, culturally, morally, and ethically."—Michelle Satterfield, from Virginia State University, is the corresponding secretary of Delta Sigma Theta Sorority, Inc. and an ROTC Scholar.

Building Multicultural Appreciation

Being an effective leader or participant in a diverse organization, or being a leader who brings diversity to the organization, requires that we know more about developing an openness and appreciation of various cultures and aspects of how others may differ. David Hoopes (1979) presents an Intercultural Learning Process Model (see Exhibit 5.1) that describes how we develop and learn to communicate clearly and understand people and cultures that seem different from our own. The first stage is *ethnocentrism*. In this stage, we believe that our own culture or way of doing things is best—even superior to others. People with ethnocentric views can be intolerant and even hostile to others from different cultures. Racism and sexism grow from this base. As we expand our experiences, we begin to move out of ethnocentrism and our *awareness* is raised. We begin to acknowledge that many different cultures exist. As awareness of culture grows, we move to some level of *understanding* derived by experiences, learning and acquiring information, and

EXHIBIT 5.1 Hoopes Intercultural Learning Process

Ethnocentrism	A human survival response that tells us our own culture is best. Individuals at this stage may exhibit intolerance and outright hostility or aggression toward other cultures. Individuals who do not move beyond this stage tend to feel their culture is superior and impose it on others.

Transition stages

Awareness	A first step out of Ethnocentrism. This stage involves the acknowledgment that other cultures exist and the awareness that they have a culture. The individual at this stage becomes aware that differences are culturally based and that they are part of a given people's way of thinking and acting.
Understanding	This stage involves the acquiring of knowledge and information about other cultures on a rational, cognitive level. The individual begins to piece together the "puzzle" of the other culture from pieces of information about values, customs, etc. Occurs in a detached and separate way.

Acceptance/ Respect (tolerance)	Individuals at this stage accept the validity of other cultures without comparing or judging them against one's own culture. A change in attitude of "It's OK for them" occurs, a relativistic approach. A "live and let live" attitude results and the value of other cultures is for others, not me.

Transition stages

Appreciating/ Valuing	At this stage, one begins to understand that cultures have strengths and weaknesses; such an understanding leads to appreciation and valuing of specific aspects of other cultures. A change occurs from objectivity to subjectivity consider-

EXHIBIT 5.1 Continued

	ing cultural aspects in terms of one's own identity and values.
Selective adoption	The individual at this stage tries and adopts new attitudes and behaviors from other cultures which are believed to be useful and desirable to emulate. Aspects of another culture which have value and worth for me personally are integrated into my way of thinking, feeling, or acting.
Multiculturalism	An ideal state and an ongoing PROCESS where a person is able to feel comfortable in and communicate effectively with people from many cultures and in many situations. Identities, self concepts, outlooks, and value formation transcends cultural considerations. Very open to new experiences.

Source: Leppo, 1987, pp. 56–60. Copyright 1987 by the National Association of Campus Activities. Adapted with permission. (Original work from Hoopes, 1979, in Pusch, [ed.] *Multicultural Education: A Cross-Cultural Training Approach,* 1979, pp. 17–20. Copyright 1979 by Intercultural Press. Adapted with permission of Intercultural Press, Inc., Yarmouth, MA.)

knowledge. Learning about other cultures is somewhat objective in this transition and is more thought about than felt.

These two transition stages of awareness and understanding lead to a willingness to *accept and respect* that others do have a legitimate cultural view. This tolerance has not led to an examination of one's own culture but to the recognition that it may be all right for others to hold the views and values they possess from their cultural view. Some would say that acceptance is still a negative attitude; it may lead to the civility of tolerance but does not yet place the same value on another's views as on one's own (Riddle, as cited in Leppo, 1987).

The transition from the tolerance step in the process toward multiculturalism moves forward with *appreciating and valuing* certain aspects of other cultures. This does not mean that everything about another culture or way of doing things is appreciated but that a recognition of the strengths, assets, and value of another cultural view has occurred. For example, we have learned to appreciate the international foods, music, and dance that are incorporated into our daily American life. This stage means comparing others to our own cultural view and becoming more subjective about this assessment. This leads to the next transition in *selectively adopting values or aspects of another culture* that are worthy of admiration. Aspects of value in another culture (for example, the role of elders or the role of the environment) are integrated into a person's own life out of admiration and choice.

The goal of this process is *multiculturalism*, which is not a final state but an ongoing process of comfort in learning about and appreciating other cultures—a lifelong learning task. This openness to new experiences enriches a person's own life and makes it possible to share aspects of a person's own culture that might be of value to others.

Imagine this model (see Exhibit 5.1) helping the aging culture to be more open to youth culture or the Black Student Union and the Jewish Student Union coming to an appreciation of each other's perspectives. Think of the lessons many could learn from Native Americans. A benefit of multiculturalism is to grow beyond seeing the world only in our own terms to seeing the legitimate views of others. This appreciation does not mean we will agree, or even find decision making easy, but it should mean that we will understand other views.

Attitudes Toward Differences

How we view others who are different from ourselves is complex. There is some evidence that this is a developmental or sequential process during which we move from complete unawareness as a child to some degree of acceptance or appreciation as a mature adult. Through the years, we begin to learn through positive and negative experiences. As a result of these experiences, some people learn to dislike and fear differences. In extreme cases, fears can lead to racism, homophobia, or sexism. Other experiences lead us to be appreciative and to embrace many differences.

"You cannot show respect by changing your behavior in front of someone or a particular group of people. Respect is shown when you change your behavior twenty-four hours a day."—Rebecca Weger received her B.F.A. from Alfred University and is co-president of Spectrum, a campus Gay, Lesbian, Bisexual organization.

In the previous section, we illustrated the progression from ethnocentrism to multiculturalism. One model that applies to attitudes toward many differences is the Riddle Scale (cited in Leppo, 1987). As depicted in Exhibit 5.2, the first four stages of the scale (repulsion, pity, tolerance, and acceptance) are negative attitudes because they come from a belief that the person who is different is somehow of less value than one's self. The second group of four stages of the scale (support, admiration, appreciation, and nurturance) are positive levels of the scale because the other person is of value just as is self. Dorothy Riddle developed this model originally as a Scale for Homophobia to understand attitudes toward gay and lesbian people, but our students have found it helpful as a conceptual model for understanding other differences, as well as attitudes toward people with physical disabilities or different religious practices.

Cultural Influences on Leadership Behavior

Awareness of how such aspects of diversity as personality preferences, value systems, gender, and culture influence our own behavior and

EXHIBIT 5.2 The Riddle Scale: Attitudes Toward Differences

Negative Levels of Attitudes

Repulsion	Viewing people who are different as strange, sick, crazy, and aversive. Anything which will change them to be more "normal" or part of the mainstream is viewed as justifiable.
Pity	Viewing people who are different as somehow born that way and feeling that is pitiful. Being different is definitely immature and less preferred. To help those poor individuals one should reinforce normal behaviors.
Tolerance	Being different is seen as just a phase of development and most people "grow out" of it. Thus they should be protected and tolerated as one does a child who is still learning.
Acceptance	Implies that one needs to make accommodations for another's differences and does not acknowledge that another's identity may be of the same value as their own.

Positive Levels of Attitudes

Support	Works to safeguard the rights of those who are different. Such people may be uncomfortable themselves but they are aware of the climate and the irrational unfairness in our society.
Admiration	Acknowledges that being different in our society takes strength. Such people are willing to truly look at themselves and work on their own personal biases.
Appreciation	Values the diversity of people and is willing to confront insensitive attitudes.

EXHIBIT 5.2   Continued

Nurturance	Assumes the differences in people are indispensable in society. Views differences with genuine affection and delight and are willing to be advocates of those differences.

Source: Leppo & Lustgraaf, 1987, "Student Government: Working with Special Constituencies," unpublished document, University of North Dakota, Grand Forks. Copyright by John Leppo. Adapted with permission from Dorothy Riddle, "Scale for Homophobia," unpublished document.

that of others in groups is a step toward being an effective relational leader. No group is totally homogeneous; we differ in attitudes, styles, values, beliefs, and opinions, based on how we have learned to be from our cultures. Relational leadership values effective leadership processes within heterogeneous groups. Many leadership practices could be described as participative because they value the empowerment of followers, but relational and pluralistic leadership seeks to change the very culture of the organization or group to see the diversity of the group as a true asset (Loden & Rosener, 1991).

It clearly would be inaccurate to describe people based on such simple differences as sex, race, ethnicity, culture, or age. Behaviors grow from a complex interaction of many salient background factors; it is more useful to observe their behaviors and seek to understand their attitudes than to presume differences among people that are based on stereotypes. It is useful to examine the range of human behaviors that are essential in leadership settings. Consider the cultural influences in such leadership processes as communications, conflict resolution, and decision making.

"I believe that every individual can provide a new perspective on a situation. No matter what your experiences are, they are different from mine and therefore we see things differently. Using this perspective in addition to one's ideas allows for better communication, better solutions, and better leadership."—Cathy Ragan is the student government president at Rowan University.

Communication

You might observe a range of behaviors in a group. Some people may be highly verbal with strong oral traditions; others may be verbally reserved, preferring thoughtful writing. Some may be outgoing, expressive, and emotional, whereas the cultural assumptions of others lead them to be thoughtful, objective, and analytical. Depending on the mix of individuals, some will be open and revealing, whereas others will be closed and guarded. Some cultural assumptions lead people to be direct and factual; others have learned to be symbolic and metaphorical. Some have been taught to value direct, bold eye contact; others find respect in indirect body language. Some have learned to be timely and to value promptness; other cultures value casual approaches. Understanding the mix of preferred communication patterns in any group helps the group be more informed in its interaction. Instead of judging another to be wrong or disrespectful, it is useful to ask yourself, Within that person's context, how do I understand this action or practice?

Conflict Resolution

You might observe individuals with a range of behaviors, from the confrontational to the very subtle. Some may encourage taking responsibility and being accountable; others will tend to blame; still others will seek harmony and face-saving. Some believe their way is right and are closed to other options, whereas others seek connections among options. Some resolve conflict by being deferential to authority, whereas others have learned to be confrontational of authority. Finally, some people will link resolution to values like harmony with nature.

Decision Making

The way decisions are made reflects those who value the power of majority rule and prefer voting to those who seek inclusion of the minority opinion and value consensus. In some groups, if the will of the group does not emerge as apparent, an issue might be dropped completely and brought up at a later time. Some believe the hierarchy and authorities should decide, whereas others think the experts or those involved should decide.

Relational leadership requires communication skills that help each person seek to understand others, not just persuade them. All communicators should constantly ask themselves, How do my perspectives and preferences shade my view? In what ways could I be understood more correctly and understand with greater insight?

Leadership and Communication

Just about everything done in life is enhanced by being a more effective communicator. Communication skills involve far more than persuasive talking or skillful writing. As one student leader told us, "God gave me two ears and one mouth; I figure that's a message to listen more than I talk." The Chinese language, like many Asian languages, includes symbols that depict related concepts to create new meaning. The Chinese pictogram for listening is made up of the symbols for ears, eyes, and heart (see Figure 5.2).

For most of us, hearing is a natural and almost automatic process. Listening, however, is more difficult and is a "purposive activity" requiring one to be intentionally "mindful" (Gudykunst, 1991, p. 38). True listening is far from a passive activity.

Listening and communicating in a pluralistic context requires one to listen with empathy. Listening with empathy is an "intellectual and emotional participation in another person's experience" (Bennett, 1979, p. 418). Empathy means you are using another person's standards and reference points to understand that person's experience. In contrast, sympathy is putting yourself in the other

FIGURE 5.2 Listening

Listening is when you use...

EYES

EARS

HEART

to give undivided attention.

Source: From *Transcultural leadership* (p. 37), by G. F. Simons, C. Vázquez, and P. R. Harris, 1993, Houston: Gulf Publishing. Copyright 1993 by Gulf Publishing. Used with permission. All rights reserved.

person's place but retaining your own perspective and still using your own standard of judgment.

You are using empathy if you are able to see yourself understanding the experiences of others from their point of view, imagining how they feel, and connecting with the emotions others are experiencing when they communicate. This means trying to see others as they would want you to see them and becoming able to understand what others are feeling without being told directly (Gudykunst, 1991, p. 122).

Imagine a friend with low self-confidence who says, "I made a comment in our meeting today and it was awful! People laughed at me." Showing *sympathy* and remembering times you have said things like that when you just needed a morale boost, you might say, "Oh, I am sure it wasn't that bad, and what you said was just humorous; no one probably even remembers." Responding with *empathy*, however, you might say, "I know how hard it is to speak up in that meeting. You don't talk much in that setting and it must have been very scary." The second response leads to more genuine dialogue than the first, which denied your friend's emotion and the apparent pain of the experience.

Renowned psychologist Carl Rogers would often require someone to restate what was said by a previous speaker to build a listening skill and an awareness of empathy. You learn to listen for empathy if you try to find a point of agreement or genuine understanding with a previous speaker and build on it instead of immediately criticizing, rejecting, or denying the point. "Seek first to understand, then to be understood" (Covey, 1991, p. 123). This requires one to pause, think, restate for understanding, then build on that point. Criticism that comes too quickly leaves the first speaker thinking he or she was not heard.

Empathic communication is difficult. Think of the complexity of processes in typical conversation. Both the content of what we say and how we say it influence the receiver in forming meaning from what we shared. Communication involves both verbal and nonverbal components. Think of the complexity in the verbal process:

What I meant to say

What I actually said

What you heard me say

What you think I mean

What you mean to say

What you actually say

What I hear you say

What I think you mean

Each element in that process is influenced by our cultural and gender lenses. For example, who would you say talks more, men or women? Common stereotypical perception is that women talk more, yet in almost any coeducational class or setting, men will likely be the first to speak, and they will speak more often for longer periods (Hart & Dalke, 1983). What men and women include in their speech varies as well. Deborah Tannen (1990) notes a difference in public speaking and private speaking. Another way of stating that is that males prefer report-talking and females engage in rapport-talking (Tannen, 1990, p. 77). Men's speech promotes their independence and is often to share information or opinions, to tell jokes, or to relate stories. Women's speech, even in public settings like meetings or classes, seeks to find connections with others and build relationships. Often, women will add a tag-line to the beginning or end of an opinion to provide bridges for others in the conversation. They do not want to stand out or apart. For example, a woman might say, "It's just my opinion, but . . . " or "I know there are many different views, but . . . " or "I think. . . . Do you agree or disagree with that?"

"I think that it is definitely important to listen to everybody. I was in a workshop, and one of the things that I learned is the word 'listen' also can spell 'silent.' I have a tendency to cut people off. Listening to people and being silent definitely lets you understand the person and lets them speak."—Marcie Avrunin is president of the Residence Hall Association at Boston University.

Assertive Communication

Socialization has clearly played an important role in how we have learned to converse with each other. Some women feel silenced, or have silenced themselves, by assuming their opinions were of less value than others or being socialized to avoid conflict. They have learned to be harmonizers or peacemakers. Some men feel it is more manly to be aggressive, assuming that their opinions are of more value and that others should acquiesce.

In every communication, each person has a right to be heard and a responsibility to listen. Each has a right to make a request or ask a question, and the recipient has the right to make his or her own decision without apology. Imagine an assertiveness continuum with three positions: a person might be unassertive, assertive, or aggressive (Alberti & Emmons, 1974). If you are unassertive, you passively give up your rights to others and let them take advantage of you. After an encounter, you might often wish you had said or done something different. Exhibit 5.3 illustrates this continuum.

Being assertive does not mean that you get your own way but that you did what you could to be understood. In a similar way, practicing relational leadership does not mean that the group will go along with what you think should happen in the group but that you would have done your best to respect their involvement, listen for true understanding, and be a productive community member.

Relational Empathy

Working effectively together requires "relational empathy" (Broome, 1993, p. 97). Relational empathy goes beyond mere understanding another "in which the emphasis is upon the re-creation in the listener of the meaning originally created by the speaker" (p. 98) and seeks shared meaning. Relational empathy recognizes the importance of context.

It may mean creating a new "third culture" (p. 103) that synthesizes the positions from the two individual perspectives, culture, and context and builds a new culture, an environment of empathy and insight. "As sharing of contexts takes place, organizations of diverse people start weaving a new context" (Simons, Vazquez, & Phillips, 1993, p. 39).

This third culture, or common context, develops its "own jargon, definitions, visions, and understandings" through which

EXHIBIT 5.3   Illustrations of Unassertive, Assertive, and Aggressive
Communication

The Question: "Could you substitute for me at the event tonight?
I have had something come up and cannot go after all."

Unassertive response: Even though you have several plans, you almost meekly reply. You deny your own rights and are intimidated into compliance. You may feel trapped or afraid to say no. You are fairly passive.	"OK, sure, I guess I can."
Assertive response: This response acknowledges that the other person had every right to ask, and you have a right to make your own decision. Being assertive means you can say no without feeling guilty or without apologizing.	"No, I have other plans and cannot do it." Depending on your style you might say, "I am sorry I cannot substitute. You might ask me again sometime when I would have a little more time to change my plans but thanks for thinking of me."
Aggressive response: This response denies the other person had any right even to ask for your help and is rarely appropriate.	"How dare you ask me to do this. You always slack off on your responsibilities and I won't stand for it."

members from different contexts can come together (p. 39). In these organizations, the culture says

- People are good, honest, and trustworthy.
- People are purposeful.
- Each individual has a unique contribution to make.
- Complex problems require local solutions.
- Me *and* you versus me *or* you. (Kiefer & Senge, 1984, pp. 75–78)

These beliefs about the goodness of people guide how we approach others. "Self-fulfilling prophecy" demonstrates that people may indeed become as you see them (Argyris in Yukl, 1994, p. 176). If you think no one will get along in the group, conflict is bound to occur and be harmful. If you believe people will avoid responsibility, then you may shape your own behavior to be controlling and negative, and you may act discouraged. Those with whom you are engaged are likely to become as you anticipate. Conversely, if you think people will try to get along, want to face their sources of conflict, be helpful, and take responsibility, then you approach your behaviors in hopeful ways that make that prophecy come true.

Imagine going to your first group project meeting thinking that people will just slack off, that you will end up doing all the work, and that no one really cares. You then look for evidence of those assumptions and at the smallest indication, you think "Ah-ha—I knew it!" Imagine instead going to your first project committee meeting thinking we are all busy so we will have to be careful about what we take on, but people will want to do their part, and we can come up with something pretty good. There are very real differences in environments, and groups may be negative in one setting and welcoming in another. The biggest difference in how a setting is perceived is the internal assumptions that guide expectations— how one will be in that setting and how being that way brings out responses in others. Building this new third culture meets the challenge inherent in the opening question, How am I like everyone else here?

Chapter Summary

The ability to understand others, be understood by others, and together create an effective organizational or group environment is the challenge of relational leadership. Truly understanding the influences of our cultural heritage, gender, and other aspects of our difference helps us work together toward change. We usually find we are more alike than we are different. Expecting commonalties, good will, and shared purposes can become a self-fulfilling prophecy. This awareness helps us create a new third culture in any group.

What's Next?

The next section of the book presents how relational leadership works in the settings of groups, organizations, and communities. Strategies for developing effective communities and the dynamics of group processes are presented to facilitate relationship building.

Chapter Activities

1. How are your communication, conflict-resolution, and decision-making behaviors or tendencies influenced by your perceptions of the gender, race, ethnicity, family practices, or other characteristics of others in the group?

2. Referring to David Hoopes's Intercultural Learning Process Model, think about where you are currently in this model. What stage best describes you now? What experiences will help you expand your openness to others?

3. Ask a friend who is different from you to take you to an event or gathering where the majority of others will be like your friend. What is easiest and hardest for you to understand about the practices in that group? Which of your own characteristics make it hardest for you to gain this understanding?

4. Refer to the Illustrations of Unassertive, Assertive, and Aggressive Communication chart (Exhibit 5.3). Think of a recent communication in which someone asked you to do something or asked for a favor. Based on this chart, what type of response did you give? Are you satisfied with that response? Why or why not? If not, how would you respond differently if you could do it over again?

Additional Readings

Gudykunst, W. B. (1991). *Bridging differences: Effective intergroup communication*. Newbury Park: Sage.

Helms, J. E. (1992). *A race is a nice thing to have*. Topeka, KS: Content Communications.

Tannen, D. (1990). *You just don't understand me: Women and men in conversation*. New York: Morrow.

PART THREE

Relationships, Environment, and the Practice of Leadership

Any leadership setting can be viewed as a community of people working together for shared purposes. Relational leadership is best practiced by framing any kind of group or organization as a community.

In the *Tao of Leadership*, Heider (1985) interprets,

The leader who understands how process unfolds uses as little force as possible and runs the group without pressuring people.

When force is used, conflict and argument follow. The group field degenerates. The climate is hostile, neither open nor nourishing.

The wise leader runs the group without fighting to have things a certain way. The leader's touch is light. The leader neither defends nor attacks.

Remember that consciousness, not selfishness, is both the means of teaching and the teaching itself.

Group members will challenge the ego of one who leads egocentrically. But one who leads selflessly and harmoniously will grow and endure. (p. 59)

This section explores how groups develop through stages, how they can be enhanced by attention to process, and how they can become building blocks for complex systems and organizations.

Leadership in groups and committees is substantially different than the complexity of leadership in organizational systems (for example, a college, a company, a hospital, a church).

Groups and organizations are best understood as communities of people working together to accomplish their shared purposes. Viewing all contexts in which leadership happens helps identify the important interdependence of people working together.

The final chapter of this section asserts that in all settings, relational leadership must be grounded in ethical processes, create ethical climates, and produce moral actions and outcomes that reflect the interests of the common good. Creating an ethical climate in all contexts is an important dimension of the Relational Leadership Model.

6

Interacting in Teams and Groups

You have just been invited to attend a meeting of a group that has similar interests as yours. You have been hearing about them for a few months. A current member who is in one of your classes asks if you'd like to attend. You get to the meeting and wonder: Does this group do what I think should be done? Will I be welcomed and valued? Can I make a contribution? Do I have enough in common with other members? Will I feel comfortable, or will things be done differently than I expect? Will the climate of this group be formal and stuffy or casual and friendly? Will this group be a community I can imagine identifying with?

The groups we join—classes, a work staff, committees, or church club or student organization—each take on a unique character or personality. Each group faces unique challenges in getting members involved meaningfully in shared work.

Chapter Overview

This chapter explores the characteristics of groups, the way groups develop, and the dynamics among group members, in order to emphasize how leadership in groups is process-oriented. The chapter presents concepts of teamwork and collaboration in group work. Leadership perspectives within groups feature applications of the Relational Leadership Model.

Understanding Groups

In an average week, you experience many types of groups. Some of these are highly structured, with clear roles and processes. Examples are a class or a student government senate meeting. Other groups are loosely structured and informal, like a discussion at a cafeteria table or a pick-up softball game. However, the kind of group that is pertinent to this discussion of leadership is not just any gathering of people. For our purposes, a group is considered to be three or more people "interacting and communicating interpersonally over time in order to reach a goal" (Cathcart, Samovar, & Henman, 1996, p. 1).

There are many different dimensions to how groups are structured, and each has implications for the leadership dynamics in that group. Three key dimensions that help us understand different types of groups are *purposes, structure,* and *time.*

1. *Purposes:* Groups exist for very different purposes; they range from friendship support groups to highly focused task groups to groups like a staff that delivers a service or a product over time. The architectural maxim that "form follows function" applies to groups as well. The purpose of a group should lead to the structures and processes needed to help the people in the group accomplish their purposes.

2. *Structure:* Structure relates to the mechanisms for how the people in the group relate to each other. Some groups are highly structured, with hierarchical roles or positions; others are undefined and evolve. Leadership roles in groups range from leaderless groups in which a group of people get together to do something but no one is the formal leader, to highly structured groups with a person in position as the formal leader—the president, chairperson, or director. In the informal setting, participants share needed roles, and leadership emerges or is all around in the group. In the formal, structured setting, the positional leader may be accountable but may use diverse styles ranging from highly autocratic (making all

the decisions and directing or controlling the followers) to engaging group members and empowering them through the relational leadership elements presented in this book.

3. *Time:* Groups exist over varying lengths of time. The group may be time-limited (meeting once to discuss a specific issue or completing a task in three meetings), or it may meet for a specified amount of extended time. Members may have a specified term of appointment, as would a representative from your major to the student senate for a year or in a class for a semester. The group may be an on-going group (like staff members at work, your family, or a fraternity). Time-limited groups are often called task forces or ad hoc committees. On-going groups use such names as committee, board, or council. The duration of the group raises different challenges. Time-limited groups with short time frames must quickly establish rapport, establish common purposes, and engage members rapidly to be active and focused on their role. On-going groups must deal with member motivation over time, establish processes to welcome and bring new members into the group, and keep the group focused on its purposes.

Think for a minute about the groups you are involved with. What are the purposes for which the groups were created? What structures help them accomplish those purposes? What roles do group members assume? How do these groups vary in time commitment? How does the length of time change the dynamics of the relationships? Those groups clearly develop differently. One challenge to leadership is to attend to the process of group development in order to facilitate the most involvement of the most members in the most effective way to make the best decisions.

Group Development

Robert is visiting his friend Sean before spring break and attends a meeting of Sean's Business Entrepreneurs Club. Sean is a cofounder of this group. Robert is puzzled at what he sees. The group argues for most of the meeting about whether they should engage in design-ing a logo for boxer shorts to sell and use the profits for a group party or whether they should design a t-shirt to raise money as a service for a local youth recreation league. There are two loud factions, with several people competing for attention and trying to be seen as leaders. Robert is puzzled by this and realizes that the group has some problems.

It would help Robert to realize that most groups, whether for-mal groups or informal groups, go through fairly predictable stages of their development as a group. One classic model labels these group development stages as *forming, storming, norming,* and *per-forming* (Tuckman, 1965). If the group can handle the important issues at each stage, it can stay vibrant and healthy. If the group is struggling, it can re-visit a stage to intentionally re-learn together how to be effective. Sean's group is struggling with the storming process, which is characterized by differing opinions and goals.

Forming

Forming is the group's initial stage of coming together and refers to such tasks as member recruitment and affiliation. What informa-tion do people need? When will the group meet? How will the group communicate? What will the type of commitment mean? What are the purposes and mission of the group? What agreement is needed to make this group functional? The forming stage of development is when team building initially occurs and trust is established. Successful strategies of this forming stage include build-ing open, trusting relationships that value inclusion.

Storming

Storming is the stage when the group starts to get in gear and dif-ferences of opinion begin to emerge. If the group is not clear about its purposes and goals, or if the group cannot agree on shared goals, then it might collapse at this stage. Members of Sean's Business Entrepreneurs Club have vastly different expectations of what they think the group should do: service or profit or both. They need to re-visit some of the processes of the forming stage and resolve that issue so they can deal with the decisions of what projects to select. In this stage, individuals engage in self-assertion to get their needs recognized and addressed.

Storming may be a short process in which the group comes to pretty clear direction, or it can be destructive. Some groups establish such trust in each other and in their process that the storming process is resolved quickly. Indeed, some members who feel like storming may never raise their issues because they are strongly connected to shared purpose and know their assertions would not be useful. Some groups exist in this storming phase and develop adversarial models of operating. They may depend on it so much that it becomes the way of getting their work done. The two-party political system and the check-and-balance processes of government are examples. Other groups have become accustomed to adversarial processes but would do better to develop more effective ways of relating. Examples include the constant conflict on some campuses among faculty and administrators or between the Greek and independent leaders in the student senate.

Norming

Norming follows storming. Once the group resolves key differences, it establishes patterns of how it gets work done. The group sets up formal or informal procedures for which things come to the whole group, which reports are needed, who is involved in what, and how people interact. At this stage, individuals in the group deal with both intimacy and identity. Members of the group begin to understand the group's culture. For example, do meetings always start ten minutes late so people can visit with each other for a few minutes first? Do members understand whether they should volunteer for new projects or wait to be invited? The group practices that evolve in the norming stage are often more obvious to outsiders than to those in the group. These practices and characteristics might also describe the personality of the group.

Performing

Performing is the fourth stage of group development. Built on the strong foundation of the previous three stages, the group now cycles into a mature "stage of equilibrium"—getting its work done (Lippitt, 1973, p. 229). Time-limited groups may need to quickly get to the performing stage to get their work done in a timely way. They need to intentionally and effectively work through the previous stages and not skip right to performing without the foundational processes. Time-limited groups still need the team-building steps so essential in the forming stage, need to encourage diversity of opinion and wrestle with common purpose in the storming stage, and clearly establish group processes in the norming stage to effectively perform their task. On-going groups with longtime durations will have to stay renewed (see Chapter Ten) and continually recycle to be effective. Otherwise, they risk becoming dysfunctional or even terminating. Even the most successful groups have to revisit this cycle when new members join (forming), when new issues challenge the group's purposes (storming), or when new processes are needed because old ones no longer work (norming). Exhibit 6.1 illustrates the aspects of the Relational Leadership Model that might help the group successfully deal with each stage of its development.

Groups exist over different time frames. All short-term groups like task forces and special topic committees need to plan on their eventual termination. Groups that intend to exist for a long time, often with no planned end in sight, need to stay vibrant and healthy if they are to continue effectively. Groups that do not engage in a continual re-visiting of the cycle to stay active and vital may find themselves moving toward a final stage of group

EXHIBIT 6.1 Relational Leadership and Stages of Group Development

When the group is. . . .	Relational leadership philosophy would encourage participants to...
Forming	Be inclusive and empowering. Make sure all the shareholders and stakeholders are involved. Seek diverse members to bring talent to the group. Model the processes of inclusion and shared leadership. Identify common purposes and targets of change. Create a climate where each person matters and build commitment to the group as a community of practice.
Storming	Be ethical and open. Be patient to give divergent views a full hearing. Be aware when you might be biased or blocking the full participation of another. Handle conflict directly, civilly, and openly encouraging participants to identify their biases. Revisit the purposes of the group and targets of change.
Norming	Be fair with processes. Practice collaboration. Keep new members welcomed, informed, and involved. Clarify individual's responsibility to/expectations of the group and the group's responsibilities/expectation of individuals.
Performing	Celebrate accomplishments and find renewal in relationships. Empower members to learn new skills and share roles in new ways to stay fresh. Revisit purposes and rebuild commitment.

development—dissolution. If a group does not maintain new members or keep up with current issues and needs, it may find itself unable to perform and might need to dissolve. A new group might need to be formed with new purposes and new members.

We visited a campus recently where the former Black Student Union (BSU) took the bold step of voting itself out of existence. Its programs had developed into social events with dwindling attendance. Most members felt that they could do social events through other avenues and that this group needed a broader scope. The circumstances on campus led many of the African American student leaders to think they needed a group with a more active educational and campus advocacy role. The key members decided to involve other non-black student leaders in a planning session and formed a new group named Umoja—a Swahili word for unity. They sought a more diverse membership around their new purposes and were widely credited on that campus for strong programs and events that attracted a wide range of participants and benefited the whole campus. Although it would have been perfectly fine for this BSU to evolve into a social organization, it was not the intent of the leaders or members that the focus be social, so they boldly reorganized to accomplish social action and campus change around racial and ethnic unity. This was indeed a strong and courageous action; few groups would vote themselves out of existence or go through such a transformation—yet many groups need to do so.

Active participants need to continually assess their group's development. We have a colleague who encourages group members always to ask, "Should we, could we, are we?" "Should we?" leads a group to clarify their purposes and direction. "Could we?" asks the group to anticipate the storming and norming stages to see if they are up to the task. "Are we?" is the constant formative evaluation cycle in the performing stage to see if the group is truly doing what it sets out to do. Evaluation is both formative and summative. Formative evaluation—Are we?—is asked at various times for the purpose of reshaping plans and directions. Summative evaluation might ask, Did we?, at the end of a task or event to see if it met original plans. When the cook tastes the soup it is formative evaluation, but when the customer tastes the soup it is a summative evaluation.

Dynamics in Groups

Groups engage in various processes that are often called group dynamics. Group dynamics is the study of the group's life (Johnson

& Johnson, 1994). Group dynamics include such processes as how the group makes decisions, how the group handles its conflict, and how the group meets its leadership needs.

Group Roles

One of the foundations for understanding group dynamics is to recognize that in any interactive setting, individuals engage in communication patterns that may signal roles they are adopting in the group. Groups depend on two kinds of roles: group-building roles and task roles. Participants engaging in both kinds of roles are absolutely essential to effective group dynamics. Group-building roles are actions that focus on the group as people, including the relationships among members. Group-building roles attend to the process of the group. These have also been called group maintenance roles. Task roles focus on accomplishing the purposes of the group, including giving information and opinions and moving the group along on tasks by summarizing and by using various decision-making strategies. Task roles are focused on the content of the group discussion.

On occasion, group members might demonstrate some individual dysfunctional roles that actually hamper the group's progress. Someone may doggedly push his or her point like a broken record, even if the group is ready to move on. A person like this is called a special interest pleader and may have a secret reason for saying things—a hidden agenda. A member may resist or block any group action by being negative and disagreeable on everything. A person like that is called a blocker. Dysfunctional roles are those that truly hamper a group's goals or progress. Participants, however, who truly are concerned about a course of action and express negative opinions are helpful to the group and should not be confused with someone who is a blocker. Someone who acts like a clown and never takes the group seriously may be exhibiting a dysfunctional role but should not be confused with someone who effectively uses humor (no matter how goofy) to relieve tension or create harmony.

Someone who sits in the back reading a newspaper and not even listening is a nonparticipant, whereas an active member (who might typically be called a follower) is someone who is actively engaged in listening and thinking and who is willing to support the group's decisions.

Each of us has a preferred set of practices we are most comfortable with in a group. This might be called our role set. You may find it comfortable or easier in a group to seek opinions from others, make sure people have a chance to share their ideas, or summarize what was discussed before a vote. Someone else might like to share an opinion or give information. To perform effectively, the group needs participants to practice both task and group-building roles. You may prefer to do mostly group-building functions or mostly task things.

While any individual participant or positional leader may not perform in all roles comfortably, it is useful to know which roles the group needs and ask someone to engage in them. For example, you might be terrible at summarizing discussions because it all seems a jumble to you, but if you know that a summary is needed before the group makes its final decision, you can intervene. In this case, you might say, "It would help me if someone would summarize the key points on both sides of this issue so I can fully understand before I vote." Someone who is comfortable with that role will provide that needed process. It is empowering for participants to be asked to contribute their preferred roles to the group process.

Examples of common roles that help us understand group dynamics are presented in Exhibit 6.2. These roles have evolved from the early group dynamics research in the 1940s and 1950s (Benne & Sheats, 1948; Knowles & Knowles, 1959). Think of examples you use or see others using.

Describe the various roles you have played in different groups. Are there any similarities between groups? Do you find yourself playing the same role no matter what the group? Or do your roles vary? Do the roles you play give you any insights into how you act when a member of a group?

EXHIBIT 6.2 Examples of Common Roles in Groups

Task Roles	Role Description	Example of Role in Use
Information seeker	Aware that the group needs more facts or data before proceeding.	"We cannot vote yet on this, we need more information first so let's ask Sharon to brief us at the next meeting."
Opinion seeker	Aware that the group needs more insight, ideas, or opinions before proceeding.	"What do you think, Roger? You have had a lot of experience with this topic."
Opinion giver	Sharing one's views, feelings, or ideas so the group has the benefit of your thinking.	"I strongly think we must increase the budget for this project if we intend to serve more students."
Summarizer	Condensing the nature of "the opinions" or discussion in a capsule format for clarity.	"Before we go further, is it accurate to say that while some of us think we should not spend much money, we all agree we should do this project?"
Clarifier	Elaborating or explaining ideas in new words to add meaning. Showing how something might work if adopted.	"Jim, did you mean we need more involvement meaning quantity or better involvement like quality?"

Exhibit 6.2 Continued

Group Building Roles	Role Description	Example of Role in Use
Gatekeeper	Inviting those who have not yet spoken or who have been trying to say something into the conversation.	"Tanya has been trying to say something on this for a while—I'd like to hear what that is."
Encourager	Welcoming all individuals and diverse ideas. A warm response to promote the inclusion and empowerment of others.	"What the new members just said about this issue was really enlightening. I am really glad you took some risks to tell us that. Thanks."
Mediator	Someone who harmonizes conflict and seeks to straighten out opposing points of view in a clear way.	"You two don't seem as far apart on this issue as it might seem. You both value the same thing and have many points of agreement."
Follower	An active listener who willingly supports the group's actions and decisions.	"I haven't said much, but this has been a great discussion and I feel really informed. I am comfortable with the decision."

Source: Based on the early work of Benne & Sheats (1948), and Knowles & Knowles (1959).

Group Norms

Imagine attending your first meeting of an on-going group. You walk into the room and begin observing other group members as a clue to what is acceptable or expected. Does the group stay focused on its agenda or wander into other discussions? Do members seem friendly and social or distant and isolated? Do people sit formally and wait to be called on by the chair, or is there a more open discussion? All of these kinds of practices are the norms or rules of conduct that lead to consistent practices in a group.

Some norms are explicit and clearly seen by all participants. When you play cards you expect to follow suit; when you play baseball, you expect to bat in order. When your group uses Robert's Rules of Order, you know you must make motions, seek a second to the motion, speak in turn, and plan to vote on the motion eventually. Other norms may have evolved through the cultural practices of the group—arranging the chairs in a circle, starting each meeting with introductions of new members and guests, congratulating group members on their accomplishments, or celebrating birthdays.

Group norms contribute to the concept of group climate. Climate is like the group's personality. Just as individuals have personality, so do groups. One group you are in is open, flexible, supportive, uses humor often, and views each person as important; another might be formal, guarded, distrusting, impersonal, and stuffy. If you want your group to have a distinct personality, it is useful to consider what group norms will lead to those desired outcomes. The Relational Leadership Model is designed to create a group in which members feel highly engaged.

Creative Conflict

The storming stage of group development can paralyze a group's progress. Unresolved conflict at any stage can create a group climate that is tense and hostile, or it can be an effective method for improving the group's outcomes.

What words or emotions come to mind when you think of the term *conflict*? For most people, the idea of conflict is uncomfortable and creates knots in their stomachs; most of us would prefer harmony. In many earlier leadership books, the term *conflict* does not even appear in the index, or the topic is handled in a power dynamics model, or in a section on how to win your own way.

Conflict might result from such things as clashes in personalities, expectations of roles (role conflict), or conflict over ideas. Personality conflicts can often be understood by returning to personality pref-erences and learning preferences that were presented in Chapters Four and Five and being more focused on listening and under-standing others. Role conflicts are best handled by thinking of what assumptions you might be bringing to the conflict about your own role or your expectations of others that clash with their assump-tions. Conflict in ideas is often called controversy, and a full airing of differences of opinions and ideas is essential for a group to make the best decisions. Such controversies need to be handled with civility and open dialogue (A *Social Change Model of Leadership Development*, 1996). Exhibit 6.3 illustrates some of the advantages and liabilities of conflict in groups.

It is not uncommon for people to want to avoid conflict, so they often ignore it or pretend it does not exist. Some say it is like hav-ing an elephant in the room. Everyone is aware of the tension that a huge conflict creates—like an elephant standing in the corner—but no one talks about it. Still others diffuse conflict by acting as if it is unimportant or can be handled at another time. True commu-nities resolve conflicts rather than avoid them. That is often the best way. When conflict is confronted, it is usually best to employ negotiation and mediation strategies instead of power strategies.

The resulting different conflict resolution outcomes have been described as win-win, win-lose, and lose-lose. In win-win outcomes, both sides are heard and are satisfied with the resolution of their dif-ferences. The group often emerges as stronger for the discussion, and the decisions made may be significantly better than they would have been without the dialogue. In win-lose outcomes, one side uses power strategies to win by out-talking, putting down, or rush-ing to a premature vote. But in the process, a loser is created. The participants who lost (and their potential allies) feel margin-alized, angry, and even resentful. The group's harmony is jeopar-dized and participants are not empowered or included. In lose-lose outcomes, both sides use power strategies and get so entrenched, rigid, or hurtful that no effective resolution is reached, even in compromise.

EXHIBIT 6.3 Understanding Conflict

Advantages of Conflict	*Liabilities of Conflict*
1. Can increase motivation and energy.	1. Can be debilitating
2. Clarifies issues and positions.	2. Can distract from goal achievement.
3. Can build internal cohesiveness and espirit. de corps	3. Can cause defensiveness and rigidity.
4. Can lead to innovation and creativity.	4. Can cause distortions of reality
5. Can increase self-awareness.	5. Often becomes a negatively reinforcing cycle.
6. May be a means of dealing with internal conflicts.	6. Tends to escalate (more serious) and to proliferate (more issues).
7. Can lead to a new synthesis of ideas or methods.	7. Efforts to resolve are often not reciprocated.

Source: Reprinted with the permission of Simon & Schuster from *The Art of Leadership* (p. 48) by Lin Bothwell. Copyright © 1983 by Lin Bothwell.

Reciprocal and relational models of leadership know that some conflict is natural and inevitable. The Relational Leadership Model encourages processes to handle conflict that will promote inclusivity and empowerment. By anticipating that when great people get together they will have differences of ideas and approaches, the group can set some ground rules (that is, group norms) to guide the openness and honesty with which they will raise issues of possible conflict. These ground rules can "create an environment 'safe' for differences" (Lappé & Du Bois, 1994, p. 251). Such ground rules might include agreeing that everyone will have a chance to be heard who wants to speak and that the group will look for points of agreement as well as disagreements. Handling all these disagreements with civility is essential. Each person should commit to making "no permanent enemies" in the group (Lappé & Du Bois, 1994, p. 255) in order to be inclusive to all members' rights to their opinions.

"When a group handles conflict within itself, the most important thing is to deal with the problem immediately. Nothing hurts a group more than allowing a conflict or problem to fester or grow for an extended period of time. It can only worsen and therefore weaken the group. Also important in dealing with conflict is to understand both sides; doing this will allow for an easier time of solving the problem. Conflict, when resolved, is very helpful to a group. In fact, having the confidence of knowing that any problem or conflict can be resolved is extremely beneficial and can strengthen the dynamic of the group."—Hunter Ruch is a third-year student at the University of Virginia. He is double majoring in architectural history and religious studies, and is active with the Intervarsity Christian Fellowship.

Conflicts are useful when they raise perspectives that need attention before the group moves to resolution. The more homogeneous a group may be, the more essential to think through an issue from multiple perspectives. Even if there is little diversity in the group, someone might say, "If there were freshmen students here, how would they see this policy, and should we reconsider any parts of it?" or "If older students were here, would they see any issues we have not yet addressed?" At least decisions are informed by the broadest possible thinking, even if no person is physically present who holds a divergent view.

Group Decision Making

Traditional views of leadership often assume that a group or organization has a formal leader with the authority and responsibility for making final decisions. Indeed, on many occasions the positional leader has to make a decision on behalf of the group. Some possible reasons for this are: there may be no time to hold a group meeting or consult with group members; the leader may be representing the group in another meeting and need to speak for the group; or the leader might judge that the decision is not a major one and not worth group time and energy. Whenever a positional leader is faced with making an individual decision, the Relational Leadership Model will be useful in guiding the decision process. The leader should ask herself:

What opinions do my group members have about this issue? (inclusive)

Will this decision heighten our involvement or limit involvement? (empowering)

Is this the right thing to do? Is it principled? (ethical)

Does this decision support our vision and mission? (purposeful)

Should I slow down making this decision so that others can get involved? (process-oriented)

In formal organizations with positional leaders, participative leadership is often thought to involve "the use of decision procedures intended to *allow* other people some influence over the leader's decisions" (Yukl, 1989, p. 83 [emphasis added]). The values in participative leadership acknowledge that a better decision is made and receives greater acceptance when those involved are part of that decision process. Group members may be empowered, learn more effective leadership skills, and sustain a high commitment to the process when others are involved. You will see a profound philosophical difference when you examine the word *allow* in the definition of participative leadership. *Allow* correctly identifies who—the positional leader—has responsibility and who can involve or not involve others, as that leader chooses. In most work settings and in volunteer organizations, for the leader to presume that she should make the decision or "allow" the involvement of others is a conventional way of looking at the situation. A more useful perception would be to assume instead that the unit (the organization, the work unit, the group) *must* be involved with key decisions—has the right to be and should be. Now the question becomes how they best should be involved, not whether they should be. Clearly, there is tension in formal settings about the authority and role of participants in the decision process. We sense a shift in people's expectations—that they want, indeed often demand, a role in decision making. Examples include parent involvement in school-based management and employee involvement in selecting benefits packages.

Yukl (1989) identifies a continuum of four possible decision-making procedures: autocratic → consultation → joint decision → delegation or participation. They range in amount of influence others have on the decision from no influence (in which an autocratic decision is made) to high influence of others in the process (in which complete delegation has occurred).

Johnson and Johnson (1994) present seven methods of decision making. Each of the decision-making methods in Exhibit 6.4 may have its own purpose, but relational leadership would promote consensus models whenever possible. When a trusting group climate exists, groups may chose other models and be comfortable using minority control or majority control.

In our view, some decisions are best made by an authority or expert. However, most groups would benefit by shifting important decisions that affect the entire community to a discussion and consensus model. More and more participants in groups expect to be involved in decision making and, indeed, involvement is essential to a relational, empowering approach. Positional leaders who make important decisions in an autocratic manner find that they alienate

EXHIBIT 6.4   Advantages and Disadvantages of Decision-Making
Methods

Methods of Decision Making	Disadvantages	Advantages
1. Decision by authority without discussion	One person is not a good resource for every decision; advantages of group interaction are lost; no commitment to implementing the decision is developed among other group members; resentment and disagreement may result in sabotage and deterioration of group effectiveness; resources of other members are not used.	Applies more to administrative needs; useful for simple, routine decisions; should be used when very little time is available to make the decision, when group members expect the designated leader to make the decision, and when group members lack the skills and information to make the decision any other way.
2. Expert member	It is difficult to determine who the expert is; no commitment to implement the decision is built; advantages of group interaction are lost; resentment and disagreement may result in sabotage and deterioration of group effectiveness; resources of other members are not used.	Useful when the expertise of one person is so far superior to that of all other group members that little is to be gained by discussion; should be used when the need for membership action in implementing the decision is slight.

continued

EXHIBIT 6.4 Continued

Methods of Decision Making	Disadvantages	Advantages
3. Average members' opinions	There is not enough interaction among group members for them to gain from each other's resources and from the benefits of group discussion; no commitment to implement the decision is built; unresolved conflict and controversy may damage group effectiveness in the future.	Useful when it is difficult to get group members together to talk when the decision is so urgent that there is no time for group discussion, when member commitment is not necessary for implementing the decision, and when group members lack the skills and information to make the decision any other way; applicable to simple, routine decisions.
4. Decision by authority after discussion	Does not develop commitment to implement the decision; does not resolve the controversies and conflicts among group members; tends to create situations in which group members either compete to impress the designated leader or tell the leader what they think he or she wants to hear.	Uses the resources of the group members more than previous methods; gains some of the benefits of group discussion.

continued

EXHIBIT 6.4 Continued

Methods of Decision Making	Disadvantages	Advantages
5. Majority control	Usually leaves an alienated minority, which damages future group effectiveness; relevant resources of many group members may be lost; full commitment to implement the decision is absent; full benefit of group interaction is not obtained.	Can be used when sufficient time is lacking for decision by consensus or when the decision is not so important that consensus needs to be used and when complete member commitment is not necessary for implementing the decision; closes discussion on issues that are not highly important for the group.

Source: From *Joining together: Group theory and group skills (Fifth edition)* (pp. 238–239), by D. W. Johnson and F. P. Johnson, 1994, Boston: Allyn and Bacon. Copyright 1994 by Allyn and Bacon. Reprinted/adapted with permission.

workers and group members, even when they, as leaders, have the authority to make those decisions.

Consensus does not mean that every single decision is made by the entire group. Not all decisions warrant the attention of the entire group. It would be absurd to waste group members' time or resources by meeting on everything. It is useful to think of two dimensions of decisions: the need for *quality* in the decision and the need for *acceptance* of the decision. Quality of the decision refers to its importance and accuracy. The film committee may decide to hold a cartoon fest, but the particular cartoons selected may not matter. A committee or individual can decide. Any decision that needs high acceptance by those involved usually has to be handled in an open and inclusive manner. The cartoon-fest committee may need help staffing the event, but to assign film committee members to time slots might be a mistake. The approach to staffing requires high acceptance; these members might need to be involved in the scheduling.

Consensus brings the highest commitment among participants, is the most informed by the diverse knowledge bases in the group, and takes the most time. Consensus requires that the group become comfortable with handling conflict and be informed by the rising controversies that can lead to a good decision. Groups that are uncomfortable with controversy or who do not handle it in a civil manner may move prematurely to vote just to get the group to move on. Consensus requires that the group be willing to use strategies like active listening, compromising, and working in a collaborative manner.

Teamwork

Many look to the sports metaphor of a team to illustrate how individuals need to work together toward a common purpose. "We can no longer afford the luxury of even a few individualists working in isolation from the rest of the organization. . . . Strength is not in the individuals, but in the team. Put a group of superstars together on any team, whether baseball, hockey, football or soccer, and they will still lose if they operate as individual superstars. But once they start operating as a team, they become unbeatable" (Taylor, 1989, pp. 124–125). Many organizations have adopted that metaphor and reconceptualized the work unit as a team. Hospitals have a team for each patient with a primary care nurse as team coordinator, and businesses have cross-functional teams that bring together staff from shipping, marketing, and manufacturing to do product advancement. This metaphor brings implications for morale, motivation, support, common purpose, diverse roles, and inclusion. Previously, we have used the metaphor of jazz and referred to participants as an ensemble. In this book, we also use community as a metaphor for groups of participants.

Whatever the metaphor, participants in the same group should share the goal of working toward being an effective team. Strong ensemble casts on popular TV shows often show the reciprocity of collaborators working together for shared purposes. Think of the appreciation of differences among the characters of the TV series M*A*S*H, who had an absolute trust in each other for their competence and commitment to quality work despite their divergent personalities and relationships. Think of the characters of *Star Trek: The Next Generation*. They knew each other's personalities and values so well that even the slightest deviation in their behavior raised questions to determine if their brains had been taken over by some microscopic alien life form because crew members knew they would not normally have behaved as they were now behaving. They had to stand together or the Enterprise would not survive. The casts of such shows as *Saved By the Bell*, *Seinfeld*, *Living Single*, *Friends*, and even *The Muppets* are strong ensembles who recognize their symbiosis as actors and as characters in their roles.

Teams and Groups.   Just as collections of people do not automatically constitute groups, all groups are not teams. Teams are, however, one kind of group. Teams are more than just a group of people working together. A team is two or more people engaging in structured interpersonal interactions who "(1) are aware of their positive interdependence as they strive to achieve mutual goals, (2) interact while they do so, (3) are aware of who is and is not a member of the team, (4) have specific roles or functions to perform, and (5) have a limited life-span of membership" (Johnson & Johnson, 1994, p. 503). Types of teams range from teams that function like working groups, in which individual accountability is high (such as a golf team), to true teams that couldn't accomplish their goals individually (such as a football team or the homecoming committee). Exhibit 6.5 shows the distinction between working groups and teams.

Team Learning.   Individual learning is the conventional norm as a college student. Only you can read that book, write that computer

EXHIBIT 6.5 Working Groups Versus Teams

Working Groups	Teams
A strong, clearly focused leader is appointed.	Shared leadership responsibilities exist among members.
The general organizational mission is the group's purpose.	A specific, well-defined purpose that is unique to the team.
Individual work provides the only products.	Team and individual work develop products.
Effectiveness is measured indirectly by group's influence on others (e.g., financial performance of business, student scores on standardized examinations).	Effectiveness is measured directly by assessing teamwork products.
Individual accountability only is evident.	Both team and individual accountability are evident.
Individual accomplishments are recognized and regarded.	Team celebration. Individual efforts that contribute to the team's success are also recognized and celebrated.
Meetings are efficiently run and last for short periods of time.	Meetings with open-ended discussion and include active problem solving.
In meetings members discuss, decide, and delegate.	In meetings members discuss, decide, and do real work together.

Source: From *Joining together: Group theory and group skills (Sixth edition)* (p. 504), by D. W. Johnson and F. P. Johnson, 1994, Boston: Allyn and Bacon. Copyright 1994 by Allyn and Bacon. Reprinted/adapted with permission.

program, or take that test. However, learning occurs in many other ways—through group projects, in experiential settings, and in study groups. Whenever a team has a shared responsibility, it has to find a way to learn together, not just learn separately. "The learning unit of organizations are 'teams,' groups of people who need one another to act" (Senge, 1993, p. 134). Approaches to team learning include accumulating the learning preference of the majority of members (for example, a scientific research group in which everyone prefers facts and details or a friendship group in which most are flexible and casual). However, intentional team learning requires intentional practices.

"Groups learn by doing. The [academic] minor I am in is going to sponsor and organize a LeaderShape Institute at Penn State, and we decided the best way to learn how to put on an institute was by being a part of one. And now after being a part of LeaderShape with the other Pennstaters who are going to set up LeaderShape, I know we have learned far more by doing than we would have any other way."—Carl Schlemmer is a civil-environmental engineering major at Pennsylvania State University and member of their 1997 LeaderShape team.

Team learning happens in dialogue with each other and through reflection on shared experiences. Dialogue is a "sustained collective inquiry into everyday experience and what we take for granted" (Senge, Kleiner, Roberts, Ross, & Smith, 1994, p. 353). Dialogue is far more than the mere words used to share meaning. It includes the tone of voice, the laughter, pauses, difficulty of finding the right words, and amount of discussion needed to come to some meaning. When a team is in dialogue, participants are aware of the process of their communication as well as its content. For true understanding to result, it is important that both teams and groups establish ground rules or norms to handle their inevitable controversies with civility (A *Social Change Model of Leadership Development*, 1996).

Dialogue and discussion are two slightly different processes. Some groups mistakenly engage in discussion in which members share their own views with minimal attempts at true understanding. This can lead to debate, which only beats down opposing views or leads to a deterioration of relationships that can unravel a group. Groups that value learning together will establish true dialogue methods, the goals of which are to learn together while engaging in change. Dialogue is built into the processes of reflection, which involve thinking together. Perhaps the best lesson for dialogue is "Don't just do something, stand there" (Isaacs, as cited in Senge et al., 1994, p. 375). Your obligation as a listener is to understand and connect. Dialogue encourages you to *clarify* your points, not *prove* them. We encourage you to refer to Chapter Five to review how different individuals learn to truly listen to each other.

"I like a saying I heard, 'Find the truth in what you oppose; find the fault in what you espouse'!"—Peter Tate is president of the Black Greek Association and aims for a career in hospital administration. He is a biology and public health major at the University of Michigan.

Leadership Implications. "In a productive work community, leaders are not commanders and controllers, bosses and big shots. They are servers and supporters, partners and providers." (Kouzes & Posner, 1993, p. 7). Leaders in teamwork settings are also facilitators of team learning. Facilitating team learning requires individual participants to understand their motivations, to advocate for their own interests while being open to hearing others' points of view, and to find common ground (Ross, 1994b).

Participants and leaders must all share the responsibility of processing any shared group experience to make it a conscious process as a team. Successes need to be understood as well as failures. Too often, groups do not reflect on why something worked really well but spend hours and hours finding errors in failures.

Chapter Summary

Groups are the building blocks of communities of practice. We function in many different kinds of groups that are at different stages of development. This chapter presented group development models and principles of group dynamics, including aspects of decision making, conflict resolution, and team learning, that inform group practices.

What's Next?

Organizations are made up of multiple groups and teams. The next chapter explores how formal organizations function and the unique role of leadership in the organizational context.

Chapter Activities

1. Analyze several groups of which you are a member according to the key dimensions of purpose, structure, and time. How are the groups similar? How are they different?

2. Think of a group of which you were a member. Using Tuckman's model as a framework, describe what it was like to be a member of the group in each of the four stages. Did the group experience any problems? In which stage? What did you do to resolve the problems? Have you ever known a group to dissolve itself? If yes, what were the situations surrounding this decision? Identify a group that should dissolve itself. Why do you think they do not take this final step?

3. Think about your personal style in conflict situations. Now read the descriptions that follow and assign a percentage to each conflict style based on how often you use it. Your total percentages should add up to 100 percent.

Style 1: I avoid conflict and stay away from issues involving conflict.

Style 2: I want to be the winner in conflict situations.

Style 3: I want to be liked so I avoid conflict.

Style 4: I believe in compromise.

Style 5: I view conflict as an opportunity to identify and solve problems.

What are the advantages and disadvantages of each style? Consider your most preferred styles and identify circumstances when these styles are most and least effective for you.

4. Consider each of the different methods of making decisions found in Exhibit 6.4. What are some benefits and drawbacks of each for a group you know best? Describe an experience when each might be a preferred method of making a group decision.

5. Think of the best team of which you have ever been a member. This could be any kind of team (newspaper staff, student government, club or organization, scouts, 4–H, sports team). What made this team special? Was there ever a time when this team had to learn something? Describe that experience.

6. Think of a group you have been a member of since it began. Turn to Exhibit 6.6 and reflect on how this group has changed over time.

Place a B on each item of the scale reflective of how the group functioned at the beginning; place an M to reflect the middle as the group began to mature; and place a T for where it is today.

EXHIBIT 6.6 Assessing Your Group

Place a check on the scale to indicate how you would assess your group's dynamics as an organization. You could ask other group members to complete this scale as well and establish a profile of group strengths and weaknesses.

1. How clear is the group's purpose?

/—————————/—————————/—————————/—————————/

Unclear or
confused

Very clear,
all understand

2. How are members valued?

/—————————/—————————/—————————/—————————/

Many feel
unimportant

All are included
and important
to the group

3. How is power distributed in the group?

/—————————/—————————/—————————/—————————/

Power is held by
one or a few

Power is shared;
members feel
empowered in
the group

4. How is leadership handled in the group?

/—————————/—————————/—————————/—————————/

Leadership comes
only from the top

Leadership
is shared
among most
participants

5. Is an ethical climate sustained in your group?

/—————————/—————————/—————————/—————————/

Members do what
they want with no
regard to others

Members have
integrity and
principles are
valued

continued

EXHIBIT 6.6 Continued

6. How are decisions made in this group?

|_____/_____/_____/_____|

A few people decide
everything with little
group input

Decisions are
not final until
consensus is
reached

7. How concerned is the group about process?

|_____/_____/_____/_____|

Pays no attention
to process

Very intentional
about process

8. How purposeful is this group about accomplishing change?

|_____/_____/_____/_____|

Often floundering

Very clear and
intentional

Additional Readings

Howard, V. A., & Barton, M. A. (1992). *Thinking together*. New York: William Morrow.

Johnson, D. W., & Johnson, F. P. (1994). *Joining together: Group theory and group skills* (5th ed.). Boston: Allyn & Bacon.

7

Understanding Complex Organizations

You, as a student, see and experience numerous organizations every day. You may get up in the morning and read the campus newspaper or tune in to the student radio station—both are important student organizations. You have undoubtedly visited some campus administrative office and had the frustrating experience of trying to work with a bureaucratic organization. Campus clinics help keep you healthy, and the campus police help keep you safe.

Different types of student government organizations represent student views and help protect student rights. Student programming boards work closely with administrative offices to provide educational, cultural, social, and recreational activities for the campus. Campus service organizations like Habitat for Humanity or Circle-K are local branches of larger, international organizations; they provide opportunities for students to help those in need. Various forms of business organizations provide opportunities for students to make money by working on and off campus. Organizations of all kinds exist everywhere in and around campus and add to the quality of life for everyone. Leadership in organizations is both prevalent and common in our everyday lives, both on and off campus.

Chapter Overview

In the previous chapter, we explored leadership within group settings. In this chapter, we expand the scope of the environment and discuss leadership in an organizational context. Within this context, the importance of focusing on the five aspects of the Relational Leadership Model (inclusive, empowering, purposeful, ethical, and process-oriented) become even more evident.

Groups and Organizations

It can be difficult to differentiate between groups and organizations. Some of the differences are obvious; some are more subtle. One way to get a sense of the difference can be shown by answering the who?, what?, when?, where?, how?, and why? questions (Exhibit 7.1). Organizations are large collections of groups that interact in a continuous manner within a complex structure to accomplish a specific purpose. Whereas proximity of location has traditionally been a determining factor for organizations, we will see that this is not always the case.

EXHIBIT 7.1   Groups and Organizations

	Groups	Organizations
Who?	Small-to-medium (3+ participants)	Large (20+ participants)
What?	Collections of individuals	Collections of groups
When?	Continuous interactions	Continuous interactions
Where?	Close proximity	Proximity unimportant (ranges from close to far away)
How?	Simple structures	Complex structures
Why?	Purpose	Purpose

Organizations have many participants. Remember when you were growing up and you played with your best friend? Although sometimes painful, it was relatively easy to work out any problems or difficulties you had with each other. As your friendship group expanded, things got more difficult. All of a sudden, you realized that not everyone wanted to play the same game you did or that they wanted to play the game differently. Now, expand your world even further to your high school or places of employment. Being associated with more and more people meant being exposed to different values, ideas, and ways of doing things. This probably made life more interesting, as well as more complicated.

Organizations are collections of groups. Imagine a college or university with students, professors, administrators, alumni, parents, a board of regents, legislators, and others—all working together to try to accomplish basically the same thing—to educate students. Yet each of these groups views the education of students in a different way. What groups participate in the life of your organization?

Interactions within organizations are continuous. The success of any organization depends on the various groups within it staying connected so they can work together easily and effectively. Becoming isolated or separated can have a negative impact not only on the specific group that has become separated but also on the entire organization.

Proximity—being physically close to other participants—is certainly helpful but not absolutely necessary in organizations. This is contrary to our conception of an organization as people working in the same room or at least in the same building. As we will discuss later in the section on "virtual organizations," a growing number of examples exist of organizations that are physically separated yet remain connected through technology and the strong belief in a mission or purpose.

Organizations are complex in their structures. There are usually many layers and departments in the organizational structure and many people involved in leadership and decision making. Think again of the college or university example. In order to successfully involve all of the different groups in the educational process, different roles, policies, and procedures must be in place. A number and variety of different leadership positions will also probably exist.

Organizations exist to accomplish a specific purpose. While we have all been participants (and possibly leaders) in numerous organizations throughout our lives, we probably have never stopped to ask, I wonder how this organization got started? Unless you were part of the core group that started an organization, it was probably just "always there." Your participation began with your showing up at a meeting and either continued or ended based on how your needs were met by the organization. If we try to formulate an answer to the question, Why do organizations exist?, we probably come up with something like, They exist to accomplish a specific purpose. This would be absolutely correct.

Organizations as Complex Systems

Organizations are also systems. Systems are defined as environments in which each interaction between members produces outcomes that affect each individual and subsequent interactions and outcomes (Tubbs, 1984). With more people and groups in the organization, interactions become more frequent, and life within the organization becomes more complicated because everything affects everything else.

In *Out of Control*, Kevin Kelly (1994) introduces "The Nine Laws of God," which he describes as "the organizing principles in systems as diverse as biological evolution and SimCity" (p. 468). Depicted in Exhibit 7.2, these "laws" also apply to organizations as systems. These qualities relate closely to the new paradigm material covered at the end of Chapter Two, yet they also apply directly (and indirectly) to organizational life. We believe that these qualities really describe life, both in and out of organizations, and will become even more visible to us in the coming century.

This is what organizations are like. They are tremendously challenging places in which to participate and lead. They are also places

EXHIBIT 7.2   The Nine Laws of God—Organizations as Systems

Distribute being	The essence of the organization exists in all of its connected members.
Control from bottom up	Empower members at all levels of the organization.
Cultivate increasing returns	Focus on what your organization does well and do it even better.
Grow by chunking	Organizations grow, not one piece at a time but in bunches.
Maximize fringes	Honor your creative members and their ideas, even if they're really "out there."
Honor your errors	It is only through trial and error that learning happens.
Pursue no optima, have many goals	There is no one right answer to complex problems; there are only many partial solutions.
Seek persistent disequilibrium	Disequilibrium brings energy into the organization.
Change changes itself	Change leads to more change, which changes the initial change.

Source: K. Kelly, *Out of Control* (extracted from pp. 196 and 468). Copyright 1994 by Kevin Kelly. Reprinted by permission of Addison-Wesley Longman Inc.

of great potential because of the large number and variety of talented people who are members with you. As a leader, you may find yourself wanting to return to the time in your life when things seemed simpler and less complicated. Try not to worry. You will probably find that those qualities that helped you be successful in your youth—enthusiasm, energy, honesty, willingness to work hard, and character—will serve you well as a leader in a complex organization.

Organizational Leadership

In the previous sections, we addressed the questions, What are organizations? and Why do they exist? It is also interesting to ask, Why does leadership exist in an organization? Because organizations are "large collections of groups that interact in a continuous manner within a complex structure to accomplish a specific purpose," leadership in an organization exists to help these groups work together to accomplish a specific purpose. While this seems simplistic, how could leadership be anything else? Regardless of how it comes into being, leadership exists for only one reason: to help an organization accomplish its stated purpose. While this purpose may shift over time, leadership must always honor its inherent commitment to keep the organization on track to pursue its mission. We believe that the Relational Leadership Model provides a usable framework from which leaders can work to accomplish an organization's purpose. By being *inclusive, empowering, ethical,* and *process-oriented,* while helping all of the organization's members be *purposeful* and embrace a common purpose, leaders and members can work together successfully to accomplish amazing things.

"Best Buddies is an international organization that provides an opportunity for college students and persons with mental retardation to become friends. When I arrived at the University of Maryland, the inactive Best Buddies chapter consisted of two members, one advisor, and a world of potential. When no one else assumed the role of president, I accepted the challenge. A campuswide recruitment effort resulted in twenty-five new matched friendships, and even generated a waiting list! The demand by the college students quickly overwhelmed the number of mentally retarded buddies, and the organization vaulted from virtual anonymity to one of the more colorful patches woven into the fabric of the campus. Best Buddies transcended the expectations of a student group and became a way of life for its members. By challenging and empowering individuals with responsibility and encouraging them to make meaningful contributions, members worked toward shared visions and gained valuable experiences. As a powerful example of what is possible if we care, if we organize, and if we empower others, members of Best Buddies continue to make a difference in the lives of people with and without mental retardation."—Reena Meltzer is a senior government and politics major at the University of Maryland. She was elected Sophomore of the Year in 1995 and assisted the authors with this book.

Organizational Structures

Just as all organizations exist for some purpose, they also have a structure that makes their day-to-day operations easier. The traditional organizational structure that is familiar to all of us is a pyramid. This structure has been adapted to show how it might look for a typical student organization (Figure 7.1). In this model, the power, authority, and responsibility for leading the organization is at the top with the president and flows downward in the structure through the other officers and committee chairs. This power and authority are delegated as needed. The "rules of the game" in the traditionally structured organization are that the members have little power, authority, or responsibility. They simply do as they are told and have little, if any, input into the decision-making process. Involving the wants, needs, and talents of the organization's membership is only done by the most forward-thinking organizations.

FIGURE 7.1   The Traditional Organizational Structure

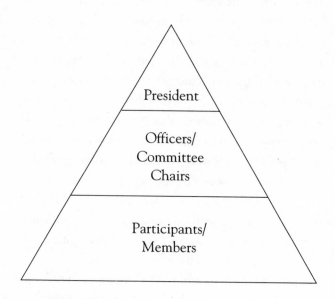

Recently, new ways of conceptualizing the organization have been proposed. Some have proposed flipping the traditional pyramid upside down so that the members are at the top and the president is at the bottom (Figure 7.2). This reconceptualization means that the work of the president is to support the efforts of the other officers and committee chairs so they can better meet the needs and wishes of the members. This can be a powerful exercise for any organization. Turn your organizational pyramid upside down. How well does your leadership help the other members of the organization work toward achieving the purposes for which the organization exists? Who are your members, and what are you as a leader doing to meet their wants and needs? How are you using the talents of your members?

Another organizational structure that has been proposed is the web (Allen, 1990b; Helgesen, 1990, 1995). The web is defined both by its pattern (similar to a spider's web) and by the idea that the shape and pattern of the web will vary over time (called series processes) (Helgesen, 1995). New members easily connect to the structure at its outer edges where the web is looser and more permeable (Helgesen, 1995). This structure works well in an environment filled with change, as the pattern is "continually being built up, stretched, altered, modified, and transformed" (Helgesen, 1995, p. 20).

Our conceptualization of the web is shown in Figure 7.3. As you can see, common purpose is at the center of the web. We believe that the purpose of the organization—the reason it exists—is more important than its leadership and is the reason people become participants. This is a different interpretation than Helgesen's (1995), which has the leader at the center of the web—surrounded by other participants and at the center of the organization's activities.

Helgesen (1995) outlines six important processes that define these webs more clearly than the patterns define them. Within the web, communication is open and happens across and between all levels of the organization. Thinking up what to do and actually doing it are not separated because information and expertise are

FIGURE 7.2   Inverted Organizational Structure

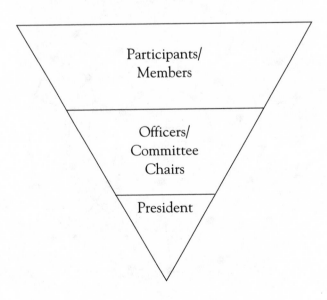

distributed all over the web. The strands of the web distribute the power throughout the network, so those who come up with creative ideas feel they have both the responsibility and the authority to follow through on implementation. Reorganization is easy, as the web can tighten around its center or become looser, and there is less emphasis on who is in what position or who holds how much power. The strands radiating out from the leader provide points of connection to the outside environment and allow new members to latch onto the organization. Finally, the web organization constantly reinvents itself through a process of trial and error. Processes that are successful continue and strengthen the entire web, whereas those that are not successful change. This change is more easily accomplished because communication and decision-making power are distributed throughout the web (Helgesen, 1995).

FIGURE 7.3   The Web Structure

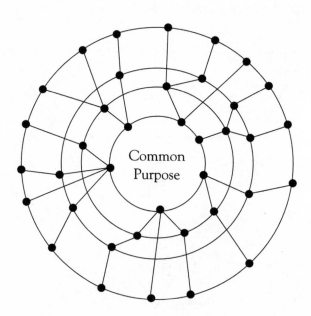

A note of caution: whichever organizational structure you have already in place, it is important to remember that the structure is not the organization. The organization is the membership who have come together for certain purposes. The structure was created to help the membership achieve the purposes for which the organization was developed. Organizations also exist to connect people to each other. When the structure ceases to do either of these things, it must be changed. It is easy to convince yourself that a change in structure will remedy an organization's problems. We have not found this to be the case. Change your organization's structure as you see fit—eliminate a position, add a committee, whatever—but realize that the cause and remedy for most organizational problems lie within the people in the organization, not in its structure.

Organizational Mission, Vision, and Core Values

Organizations exist for a specific purpose—to represent the views of the membership, to produce some product, to provide activities for its members, or countless other reasons. This is what causes people to want to join and participate in organizations. A critical aspect of success or failure of any organization will be how its purpose (or mission) comes to life in its vision and actions. The importance of mission, vision, and core values of an organization cannot be overestimated, and this section will explore these concepts in greater depth.

The mission of the organization is, quite simply, why it exists. Jones and Kahaner (1995) have collected the mission statements of fifty corporations, and they make fascinating and insightful reading. Avis's mission statement reads, "Our business is renting cars; our mission is total customer satisfaction" (p. 12). Southwest Airlines vows, "The mission of Southwest Airlines is dedication to the highest quality of Customer Service delivered with a sense of warmth, friendliness, individual pride, and Company Spirit" (p. 218). Finally, the mission of Levi Strauss & Co. reads like much more than a statement from an ordinary maker of jeans:

The mission of Levi Strauss & Co. is to sustain responsible commercial success as a global marketing company of branded casual apparel. We must balance goals of superior profitability and return on investment, leadership market positions, and superior products and service. We will conduct business ethically and demonstrate leadership in satisfying our responsibilities to our communities and to society. Our work environment will be safe and productive and characterized by fair treatment, teamwork, open communications, personal accountability and opportunities for growth and development (p. 227).

Ben & Jerry's, the ice cream manufacturer, has a product, as well as an economic and social mission included in its statement. Whereas the product and economic mission contain fairly typical statements (for example, "make, distribute, and sell the finest quality all natural ice cream" and "operate the Company on a sound financial basis" (http://www.benjerry.com/mission.html)), the social part of the mission is truly inspiring in its assertion of their commitment to

operate the Company in a way that actively recognizes the central role that business plays in the structure of society by initiating innovative ways to improve the quality of life of a broad community—local, national, and international (http://www.benjerry.com/mission.html).

This mission statement concludes with the following statement:

Underlying the mission of Ben & Jerry's is the determination to seek new and creative ways of addressing all three parts, while holding a deep respect for the individuals, inside and outside the company, and for the communities of which they are a part (http://www.benjerry.com/mission.html).

The mission statement should answer the question, Why does this organization exist? The mission statement must be written in clear, concise language and include input gathered from throughout the organization so that it reflects the personality of the organization. Once written, the statement should be shared widely and in as many forms as possible so that it can be used to truly guide the actions of the organization (Jones & Kahaner, 1995).

The mission statement should do something else. It should offer a compelling reason for the organization's existence. The contribution the organization makes to the campus, community, or world needs to be articulated in a way that is enticing to potential participants and motivational to those who have already joined the organization.

As you might imagine, many definitions could describe the vision of an organization. Kouzes and Posner (1995) call a vision "an ideal or unique image of the future" (p. 95). Albrecht (1994) terms it, "an image of what the people of the enterprise aspire for it to be or become" (p. 150). The vision answers the questions, "What do we want to be? What is the best we can be?" (Jaffe, Scott, & Tobe, 1994, p. 146). We believe that the vision answers the question, What is the ideal future for this organization? As such, it must motivate and inspire, be a stretch, be clear and concrete, be achievable, reflect high values, and be simple (Jaffe, Scott, & Tobe, 1994). The vision that the organization embraces challenges both the leader and the membership to do its very best, sometimes even more than believed possible, to move toward the mission for which the organization exists.

"[It is important to listen] when someone is describing their vision—because it is important to know someone else's thoughts on a subject; then it becomes less difficult to communicate and know the direction your group is going."—Dawn R. Marlette is a nursing major at the University of Delaware and an officer in her sorority.

Getting the members of your organization to share this vision can be very challenging, but unless it is shared and owned by the members, nothing of significance will ever happen. The vision must tap into the motivational systems of the people in your organization. This is why it is so important for the mission and vision statements to be clearly stated and inspiring. It is also the reason why these two statements must constantly be in front of all leaders and members and used to guide the actions of the organization. As Margaret Wheatley (1992) notes, "We need to be able to trust that something as simple as a clear core set of values and vision, kept in motion through continuing dialogue, can lead to order" (p. 147). In other words, the mission and vision need to come alive and be kept constantly alive through the actions of the leaders and members of the organization.

The final concept we explore in this section is that of core values. Without core values, any behavior would be justifiable as long as it moved the organization toward its mission or vision. We have all seen examples of this where people say that the ends justify the means. In their examination of visionary companies, Collins and Porras (1994) described core values as, "The organization's essential and enduring tenets—a small set of general guiding principles; not to be confused with specific cultural or operating practices; not to be compromised for financial gain or short-term expediency" (p. 73). These core values are small in number (usually three to six values) that are "so fundamental and deeply held that they will change or be compromised seldom, if ever" (p. 74). Core values answer the question, How do we, as organization members, agree to treat ourselves and others as we pursue our mission and vision? While core values are very important to the success of any organization, they are seldom discussed or shared among the membership. We think they are so important that the next chapter focuses on the moral purposes of organizations. We encourage you to take some time, both individually and as a group, to reflect on the core values for which your organization stands. It will be time well spent.

Organizational Culture

Many people believe that organizations are so powerful and influential that they take on a culture of their own. Edgar Schein (1992) defines this form of organizational culture as, "a pattern of shared basic assumptions that the group learned as it solved its problems of external adaptation and internal integration, that has worked well enough to be considered valid and, therefore, to be taught to new members as the correct way to perceive, think, and feel in relation to those problems" (p. 12). James Carse (1986) defines culture in a little different manner. "Culture . . . is an infinite game. Culture has no boundaries" (p. 53) . . . "for this reason it can be said that where society is defined by its boundaries, a culture is defined by its horizons" (p. 69).

Edgar Schein (1992), in his classic work *Organizational Culture and Leadership*, proposes that culture has three different levels. The most visible level is the *artifacts*—the organization's structures and processes. The *espoused values* of the organization make up the next level. These are the strategies, goals, and philosophies that the organization claims it embraces. At the final, deepest level are the *underlying assumptions*. These are the beliefs, thoughts, and feelings that are assumed to be true by members of the organization. It is these underlying assumptions that really drive the values and actions of the organization.

"If the group has the same core beliefs that I have and the same vision, I would want to stay. I would want to leave if they violated that set of beliefs."—Lora Klaviter is service chair of her sorority at Tulane University.

Terrence Deal and Allan Kennedy (1982) offer a different framework from which to examine organizational cultures. They stress the importance of the organization's *values, heroes, rites and rituals*, and *communications network*. Values are important because they provide the "core" of the organization and a guide for the behaviors of the members. Heroes are critical because they make success human and attainable, provide role models, symbolize the organization to outsiders, preserve what makes the organization special, set a standard of performance, and motivate members (Deal & Kennedy, 1982). The rites and rituals provide the formal and informal guidelines for how the everyday occurrences within the organization are to proceed. They include how members should communicate, socialize, work, and play, as well as what actions should be recognized and how they will be rewarded. The rites and rituals also govern the intricacies of how the organization operates, for example how its meetings are conducted. Finally, Deal and Kennedy analyze the organization's communications network by examining how information is gathered and disseminated, both formally and informally. As they note, "The whole process depends on people, not on paper" (p. 87).

Deal and Kennedy (1982) describe various characters within the organization and outline how they contribute to the communications network. Storytellers interpret what is going on in the organization; what they say may or may not be the truth, because it is their perception of what is happening. Priests worry a lot and see themselves as guarding the values of the organization's culture; another of their roles is to keep the membership of the organization together. Whisperers work behind the scenes and have power because of their close connection to the leadership of the organization. Gossips can provide detailed information about what is currently happening within the organization; sometimes the facts they provide are correct, sometimes they are not. Secretarial sources can tell members what is really going on in the organization because of their access to important information. Spies are loyal to the leaders of the organization and provide information to them about what is happening. Finally, cabals are groups of two or more people whose main purpose in joining together is to advance themselves within the organization; their alliance is often kept in secret.

It is important to have a sense of the culture of your organization because it provides clues into how your organization "really" operates. This may seem silly because we all think we know how it operates. But veteran members' experiences in an organization can be very different from those of new or prospective members. Consider the general concept of change. In some organizations, "If it ain't broke, break it" could define the culture, whereas in other organizations, "If it ain't broke, don't worry about it" may be the way things operate. Being a new member of a change-oriented organization can be very exciting because your opinions may be listened to more closely than in the organization that embraces the status quo. Veteran members, however, may think things are just fine the way they presently are and see no need for much change at all.

An organizational culture can also negatively affect life within an organization. As Stacey (1992) notes, "Strongly shared cultures inevitably block new learning and cut down on the variety of perspectives brought to bear on an issue" (p. 143). In other words, "The more norms we strongly share, the more we resist changing them" (Stacey, p. 143). While the development of a culture that supports the pursuit of the organization's mission, values, and goals is very important, everyone must be aware of how the culture may also be inhibiting the organization. People must also realize that trying to change the mission, vision, and values of the organization without paying attention to changing the culture may meet with resistance. Think about how something as "simple" as eliminating hazing from the initiation process of an organization should be. Hazing is against the law, causes harm, and does little to benefit the organization. Yet the culture of many organizations strongly embraces the need for such rites of passage in order for new members to show their dedication to their new organization. Changing the mission and values of the organization to embrace non-hazing principles is often relatively easy. Changing the culture of the organization so that it does not haze is often more difficult. Planning a rewarding substitute activity to celebrate the transition of new members to full membership can enrich the culture.

Organizational Networks

Jessica Lipnack and Jeffrey Stamps (1993) define networks as "where disparate groups of people and groups 'link' to work together based on common purposes" (p. 7). These groups of people may be participants in your organization and may also include others from outside the organization. The keys are that they work together and have a common purpose. Networks are important because they provide the chance to bring together a wide range of individuals. The network may address either a specific issue, such as when a wide range of students, faculty, and staff members are brought together to plan an institution's one-hundredth birthday celebration, or it may work on an on-going concern like student retention. Key issues in the formation of a network include agreement on the network's purpose, creating as many links as possible between members of the network and making sure that multiple leaders exist within the network (Lipnack & Stamps, 1993).

Lifecycles of Organizations

Although the emerging paradigm described in Chapter Two would suggest that organizations cannot be controlled, we believe that a critical point in the success of any organization is its ability to adapt to change—changing conditions, changing membership, and changing leadership. This ability to adapt enables an organization to renew itself and maintain its vibrancy. A small group of skilled and determined individuals can move an organization into greatness by their focused actions. This sometimes happens with new organizations. A group of students gets excited about an idea and, with the help of a few other students, forms an organization dedicated to a specific purpose. The energy, excitement, and dedication of this small group often helps them accomplish amazing things. However, this success can be short-lived unless the organization makes plans for what will happen next—specifically, who will be recruited as new members and who will be groomed for future leadership positions.

John Gardner (1990) and Ichak Adizes (1988) present the concept of "lives" of organizations. Gardner uses the terms *infancy* and *maturity* to differentiate organizations that are in their early lives from those that have evolved into something more orderly and with more of a sense of direction. Adizes goes into more detail and uses the terms *courtship, infancy, go-go, adolescence, prime, stable, aristocracy, early bureaucracy, bureaucracy,* and *death* to describe a similar change process. As Gardner notes, "At each stage something is gained and something lost" (p. 122). When organizations are young, they are very flexible and motivated, willing to try new things, and have the ability to respond quickly to new challenges. Yet they may expend much energy to accomplish relatively little. As organizations mature, this flexibility lessens, and they become more orderly and are more satisfied with slow, steady advances (Gardner, 1990). These stages in the life of organizations are similar to the stages of group development presented in Chapter Six.

It has been said that when asked about the early days of the Peace Corps, Sargent Shriver, its director, noted that the leadership of the organization didn't meet—they were too busy doing things. This dedication is often felt early on in new organizations and is exciting—even intoxicating—but it will always end. The model of Adizes is critical for student leaders to understand because of its focus on how an entire organization changes. Take a hard look at your organization. How would a random sample of students on your campus describe the student government? Would they be positive? Negative? Indifferent? Could they identify any recent accomplishments of the government?

Your organization needs to ask itself two questions on a regular basis: What have we accomplished recently? and How does what we've accomplished reflect our organization's mission? If you are having trouble formulating answers to either of these questions, you may need to reexamine what you are doing and how you are doing it. Remember that the purpose of meetings and standard operating procedures is to help your organization *do things* in the most expedient manner. They are not designed to become ends unto themselves. As a leader, you must identify and describe significant accomplishments that you helped your organization achieve, not that you attended or ran a lot of meetings.

Organizational Transformation. Organizational development or, as we have chosen to call it, organizational transformation, means the process of making your organization into something new, something better than it was before. While Rhinesmith's (1993) work focuses on a global context, he also has much to offer in our discussion of organizational transformation as a change process. As he notes, "The basic dilemma of organizational change is that it must be freely adopted by the people that it affects who are many times against its introduction" (p. xii). He goes on to say that it is important for the organization's membership "to identify and become committed to changes that will meet the best long-term interests for themselves, their organizations, and society" (p. xii). Although these words may sound simple, several points must be remembered. First, change will not usually be embraced by the members of an organization. People tend to like for their lives to be predictable, and change disrupts this predictability. Second, for change to work, the organization's membership must be committed to making it work. Finally, the change needs to be in the interests of not only the individual members but also of the organization as a whole and of the society in general.

John Kotter (1995) provides an excellent model from which to work to initiate change in your organization (Exhibit 7.3). As you look at Kotter's model, note the presence of the concepts of empowerment, common purpose, and a process orientation—all aspects of the Relational Leadership Model. Kotter also stresses the importance of having a sense of urgency. Because change is not something that people naturally will embrace, this is absolutely critical to the success of any transformation process.

Multicultural Organizational Development. The concept of multicultural organizational development has been used by Armour

EXHIBIT 7.3   Transforming the Organization

1. Establish a Sense of Urgency.
2. Form a Powerful Coalition.
3. Create a Vision.
4. Communicate the Vision.
5. Empower Others to Act on the Vision.
6. Plan for and Create Short-Term Wins.
7. Consolidate Improvements and Produce Still More Change.
8. Institutionalize New Approaches.

Source: Reprinted by permission of *Harvard Business Review* from "Leading change: Why transformation efforts fail" by J. Kotter, 73, 1995. Copyright © 1995 by the President and Fellows of Harvard College; all rights reserved.

and Hayles (1990), Jackson and Holvino (1988), and Pope (1993) to mean a specific approach to organizational transformation. This process emphasizes the full participation of members from all cultural and social groups and a commitment to end all forms of social oppression that might exist within the organization. This emphasis on diversity and social justice offers a fresh perspective from which to approach organizational transformation. Because the Relational Leadership Model emphasizes being inclusive and empowering, understanding how an organization might transform itself to be multicultural is essential. What do you think the impact would be if every organization on your campus made a commitment to end all forms of social oppression? This would clearly be a transformation, and the campus would become a better place for *all* its students, faculty, and staff.

Armour and Hayles (1990) and Jackson and Holvino (1988) offer similar models for multicultural organizational development. Their models show the organization moving from a perspective that is monocultural and exclusionary, to one that is compliant and nondiscriminatory, through a redefinition process, and finally to a multicultural perspective. Of particular importance in Jackson and Holvino's (1988) work is their elaboration of the assumptions that change agents make, depending on whether they come from a monocultural, nondiscriminatory, or multicultural perspective (see Exhibit 7.4). Whereas those coming from a monocultural perspective view society as basically harmonious and doing all right, those having a multicultural perspective see society as filled with conflict and in need of radical change. You may already see examples of these two opposing perspectives on your campus. Learning to understand, respect, and work effectively with others who have strongly held views that differ from your own is one of the great challenges of being a leader. It is also absolutely necessary as you work to make your organization and campus a better place for *all* people.

Learning Organizations. Peter Senge (1990), Watkins and Marsick (1993), and others have proposed a way to conceptualize organizations that will help them operate successfully in the chaotic world described in Chapter Two. They used the label, "learning organizations" to describe organizations that have the capacity to grow, change, and develop in order to adapt to the challenges of their constantly changing environments. In his conceptualization of the learning organization, Senge included the modules of personal mastery, mental models, shared vision, and team learning. These modules make up a framework of systems thinking; each is interrelated with the others. We believe that the concept of the learning organization and its guiding principles of the primacy of the whole, the community nature of the self, and the generative power of language (Senge, 1994) have much to offer in our discussion of organizations.

Personal mastery involves individuals doing the best possible job. For a treasurer in an organization, it might include knowing how to use computer spreadsheets, being able to follow the steps needed to purchase something, and having budgeting skills. For a vice president, it might include skills in working with committee chairs so that their respective groups can get organized and be productive. Everyone in an organization—officers and members—has skills and abilities that can be contributed to the organization. It is

EXHIBIT 7.4 Change Agent Assumptions in Multicultural Organizational Development

	Monocultural	Non-Discriminatory	Multicultural
Nature of Society	Harmonious Similar interests Needs to improve, but basically OK		Conflict Different interests Oppressive, alienating, needs radical change
Oppression	Dominance	Desegregation	Pluralism
Liberation Model	Assimilation	Integration	Diversity
Self-Interest in Change	Survival and social acceptability	Adaptation and full use of human resources	Equity, empowerment, collective growth
Values and Ideology	Basic rights of individual Best person is rewarded Efficiency and economic survival		Interdependence Ecological survival Development of human and societal potential

Source: Jackson & Holvino, 1988, p. 18.

important for leaders to work with the group's membership so that individuals can gain the skills needed to be effective, not only in their current roles within the organization but also as a way of preparing them for future positions. When members are skilled and empowered to use these skills, the whole organization benefits.

Mental models are the assumptions that people make about the various aspects of the world. For instance, when someone says the words *leader* or *conflict* or *diversity* or *meeting*, what images pop into your head? These mental models are often difficult to grasp and, therefore, are sometimes difficult to change. But these models must be changed if any real change is to occur in the world. Disagreements sometimes occur because these differing mental models are not brought to the surface so they can be examined and, if needed, changed. Consider for a moment the concept of "adviser." If your organization has an adviser, you may assume that this person will make sure details do not fall through the cracks when you are planning a big event. When this turns out not to be true, everyone loses. It is important to compare the mental models that you have with others in your organization. In this way, false assumptions can be minimized. Mental models can also be empowering for a whole organization. Consider what would happen if, when members thought about your organization, the concepts of inclusion, empowerment, process, ethics, and common purpose immediately came to mind. These images could do a lot to guide the organization in a way that would help make it strong and successful.

"Organizations that take the time to train their members in areas such as diversity, cross-cultural relations, and interpersonal communication can't help but change for the better."—Christina Cruz is an environmental science/anthropology major and president of Associated Students of Occidental College.

Shared vision focuses on the idea that the mission, vision, and purpose of an organization must be shared by all members. Shared vision—or common purpose—is especially important given the current emphasis on empowerment. People can be empowered and their personal mastery level high, yet without some shared sense of direction, everyone will be pushing hard in different directions. The result will be an organization that moves haphazardly, if at all. Although vision is certainly important, Helgesen (1990) notes that feeling confident in one's "voice" may be just as critical because this is how the vision is related and shared with others.

The concept of team learning is also vital in any learning organization. As Senge and others (Kline & Saunders, 1993; Watkins & Marsick, 1993) note, learning at the individual level (Senge's concept of personal mastery) must be supplemented by learning at the team, organizational, and societal levels if any true learning is to occur. This might include learning how to make decisions, how to really communicate, and how to disagree—aspects of organizational life that we usually take for granted, yet do very poorly. The concept of team learning also underscores the need to consider leadership as an on-going process rather than an end result or product. Just as team members are constantly engaged with each other in learning new approaches or methods, leaders must be continually engaged in dialogue with members of their organizations.

Finally, a systems approach governs the thinking in a learning organization. When people think systematically, they share responsibility for the good and bad things that are happening. Rather than looking for someone else to blame, members of a learning organization hold up the mirror and ask what they have done to contribute to the problem. Think of how many problems we blame on someone or something else rather than accepting responsibility for them ourselves and working toward a solution. Senge (1990) calls this specific "learning disability" a belief that "the enemy is out there." As in our earlier example of the organization as a weather system, all aspects of a system are constantly working together to create the reality of the system. All of these aspects—personal mastery, mental models, shared vision, team learning, and systems thinking—combine to create a learning organization.

We have gone into so much detail about the learning organization because the capacity for an organization to continuously learn enables it to continuously recreate itself as it faces new challenges. Consider the following example. A student government organization needs to appoint a student member to its college's board of trustees. What qualities should such a representative have? How should that person be selected? What issues should this representative bring to the board? All of a sudden, the student government has moved from being an organization that may have a programming emphasis to providing students with a voice within the group that makes the major decisions regarding campus life. This is a major change in focus. To take advantage of this opportunity, the organization must be able to learn how the board operates, what issues will be of most interest to the board, and what approaches will be most successful. Much of this learning will have to be "on the hoof" (Stacey, 1992). Only an organization that is truly open and embracing of learning new approaches will make optimal use of this opportunity.

Virtual Organizations

One of the more interesting developments of recent years has been the impact that technology is having on our lives (see Postman, 1992). Organizations have not been exempt from this impact. The growth of virtual offices and virtual organizations has been chronicled in a number of publications (for example, Davidow & Malone, 1992; Grenier & Metes, 1995; Handy, 1996; Lipnack & Stamps, 1993; Petersen, 1994; Pickover, 1991; Rheingold, 1993). Charles Handy defines virtual organizations as "organizations that do not need to have all the people, or sometimes any of the people, in one place in order to deliver their service. The organization exists but you can't see it. It is a network, not an office" (p. 212).

So what will these virtual organizations be like? Charles Handy (1996) believes that trust will be very important and very difficult to develop when people do not often see each other face-to-face. He also stresses the need for a common purpose and values to be shared by all the organization's members. Davidow and Malone (1992) note that organizations will certainly be flatter (multiple layers of hierarchy will be a thing of the past), built on the need for the organization's members to believe and trust in each other, and involve members at all levels more and more in the decision-making process.

Your organization may already seem a lot like a virtual organization, with members coming and going at all hours of the day or night and spending very little time together in the same place. You may already be involved in other examples of virtual organizations on your campus. Your student government organization may also be a member of a state, regional, or national coalition with other student government groups. You may plan a leadership conference with students on other campuses via e-mail, phone, and fax and never actually meet face to face in the same room until the conference begins. On your campus, you may find that you communicate more often with the members of your own organization through the use of e-mail or other technologies than in face-to-face meetings.

New Paradigm Leadership in Conventional Paradigm Cultures

One of the most challenging results of reading a book like this is realizing that you may embrace the principles of new paradigm leadership but find yourself mired in a conventional culture. This can present a dilemma, but you can take actions toward continuing to use this information. First of all, share what you know with other leaders, members of your organization, advisers—anyone who will listen. By sharing, you do two things: you learn the information better yourself, and you may find some other interested people with whom you can continue to connect. Accept personal responsibility for finding ways to use the information rather than always saying "Well so-and-so won't let me do that." Maintain a positive outlook and try to find areas in which you *can* use this information rather than focusing on areas that seem out of bounds. Continue to try new things, even in small ways. You will find a number of different exercises and thought pieces in *The Fifth Discipline Fieldbook* (Senge et al., 1994) that you can use in a variety of settings, both in and outside of your organization. Volunteer to do programs or activities with other organizations or to be a guest speaker or teacher. Finally, continue to read and explore. A number of resources are listed in this book. Continue to develop your own leadership library. It will serve you well for your entire life (Allen, 1990a).

Chapter Summary

In this chapter we have discussed complex organizations. We have discussed why organizations exist and how they are structured. We have stressed the importance of mission, vision, and core values. We have also presented what the virtual organization of the future might be like. Throughout this chapter the importance of the Relational Leadership Model has been evident. It is only by being *inclusive* that organizations can creatively use the talents and abilities of all of its membership. By being *empowering* and *process-oriented*, all members are encouraged to take an active role in the life of organization. By being *ethical*, members can hold each other to a higher standard of behavior that is more closely aligned with the organization's mission, vision, and core values. Finally, it is only when this vision or common purpose is truly shared by the entire membership that an organization can reach its potential and be *purposeful*. Organizational life need not be an endless series of meetings run by *Robert's Rules of Order*. There can and should be excitement and energy there. We hope you will find it.

What's Next?

So far in this section we have presented leadership in the context of groups and organizations. In the next chapter we introduce the community context. The term *community* can be used to describe a spirit that encourages a collection of people to work and act collaboratively (sense of community). It can also be used to identify the population of a geographic area (the community of Smallville). The spirit of community and the principles of community development are explored further in the next chapter.

Chapter Activities

1. *Groups and Organizations:* Identify a group and organization in which you are currently a participant. Now look at Exhibit 7.1. How do your experiences support the way we differentiated among these three concepts? How do your experiences differ from our framework?

2. *Organizational Mission:* Find your organization's mission statement or an example of a mission statement not described in this chapter. Does it meet the criteria suggested by Jones and Kahaner? What are your statement's strengths? Where does it fall short? How could you change it to make it more reflective of both the purpose and personality of your organization? How compelling is it? If you don't have a mission statement, write one now. How did you do? Would you be inspired by your statement if you knew nothing of your organization?

3. *Organizational Vision:* Imagine an ideal future for your organization. Try to capture this image on paper. Be creative. You can make a collage, a drawing, use words—whatever works for you. When you are finished, look at your image. Is it inspiring? Would it motivate your members? How could it be improved?

4. *Core Values:* Reflect for a couple minutes on the core values of your organization. Write down what these values are. Do not worry about the number you have, but try to come up with at least ten. Do not worry about putting them into any order. Once you have your list, pick the top five—the five most important core values. Again do not worry about prioritizing your choices. From this list of five, pick the three most important values. Finally, pick *the* most important core value for your organization. Repeat this exercise with all members of your organization.

5. *Organizational Culture:* Answer the following questions about your organization.

   Values: What basic values do the members of your organization embrace?

   Heroes: Who are the heroes of your organization? Why are they famous or infamous? What qualities do the exemplify?

   Rites and rituals: How do members of your organization work together? How do members of your organization play together? What actions or behaviors are recognized? How are they rewarded?

6. *Organizational Transformation:* Think about a change that has been made, either successfully or unsuccessfully, within your organization. Why do you think it succeeded or did not succeed? Now look at Exhibit 7.3. What clues does this figure offer about why your change effort succeeded or did not succeed?

7. *Multicultural Organizational Development:* Think about the concept of multicultural organizational development. How committed is your organization to full participation by members of all cultural and social groups? How committed is your organization to end all forms of social oppression that might exist within the organization? What could you do to increase this commitment?

Additional Readings

Deal, T., & Kennedy, A. (1982). *Corporate cultures: The rites and rituals of corporate life*. Reading, MA: Addison-Wesley.

Handy, C. (1996). *Beyond certainty: The changing worlds of organizations*. Boston: Harvard Business School Press.

Helgesen, S. (1995). *The web on inclusion: A new architecture for building great organizations*. New York: Currency/Doubleday.

Schein, E. (1992). *Organizational culture and leadership* (2nd ed.). San Francisco: Jossey-Bass.

8

Building Coalitions and Communities

Denise is at home not feeling well. She is sorry to have missed the commencement committee meeting this morning. The phone rings and Jason is on the line. He has Stacy and Carl in his room, and they are worried because Denise did not come to the meeting.

JASON: Denise, it's Jason and I'm here with Stacy and Carl. Our committee was really worried when you didn't show up this morning. Dean Jacobs asked if anyone knew if you were OK since you are always right there. You sound terrible! Are you OK?

DENISE: (clearing her throat) Thanks Jason. It feels really good to know you all noticed. I have a killer cold. It hit me late last night. Sorry I didn't call so you wouldn't worry.

JASON: That's OK, Denise. Hope you feel better. Stacy says she'll drop some résumés of the possible commencement speakers by your house tonight because we are all supposed to be ready to vote on one of them as our recommendation to the senior class council for Friday. . . . Oh, Stacy says to ask if you need anything she can bring when she comes by.

This committee appears to be a good community. Denise's absence was noticed by committee members and by the adviser. They cared enough to check on her and to pick up copies of materials in her absence. Denise knows from this encounter that she matters.

Chapter Overview

Envisioning each group or organization you are in as a community is a mental model that will respond to the relational needs of these rapidly changing times. Individuals function concurrently in many different kinds of communities. Thinking of each of your formal and informal groups as communities provides a frame for the interdependence of relational leadership. This chapter discusses the nature of communities, principles of community development, and the importance of coalitions in communities of practice.

The Importance of Community

Knowing about community, philosophically believing in the worth of community, and being skilled at developing and sustaining community are essential aspects of relational leadership. Ideal, perfect communities rarely happen. We all live, work, and learn in imperfect communities, which, if they are striving to be better, become supportive environments for individual and group growth.

Gardner (1990) asserts that *"skill in the building and rebuilding of community is not just another of the innumerable requirements of contemporary leadership. It is one of the highest and most essential skills a leader can command"* (p. 118, emphasis in the original). Relational leadership calls for attending to community as a discipline. The term *discipline* in this case refers to a concept to be studied, learned, and practiced, as one would learn academic disciplines such as biology, English, or history (Gozdz, 1993). It is not enough to understand self and others; understanding is essential to creating and nurturing the context in which the group or organization functions. Thinking of the relationships in that setting as a community focuses participants' attention on the responsibilities, processes, and the spirit of working together.

Think of the most effective and meaningful classes, clubs, committees, or groups you have experienced. You probably felt a commitment to the whole and felt like you mattered and were meaningful to others in that setting. Not all groups feel that way. You can probably imagine a group you had to be a part of and felt little in common, little value, or little commitment to the task or to others in that setting. That group might have accomplished its goals, but few would say they enjoyed working together; they probably would not want to work together again if given a choice. Relational leadership asks you to think of the context of the setting as a healthy community, which brings a whole paradigm of expectations and norms for working together effectively as participants in shared leadership.

"I feel part of a community within a family group at church camp. Each group I have been a part of has been characterized by the formation of a group covenant, a common purpose, trust, acceptance of people's emotional levels, willingness to share, security to reveal emotions, thoughts, and opinions without criticism, strong role models within the surrounding group, and time for both fun and serious activities."—Trisha Fields is chair of the Spring Leadership Trip at Texas A&M University.

Elements of Community

A community is most often described as "a social group that not only shares an identity and structured pattern of interaction, but also a common geographical territory" (Goodman, 1992, p. 48). It is not just a place where interaction occurs, but a spirit of connection and commitment that sustains relationships and purpose. Sharing that community commitment is the essence of relational leadership. Denise's phone call might not seem to illustrate leadership on the surface, but imagine a small committee or class where members matter so much to each other and to the adviser or professor that someone's absence is not only noticed but becomes a matter of concern and members look out for the person's needs. In that environment, each participant feels a sense of shared leadership.

Communities know they are a collection of individuals who accomplish their goals through trust and teamwork. Teamwork requires processes to make decisions, methods of communication, and a commitment to some level of participation by community members. Gardner (1990, pp. 116–118) extends the traditional definitions of community to refer to effective communities as those that practice these eight elements:

1. Wholeness incorporating diversity

2. A shared culture

3. Good internal communication

4. Caring, trust, and teamwork

5. Group maintenance and governance

6. Participation and shared leadership tasks

7. Development of young people [or new members]

8. Links with the outside world

Through their work together, community members develop a shared culture that is concerned about new members. Effective communities realize they are not insular but are in a constant, dynamic interaction with their broader environment. Binding all of this together is the awareness that a group *is* a community—the shared culture may reflect that spirit of community. The *spirit* of community makes many other relational processes possible.

Many traditional views of community are changing. Conventional views present communities as homogeneous groupings of people who have much in common and may even resemble each other in ideology, race, or class. Those may indeed be communities, yet "cultural and ethnic diversity (and all other forms of diversity, as well) are necessary resources for building community. A true community cannot exist without diversity" (Gudykunst, 1991, p. 146). Diversity of ideas, diversity of skills, diversity of experiences, and diversity of worldviews bring the many talents of a community to its shared goals. If all community members saw things the same way, had the same skills, and had the same life experiences, their ability to be resilient and face change would be limited.

Other traditional views have held that communities need face-to-face interaction, which is possible only through close geographic proximity. Increasingly however, the term *community* also describes those with common identity and interaction but without geographic proximity. References to "the medical community" or "the spiritual community" reflect their common frame or perspective and not their physical daily interactions. Many members of these communities do find ways to meet and think together. Professional society meetings through associations and conventions provide a forum for the development of community connections. Electronic networks have provided a creative way for communities of common interest to interact. Internet chat rooms are linking people across the globe into selective communities where minds meet. Many feel that electronic communications like e-mail and chat rooms diminish community. Indeed, it is possible to become isolated from face-to-face interaction when using the computer for most of your interactions, but the effective and responsible use of electronic communication can facilitate community.

You can also find identity and feel a sense of community with others without interacting. For example, if you are an avid environmentalist, you feel a close connection to the struggles of Green Peace or the Sierra Club when you read about them in the news. If you do community service with abused children, you feel anguish over the latest tragedies reported on the radio. If you are a member of a national organization like a sorority, you may feel immediate kinship with a sister from another chapter whom you met while you were both on vacation. You might even seek out certain communities when you move to a new town because you know you will be welcomed as a new member.

As human beings, we all want meaningful connection to others. Settings that are inclusive and empowering, where there is purposeful change being accomplished through ethical and collaborative processes, are the epitome of effective communities. Relational leadership flourishes in settings that value the elements of community.

A Common Center

In his 1958 classic *I and Thou*, Martin Buber contends that in our life together, some form of community is what makes life worth living. He describes community as a group of people who have made a choice around a common center. A true community is not a collection of people who all think alike but people with differing minds and complementary natures.

We participated in a group of leadership development educators who struggled with the role and importance of community in shared leadership. This group eventually defined community as the "binding together of diverse individuals committed to a just, common good through shared experiences in a spirit of caring and social responsibility" (National Invitational Leadership Symposium, 1991, p. 19). Developing communities like this depends on relational leadership that deeply values the inclusion of all members, empowered to work together toward common purposes.

"My residence life staff . . . really felt like a community.
There were nine of us, including me, and I think a
few things really bonded us together. For one, we were
all in the same boat when it came to our job duties.
Being an RA is a challenge but not one that has to be
faced alone. Our staff stood by one another when the

job became challenging. . . . It's really neat how a group of people can come together when they're required to depend on one another—not just in times of need but in times of silliness as well. For example, our staff bonded the most over the Residence Life Lip Sync Contest, where we were required to perform in front of others. Laughing together while planning our 'act' was a truly community-building activity."—Vanessa M. Helsing is a recent graduate of the Jepson School of Leadership Studies at the University of Richmond. She works in the change management division with Anderson Consulting in Washington, D.C.

In these communities, openness is a central practice. True dialogue requires listening and being willing to give up the need for control, even when your ideas and thoughts are in conflict with those of another. Without the willingness to give up control, you engage in monologue that cannot promote community. Being in community requires the realization that a member's own needs will not always prevail. Buber (1958) reminds us that this does not mean accepting views of others just to create a false peace but to keep the commitment to greater values in mind. "Communities speak to us in moral voices. They lay claims on their members. Indeed, they are the most important sustaining source of moral voices other than the inner self" (Etzioni, 1993, p. 31).

Communities of Practice

It is not sufficient to think of yourself as being a mere member of multiple communities; membership may mean having a passive connection or being a name on a roster. You might be highly involved and committed to the success of your fraternity, the senior class council, or the scout troop you co-lead. However, because of limited time, disinterest, or shifting priorities, you may become affiliated with only one of those communities and not highly active.

No one has enough time or energy to be highly involved in every community with which they identify. Being a member of a community in practice, however, implies an engagement with others who are working toward some action. The people in that community are doing something, and you are a part of that in some meaningful way. "Each person belongs to many communities of practice but with varying degrees of centrality. In some communities of practice we are only peripherally involved; in others we are centrally involved" (Drath & Palus, 1994, p. 11). You may have intentionally decided that this is the time to devote more time and energy to your family, some special needs in your job, or to your senior thesis project, so you cannot do as much as you might like in your worship community or in your other organizations.

Just as there are residence hall floors where residents keep their doors shut and do not even talk on the elevators going down to classes in the morning, there are also floors where residents are in and out of each others rooms, gather in the floor lounge to watch a favorite TV show, and cluster in the same section of the cafeteria for dinner each evening—and dinner companions are always available. A person can lead an isolated life while surrounded by people in classes, in the snack bar, or at work—or a connected life when meaningfully involved in a community. Even within the larger environment, one can find what Harvard sociologist Herbert Gans calls "urban villages" (cited in Etzioni, 1993, p. 120). Urban villages are the many small communities within larger systems. The giant lecture class can become an urban environment of small villages by such class structures as discussion groups and team projects.

Being in community requires an awareness of reciprocal processes. An individual has to decide to be part of the larger community, and the community has to involve and welcome individuals. Harvard sociologist Charles Willie (1992) asserts that in any community (that is, work group, classroom, neighborhood, or volunteer organization) there are concurrent obligations of *contributive justice* and *distributive justice*. Each individual in the community must practice contributive justice. Individuals contribute to the group's belief that it is fair and reasonable for each to do his or her part in the greater whole, uphold obligations, and feel a commitment to shared purposes. Conversely, the community must practice the distributive justice of caring for all community members and ensuring that each is included, is heard, and is not hurt or disadvantaged through community membership.

The Development of Community

The first day you and thirty other residents move into your new residence hall floor, or fifty students come to a first class, or a committee of twelve convenes its first meeting does not mean that community magically happens. The development of a spirit of community must happen intentionally.

Scott Peck (1987) has identified four stages of developing true authentic community. The first stage is *pseudocommunity*. In this stage a group may feel like things are just fine, people seem to be getting along, relationships are courteous, but it is in reality a superficial, underdeveloped level of community. For example, "pseudocommunity is conflict-avoiding; true community is conflict-resolving" (p. 88).

The second stage of community building is *chaos*. During this stage there is a noisy din of different views. Different people or factions are asserting their perspectives from which to set the community's agenda or determine important processes. Committee members promote individual agendas, or cliques form on the residence hall floor. This stage can be dangerous because some give up and retreat instead of working through this stage. It is important to find meaning in the idea that "fighting is better than pretending you are not divided" (p. 94). This stage is similar to the storming stage of group development presented in Chapter Six. Peck observes that groups take one of two paths out of chaos: organization or emptiness. Organization leaves the source of fighting untouched by establishing structures and systems to manage and handle the differences of opinion. For example, the residence hall floor makes a new policy to rein in those who are misusing the floor lounge, or a committee, faced with long debates, decides to vote on decisions and let the majority rule. Although it is counterintuitive to think of the term *empty* as good, *emptiness* is Peck's term for the process of community members emptying themselves of their barriers to true communication.

This third stage of *emptiness* is the realization that many personal feelings, assumptions, ideas, stereotypes, or motives become barriers to truly listening and understanding (and being understood). It may mean someone saying, "Wait a minute. This argument is beginning to sound like the freshmen think all the seniors are money-hungry, selfish egoists, and the seniors think the freshmen are unrealistic idealists. We need to let go of those assumptions and look at the good thoughts each group is raising." In the fourth stage of *true, authentic community*, conflict still arises, but there are ways to be heard, and the community knows usually they cannot reach consensus or any level of agreement without dissensus or disagreements to create truly better decisions. Building community is creating a feel of "we" out of lots of "I's." Many groups never get past pseudocommunity and find ways to courteously interact and get their work done. That may be sufficient for their purposes, but ongoing groups that are doing difficult work would benefit from recognizing Peck's stages and work toward authentic community.

Communities that engage in this developmental process and reach a stage of authentically functioning as a community often err by not recognizing that being a community is a process, not an end state. Communities are not static—they constantly change. New members join the group, external crises cause new levels or types of conflict, and key members leave who had been instrumental to nurturing community. Communities must recognize when they need to attend to the cycle of rebuilding a genuine community.

Participants who want to be highly engaged in the work of any community need to assess the ways in which they can become effective community members. Gudykunst (1991, pp. 147–148) proposes that individual participants practice these seven community building principles:

1. *Be Committed:* Commitment to others is prerequisite for community to exist.
2. *Be Mindful:* Think about what we do and say. Focus on the
   process, not the outcome . . . be contemplative in examining
   our own behavior.
3. *Be Unconditionally Accepting:* Accept others as they are; do not
   try to change or control them . . . minimize expectations, prejudices, suspicion, and mistrust.
4. *Be Concerned for Both Yourself and Others:* Engage in dialogue
   whenever possible . . . consult others on issues that affect
   them and be open to their ideas . . . fight gracefully.
5. *Be Understanding:* Strive to understand others as completely as
   possible.
6. *Be Ethical:* Engage in behavior that is not a means to an end,
   but behavior that is morally right in and of itself.
7. *Be Peaceful:* Do not be violent, deceitful, breach value
   promises, or be secretive . . . strive for internal harmony . . .
   and harmony in relations with others (emphasis in the original).

If each participant has the mental model of their organization
as a community and practices community-building skills, groups
will be enriched. They will listen more keenly, seek resolution of
differences, respect each other even when there are disagreements
on specific issues, and be generous and patient. Etzioni (1993) challenges us to "lay claims on others to be similarly involved in, and
dedicated to, community" (p. 142).

Modeling and practicing this kind of participation is essential
to being a contributing community member. Relational leadership
is directly linked with building community. Exhibit 8.1 illustrates
the connections among the elements of relational leadership, with

the understandings of the elements of community from Gardner (1990) and the advice on community-building principles from Gudykunst (1991).

Coalitions for Community Action

Margaret Mead said, "Never doubt that a small group of thoughtful, committed citizens can change the world; indeed it is the only thing that ever has" (cited in Mathews, 1994, p. 119). Individuals who decide to engage fully in their group and join with others around common needs can make a difference. Making a difference these days requires that several groups form coalitions and work together toward shared outcomes.

Today's organizational and societal problems are complex and thus require community-based solutions. Whether these are campus community problems, problems in your apartment building, or problems facing the Greek life system, they need the involvement

EXHIBIT 8.1 Connecting Relational Leadership to Elements of Community

Relational Leadership (see Chapter Three)	Elements of Community (Gardner, 1990; Gudykunst, 1991)
Inclusive	Wholeness incorporates diversity; links with the outside world; *be committed; be unconditionally accepting.*
Empowering	A shared culture; group maintenance and governance; development of young people [or new members]; *be understanding; be concerned for both yourself and others.*
Ethical	Caring, trust and teamwork; *be ethical.*
Purposeful	Participation and shared leadership tasks;
Process-oriented	Good internal communication; *be mindful; be peaceful.*

of several groups, not just one. "If there is no sense of community, it stands to reason that it will be difficult to solve community problems. . . . People in a community have to have a public spirit and a sense of relationship" (Gudykunst, 1991, p. 128).

Rarely is one group or one organization solely responsible or does it possess sufficient resources (including information) to create, implement, or sustain a complex change. This reality necessitates a commitment to coalition building. "Coalitions are often a preferred vehicle for intergroup action because they promise to preserve the autonomy of member organizations while providing the necessary structure for united effort" (Mizrahi & Rosenthal, 1993, p. 12). The approach to changing campus parking policies would not be nearly as meaningful if, for example, a residence hall government complained that change was needed instead of joining with the Commuter Student Union and Graduate Student Housing to work together toward that change.

Joining with other interested groups and organizations can create impressive change. "Through coalitions, separate groups can develop a common language and ideology with which to share a collective vision for progressive social change" (Mizrahi & Rosenthal, 1993, p. 12). They define a social change coalition as "a group of diverse organizational representatives who join forces to influence external institutions on one or more issues affecting their constituencies while maintaining their own autonomy. It is (a) an organization of organizations who share a common goal; (b) time limited; and (c) characterized by dynamic tensions" (Mizrahi & Rosenthal, 1993, p. 14).

Mizrahi and Rosenthal (1993) have identified four distinct types of goals and time durations of coalitions: "*specific goal, short-term groups* (e.g. organizing demonstrations or forums), *specific goal, long-term* (e.g. banishing domestic violence, housing court reform); *general goal, short-term* (fighting crime or drugs), and *general goal, long-term* (neighborhood improvement coalitions, anti-racist networks)" (p. 14–15). Imagine some examples of what this might look like regarding campus issues (see Exhibit 8.2).

EXHIBIT 8.2 Campus Coalitions

| GOALS | TIME FRAME | |
	Short-Term	Long-Term
Specific	Homecoming; Thanksgiving canned food drive	Reducing incidents of date rape
General	Freshman community building	Diversity initiatives; revising general education requirements

Coalitions are not easy to build. Mizrahi & Rosenthal (1993) propose that each of these types of coalitions experience a cooperation-conflict dynamic; four dynamic tensions arise in varying degrees.

1. *The tensions of mixed loyalties* result from the dual commitment the members feel between their own sponsoring organization and the growing loyalty to the coalition. For example, a member of the Campus Safety Committee may come to learn the realities of improving campus lighting and see the need to have a phased program but be pressured from the women's group she is representing to make it all happen at once.

2. *The tension between autonomy and accountability* in which the coalitions need the independence to act, yet each member needs to connect back to their organization to maintain organizational commitment and endorsement. The Campus Environmental Action Coalition just discovered a state grant they can apply for, but they

must set a focus for the grant and meet a one-week deadline. There is not time to fully consult with other organizations, which might cause those organizations to feel excluded.

3. *The tension between the amount of emphasis to place on the coalition* being seen as a means to achieve a specific goal or as a model of cooperation. Tension results between those who support the coalition as a means for achieving desired results and those who want to preserve the relationships regardless of the results. The coalition probably needs to be both. It needs to be the way some goal is actually addressed and also serve as a model of how various groups can work effectively together. For example, think of a coalition of Asian American Student Associations on campus who have come together to work for an Asian studies program. Some in the group will see the potential of working together for other purposes as well and be hopeful that the various Asian American student groups are in dialogue. Others in the group just want this one goal accomplished and see no need to preserve the coalition.

4. *The tension between unity and diversity* in which members of the coalition need to find ways to act with common purpose, recognizing the differences they bring to the goal. "The more one favors strengthening communities . . . the more one must concern oneself with ensuring that they see themselves as parts of a more encompassing whole, rather than as fully independent and antagonistic" (Etzioni, 1993, p. 155). The homecoming committee might work hard to keep a balance among the athletic emphasis, social reunions, cultural events, current student celebrations, and academic updates that are planned, even if those behind any one kind of event think it should be preeminent.

"Serving as president of the student body and also
president of the disabled student organization, I have
had the opportunity to see both sides. Administration
is concerned with cost effectiveness, being politically
correct, community support, and a positive

representation of the college at a community level.
The student is concerned with pursuing and
fulfilling the needs of fellow students, environment,
community, and dealing with issues. Working
together allows results that benefit both sides."—
Dawn M. Roberts is a returning adult learner at Gulf
Coast Community College majoring in social work.

Coalitions face unique challenges when forming alliances between groups that differ in fundamentally different approaches or worldviews that are reflected in their sex, race, sexual orientation, or class. "Minority groups have many reasons to mistrust majority groups who have historically exploited, coopted, and dominated them" (Mizrahi & Rosenthal, 1993, p. 31). Majority groups (those who have been in the dominant culture) have been used to being in control and have most often seen decisions made and problems approached in ways they are comfortable with. For marginalized group members to follow the methods of the dominant culture leadership may feel like being co-opted; to bring up issues of interest may seem like having a special agenda; and teaching the dominant culture about the issues salient to those who have not been heard in the past takes energy and can build resentment. The dominant culture may be administrators, those with resources, or the white culture. Marginalized culture may be students, the poor, or historically peripheral groups. While this may not be true of the group experiences of all those who have been underrepresented, marginalization should be addressed as if it were a true problem. This will help build sensitive coalitions.

Building effective coalitions among diverse members is important to producing successful results. Mizrahi and Rosenthal (1993) recommend that all coalition members (notably what they identify as the minority groups) be involved in the design of the coalition goals and methods from the beginning and not brought in at a later point, which can be seen as tokenism. Further, the coalition must keep a top priority on enhancing diversity and insist on the involvement of those who will be affected by the change outcome. Relational leadership values doing things *with* people, not *to* them.

College Communities

For hundreds of years, college campuses have been described as communities of scholars or as learning communities. Yet in reality, a sense of true community is not often a shared experience. The Carnegie Foundation (1990) conducted a major study of what students, faculty, and staff would like to change about their campuses. All groups agreed that they need a renewed sense of community—not a return to an older, homogeneous model but a kaleidoscope community that embraces differences and finds common purpose. How we treat each other speaks loudly about the nature of a community. We might all accept the challenge of practicing the discipline of community in all groups, classes, organizations, as well as in systems on campus where common purpose and diverse talents abound.

As microcosms of the society, the entire college campus is a community and includes multiple communities. There are communities within the various positions on campus (for example, students, faculty, administrators, staff, alumni). Within those groups are smaller community clusters (for example, seniors, the Asian Student Association, graduate students); each cluster has unique needs and shares community issues. There are communities by departments and by the programs of functional units (for example, the history department, the engineering college, the student activities office, the intercollegiate athletics program, the women's center). All of these communities are bound together by the common goals of being a community of people committed to learning and to advancing their own education and the education of others.

Different organizations have different purposes and focus. Higher education communities emphasize such elements as collegiality, learning, scholarship, academic freedom, and student development. A social organization might emphasize friendship, fun, and enriching experiences. A sports team stresses competence, teamwork, and responsibility. Regardless of the special mission and focus of those groups and organizations, the people in them will experience healthy communities if they intentionally practice the discipline of community.

Chapter Summary

Relational leadership is enhanced by understanding any group or organization as a community of people working together for shared purposes. Thinking of that group as a community connects participants to a shared paradigm of expectations and obligations. Communities require relational leadership to flourish. Relational leadership practices value community as the context in which meaningful change can occur.

What's Next?

Relationships within community contexts are all grounded in trust. Sadly, too many people observe a lack of integrity and find violations of the public trust all around them. The next chapter focuses on leadership that is committed to creating ethical environments. Trust, integrity, ethical practices, character, and moral purpose are so important that they deserve more of our reflection than often happens when learning leadership. The next chapter presents a case for moral purpose and explores the related foundational dimensions of ethical and moral reasoning.

Chapter Activities

1. Think about a particular community of which you are, or have been, a member. Which of Gardner's eight elements of community were especially visible in this community? Which were missing and why?

2. Describe a community of which you were an active member. Try to relate this community to the four stages of community development as outlined by Peck. Did you experience each stage? If not, why not? What was each one like? How were they similar? How were they different?

3. Consider the different types of tensions in coalition building outlined by Mizrahi and Rosenthal. Have you experienced any of them? Which ones? How did they feel? How did you address that tension?

4. To what degree is some kind of community awareness essential for the Relational Leadership Model? Can the model still be a helpful frame to guide your leadership role (as a participant or as a positional leader), even if a sense of community does not exist in your groups or organizations?

Additional Readings

The Carnegie Foundation (1990). *Campus life: In search of community*. Princeton, NJ: Carnegie Foundation for the Advancement of Teaching.

Etzioni, A. (1993). *The spirit of community*. New York: Crown.

Peck, M. S. (1987). *The different drum: Community-making and peace*. New York: Simon & Schuster.

Rheingold, H. (1993). *The virtual community: Homesteading on the electronic frontier*. New York: HarperCollins.

9

Leading with Integrity and Moral Purpose

Imagine yourself in the following situations:

• Your campus has policies that govern how organizations can recruit new members. You are the newly elected president of a student organization with a dwindling number of current members. If you do not recruit a large number of new members this year, your organization will be forced to disband. Current members are prepared to do anything necessary to recruit enough members to keep your organization in existence. What do you do?

• You are a new participant in a residence hall programming committee. Your committee rents videos from one of the major distribution companies to show in the halls on a rotating basis during the semester. The committee's regular practice is to copy all of the videos that are used. When you ask about this practice, you are told, "Everyone does it." What do you do?

• You are in charge of the election's committee in your organization. Your by-laws note that all officers must have a minimum grade point average at the time they are elected. Candidates must sign a statement verifying that they have good enough grades to be eligible for office, but these statements are never checked or verified. Your best friend is running for office and has signed such a form. You know his GPA is lower than the required minimum. In the past, other candidates have signed such a form without having the necessary grades, and this by-law is considered a joke by the organization. What do you do?

Too often, we find ourselves in ethical dilemmas like these, and our tendency is to react quickly to resolve them. However, quick decisions preclude careful thought about all the aspects of the situation, which could raise questions of character and ethics if participants rush to decisions that are void of ethical considerations. Participants might get caught up in competition that causes them only to focus on the bottom line or on winning at all costs. They may feel the need to please others, without stopping to think about the implications of the decisions and their long-term effects. They may tend to shove problems under the rug to avoid tarnishing the organization's reputation or to avoid causing conflict in the group. But we need to learn to slow the process down and reflect on the ethical and moral aspects of actions and decisions. If you are used to quickly resolving ethical dilemmas, then it might be a challenge for you to stop, reflect on the situation, involve others in helping to address it, and weigh all possible alternatives of action. The key is to allow yourself and others some time to work through complex problems and engage in a process that includes reflection before action.

Chapter Overview

In Chapter Three we introduced the ethical component of the Relational Leadership Model, emphasizing the importance of ethics in the leadership process. In Chapter Four we explored essential elements of personal values and character. This chapter includes (1) a discussion of the process of creating and sustaining ethical organizational environments, (2) an analysis of the moral dimensions of transforming leadership theory, and (3) an examination of the ethical influences that participants have on their organizations through behavior modeling. Practical applications of ethics and leadership are highlighted using ethical decision-making models.

Creating and Sustaining an Ethical Organizational Environment

Understanding and applying ethical theories and models that operate from organizational values or codes of conduct, as well as being aware of your own moral development, helps to create and sustain ethical organizational environments. Nash (1990, pp. 43–47) proposes four qualities that are necessary for participants to advance ethical standards in an organization.

1. Critical thinking skills to analyze and convey the ethical components of a problem or dilemma
2. Possessing a high degree of integrity to stand up for your personal and professional ethics
3. The ability to see situations from others' perspectives (showing concern for others)
4. Being personally motivated to do the right thing

It is important when using these ethical decision-making models and principles that you are prepared to receive criticism, see members revolt, and perhaps experience a decline in membership. Not everyone in an organization is prepared or willing to do the right thing or has a moral orientation. Some would prefer to take the easy way out, do what is more economical, or take the path of least resistance. Nash's idea of having personal courage is of utmost importance when trying to make the right decision for the good of an organization in the face of opposition from the membership. Part of the leadership process is to fully explain to others the problem at hand and the basis for the action or decision.

These four qualities of leadership, when translated into behavior and action, help create an ethical organizational environment. When you identify a problem as having moral or ethical implications and involve others in the decision-making process, you provide another example of how an ethical environment is established. Several strategies and interventions can be used to create and maintain an ethical climate in a group or organization setting. The process of doing so should be intentional and include all the elements of the Relational Leadership Model.

All participants—positional leadership and members alike—should be equally empowered to set a tone in the organizational climate that will foster and support ethical and moral actions and sensitivities. The organization's mission or the group's common purpose should be the driving force for identifying its values. Participants should identify and operate from a shared set of core values that guide the organization's activities, actions, and decisions. These core values will enable individuals to work toward a common purpose and provide a common understanding of the organization's principles and standards. Members are empowered to hold each other accountable, participate in moral talk or dialogue, and work together to sustain an ethical environment. Appointing one person to be the group's ethicist or standard bearer will not achieve the same degree of ethical climate as when all participants are concerned with doing what is right. In fact, it may be counterproductive when a leader handles ethical dilemmas alone or in isolation from other members of the organization.

What is rewarded and recognized often teaches others about what is acceptable and unacceptable behavior within an organization. Creating awards and recognition for members who help sustain an ethical environment by taking risks to do the right thing is an excellent way to publicly acknowledge and promote ethical behavior. One example is the Giraffe Project, which is located in the state of Washington. The project was founded to provide higher visibility in the media and through other venues for individuals who take risks for a cause or for furthering ethical standards. Recipients are given a Giraffe Award certificate and a carved wooden giraffe at a public recognition ceremony. Similarly, Outstanding Student Leader of the Year awards, which emphasize the recipient's commitment to moral or ethical action, are an example of a way to recognize ethical behavior.

On the other side of the award continuum, unethical behavior should be addressed, but in a different manner. Public humiliation was a practice commonly used in the past to confront and punish violators of the law or ethical standards. Some cultures continue this practice today. Participants have the shared responsibility of confronting individuals who violate the organization's standards and practices. Although we do not condone public humiliation as a motivational method, members need to know that they will be held accountable for such breaches. Participants have an obligation under the principle of "doing no harm" to protect an individual's right to confidentiality when addressing a violation of rules or standards and ensuring that due process is provided and safeguarded.

Some organizations lack a positive ethical environment because leaders and participants are not committed to a moral orientation. These types of organizations may, in fact, reward unethical behavior because it is seen as "improving" the organization. An example of this would be an organization that uses unethical practices during membership recruitment to increase its membership. This type of organizational environment would support short cuts, poor-quality work, cover-ups, and a lack of personal responsibility for mistakes or problems. Individuals committed to leading with integrity are faced with their own dilemma of what to do when their values and principles clash with the organization's standards. This is a very difficult situation and offers only three choices: (1) ignore or put up with the situation; (2) address the situation and work to change the organizational climate into one that is ethical in nature; or (3) leave the organization. This is a difficult situation and one with which leaders struggle every day.

Moral Purpose as an Act of Courage

During the time this book was being written, our nation witnessed an extraordinary moral dilemma involving an ordinary citizen. In April of 1996, David Kaczynski turned his brother, Theodore Kaczynski, in to the authorities because he suspected him of being the Unabomber—the man who plagued the country for more than two decades by sending bombs through the mail, killing or permanently harming several innocent victims. David Kacyznski is an example of a courageous individual who did what he believed was right for the greater good of people. He did so at the painful expense of knowing that his brother, if found guilty, would be given a serious criminal sentence, perhaps even the death penalty. David Kaczynski acted with emotional agony because he wanted to believe that his brother was not the Unabomber. In the final analysis, David Kaczynski acted with moral purpose. This incident illuminates the difficult human struggle of discerning what is right and what is wrong when there are no easy answers or solutions. Under this circumstance or a similar one, ask yourself, Would you turn one of your siblings or your best friend in to the FBI if you thought he or she was the Unabomber?

More in-depth examination is needed of leaders and participants who are ethical in their dealings and who model good leadership—leadership that is moral, courageous, and responsible. Usually, we start searching for ethical leaders who were national or historical figures. But we know leaders like that in our everyday lives—local business leaders, faculty and administrators, religious leaders from the local community, committed citizens of a neighborhood organization, your peers, and nonprofit leaders who often work quietly and with humility to serve others. As was the case with David Kaczynski, good leaders can be ordinary people from our local communities.

Assumptions About Ethical Leadership

There are many myths and misunderstandings about "good" leadership—leadership that is both ethical and effective (Ciulla, 1995). Lucas and Anello (1995) propose eight assumptions about ethical leadership, which are central themes in the study and practice of ethical leadership:

1. *Ethics is the heart of leadership.* It is the central issue in leadership (Ciulla, 1995). You cannot have a complete discussion about leadership without including the ethical components associated with leadership processes. "Good leadership" means leadership that is effective, in that goals were achieved, and that follows a sound

and ethical process. The means do justify the ends when leading with integrity.

2. *All leadership is values-driven.* We need to reframe leadership so that it represents values that reflect good (ethical) leadership. Participants and leaders bring to the organization their own values and beliefs about how people should be treated, notions of what is right versus what is wrong, and ideas about what is just and fair. Organizations and communities are values-driven as opposed to values-neutral.

3. *The journey to ethical leadership begins with an examination of personal values,* as well as ongoing reflection of personal core values and how these values are related to the values of an organization or community. Your personal moral compass will guide you in wrestling with ethical dilemmas and eventually will point you in the direction of making a decision based on ethical analysis, consideration of opposing viewpoints, your personal values, and the values of your organization.

4. *Ethical leadership can be learned in a variety of ways* through a process involving experience, reflection, conceptualization, and application. Trial-and-error experiences can sharpen your ethical analysis, as well as your reflection about notions of what is just and fair in a given situation. You can learn this before you must act or make a decision. The life experiences you gain over time will affect your development as an ethical leader.

5. *Ethical leadership involves a connection between ethical thought and action.* Linking moral reasoning with values and action is imperative in leadership. The point of this chapter is not to have you memorize dozens of ethical theories. The goal is to engage you in ethical analysis and insights based on theories and concepts applied to real-life experiences.

6. *Character development is an essential ingredient of ethical leadership.* A leader's character is defined by his or her actions and behaviors, not simply by the values that are espoused. Leaders can be popular yet not be respected by the public because they lack congruency between their values and actions. In other words, they don't walk their talk.

7. *Members at all levels of an organization or community have the opportunity and responsibility to participate in the process of exercising ethical leadership.* Ethical leadership is a *shared* process, not just the responsibility of a positional leader. Leaders and participants share the responsibility of advancing core organizational values and of doing the right thing. Members often are called upon to be courageous and to advocate for what is right, despite risks such as losing a job or alienating friends. Organizations that are empowering and inclusive involve members in wrestling with ethical dilemmas and seek their advice on how to resolve problems.

8. *Everything we do teaches.* Role modeling is a powerful way to influence the ethical climate in families, organizations, and communities. We learn by watching others, and we make judgments about what is acceptable and unacceptable behavior in organizations. If any member (including the positional leader) routinely discriminates against other students in a membership recruitment process, then others in the organization might believe it is acceptable to exclude students of color in extending invitations to join the group. Conversely, if a leader values diversity and decides to increase the number of minorities by 50 percent on her senior staff, then other managers of the company will most likely follow her strategy.

Leading with moral purpose calls for an examination of your assumptions about what is ethical and what is unethical, how far you are willing to go to advance your core values and do the right thing, what you are willing to risk to achieve the values of justice and fairness, and how you will wrestle with an inconsistency between your values and the values of your organization. The goal is not to discover easy answers or quick fixes to these issues but to engage in an ethical analysis and to use your moral imagination in solving problems and dilemmas.

"I think being ethical is absolutely necessary when
talking about leadership. You have to have some
moral code from which your ideals come. If you act

unethical in any way, you are hurting not only
yourself but those who look up to you. In the 'real
world,' not everyone operates in an ethical manner,
but I truly believe that those who do end up being
winners in the long run."—Tim Slaughter is vice
president of Leadership Development and a member
of Student Senate at Texas A&M University.

Cultural Assumptions

Ethics also are culturally bound or culture-specific. There is no uni-
versal agreement on what behaviors or practices are considered
appropriate, legal, ethical, or moral across cultures (Henderson,
1992; Toffler, 1986). For example, the intentional oppression and
discrimination of women in Saudi Arabia is considered ethical,
legal, and moral in that country but is unethical, illegal, and
immoral in the United States. Ethics are also temporal in nature,
especially in light of changing laws and legal norms. What was considered by many to be an ethical and legal, standard practice in the
1960s—having separate water fountains for whites and African
Americans—is considered illegal, unethical, and immoral today.
Laws and regulations influence the changing nature of ethical practices and behaviors, especially in the business world.

Anthropological studies have documented the divergent moral
views and practices interculturally and intraculturally (De George,
1986). Abortion in one country may be considered morally acceptable, whereas in another culture it is considered immoral. Notions
of right and wrong or justice and injustice are validated by the values and attitudes of a given culture (Donaldson, 1989). To place
worth on moral concepts through intercultural comparison is futile.
For example, many American women believe the veil worn by
Moslem women constitutes sexist behavior and practices. What is
socially practiced and acceptable in one culture is repudiated in
another. This brings up the painful or perhaps sobering reality that
there is no moral consensus in international affairs. Ethics and

morals differ not only among various countries but among individuals in the same country.

Cultural tolerance implies that differences in practices are recognized, but not for the purpose of imposing or changing the practices to suit a particular cultural belief (Donaldson, 1989). Cultural relativism is germane to a specific culture, society, or community. The goal in comparing cultural practices is to understand them, not to judge them as good or bad. For example, leaders of multinational business organizations must follow the local laws, norms, mores, and practices associated with the country in which they are conducting business.

Many of these ethical assumptions emanate from various leadership and ethical theories and models. The following section provides an overview of ethical theories and foundations in leadership.

Ethical Theories and Moral Purposes

The study of human behavior as it relates to ethics and ethical development reaches back to the philosopher kings (Aristotle, Plato, Socrates), as well as to eighteenth- and nineteenth-century philosophers and scholars such as Immanuel Kant and John Stuart Mill. Ethical theories provide a glimpse into how human judgments are made and the thought processes individuals engage in to solve ethical dilemmas and other problems. In the next section, transforming leadership theory is described as the foremost theory that incorporates a moral component as its foundation for leadership.

Transforming Leadership Theory

The leadership theory that includes a strong component of ethics and morals is James MacGregor Burns's transforming leadership theory. As noted in Chapter Two, transforming leadership is a process in which "leaders and followers raise one another to higher levels of morality and motivation" (Burns, 1978, p. 20). Transforming leadership reaches moral dimensions when the leaders' and participants' behavior and ethical aspirations are elevated by mutual influences on one another (Burns, 1978). Transforming leadership involves persuasion, a desire to change something, and multidirectional influence relationships between leaders and participants (Rost, 1991). In any leadership situation, participants can, and often do, influence leaders to higher ethical ends.

Values or ideals such as peace, justice, fairness, liberty, equal opportunity, and people's general welfare are expressed by transformational leaders. Burns labeled these ideals as "end values" (Burns, 1978, p. 43). Leaders, superiors, participants, peers, followers, and others influence these values through specific behaviors. "The leader's fundamental act is to induce people to be aware or conscious of what they feel—to feel their true needs so strongly, to define their values so meaningfully, that they can move to purposeful action" (Burns, 1978, p. 44).

Transforming leadership theory is about the relationship and influence between leaders and followers. Burns describes this symbiotic relationship as an interaction of power and shared values. "It is the power of a person to become a leader, armed with principles and rising above self-interest narrowly conceived that invests that person with power and may ultimately transform both leaders and followers into persons who jointly adhere to modal values and end-values" (Burns, 1978, p. 457). The moral purposes of both leaders and participants are the key factors in the transforming leadership process. Change results from these shared moral purposes.

Of the seven characteristics Tichy and Devanna (1986) use to characterize transforming leaders, two relate to ethical and moral dimensions of leadership: courageous and value-driven. Transforming leaders have the courage to "confront reality even if it is painful" (p. 30) and have healthy egos to withstand peer pressure. Possessing positive self-esteem (not needing to please others to win their favor) is a necessary element of leading with moral purpose. This contrasts with leading to win a popularity contest (needing to be liked by others). For example, the president of Habitat for Humanity decided to follow her school's alcohol policy and not permit members to take cases of beer on the spring break trip, despite the fact that the membership had unanimously voted to take alcohol on the trip. In this case, the president decided to do what was right despite popular sentiment and knowing that most people would be upset with her decision.

Transformational leaders also are value-driven. They have a core set of values that are consistent with their actions. There are several ways in which a leader can inspire others to higher levels of morality—through influence and through modeling behaviors that become the standards for others to follow.

Modeling a Moral Purpose

If participants admire or identify with another member or leader, they will be more likely to imitate that person's behavior. Social learning theory provides a framework for understanding how individuals learn from others (Sims & Lorenzi, 1992). Bandura, the pioneer of social learning theory, postulated that people can learn indirectly from observation or by vicarious learning (Bandura, 1977; Manz & Sims, 1981; Rosenthal & Zimmerman, 1978; Sims & Manz, 1981). Observational learning has its history in the practices of ancient Greeks, who referred to this concept as imitation or *mimesis*. Greek scholars selected the best models in Greco-Roman literature to teach their young students (Rosenthal & Zimmerman, 1978, p. 33). Behavioral modeling by leaders and participants offers a type of vicarious learning stimulus in organizational settings.

Models in organizations are capable of eliciting ethical or unethical behavior. Referent others significantly influence the ethical decision making in organizations. For example, a student president of the Latino Student Union who wants everyone in the organization to feel empowered will practice sharing power and authority with leaders and members and will create opportunities for members to make meaningful contributions to the organization. Through observing the president, other organizational leaders empower committee chairs and members and involve them in the decision-making process.

Vicarious learning or behavioral modeling has important implications for the leadership process. Organizational and community members can learn ethical practices by observing those who model these practices in their leadership approaches. For example, members of the marching band who substitute a new activity for their traditional fund-raiser—showing an X-rated movie—because such movies are degrading and offensive to women *model* social responsibility to other members of the campus community.

Another illustration of behavioral modeling by leaders occurs when a football coach benches the star player for violating an NCAA rule, even though the coach needs that player to clinch the final playoff game. Organizational and team members learn that negative consequences result from such behavior by observing how a peer is treated. Sims and Lorenzi (1992) refer to this phenomenon as "outcome expectation" (p. 143). Participants also might infer that the leader possesses a high degree of integrity and is motivated to do the right thing. The behavior of the leader, or the coach in the example, then influences team members to act ethically because that is what is reinforced or because they want to avoid punishment for unethical behavior—or both.

Participants also model behavior that inspires leaders' ethical awareness (Chaleff, 1995). For example, the members of a student-owned food co-op influenced the student-manager to use empathy in deciding whether to dismiss an employee who missed work three days in a row to care for his ill, elderly grandmother. The members asked the manager to consider the fact that the employee was putting himself through school and that he was the only relative who could care for his grandmother. They suggested that the manager revise the work schedule to allow the employee time to help his grandmother and still maintain some hours at the co-op. In this example, the members were modeling how empathy could be used by putting themselves in the employee's situation and realizing what the impact of dismissal would be.

Modeling can also have external effects that extend beyond organizational boundaries. Ben Cohen and Jerry Greenfield, of Ben & Jerry's Ice Cream, modeled a type of socially responsible behavior in the business world when they donated pretax profits to social programs. By doing this, Ben and Jerry attempted to model a moral standard for other business leaders to follow (Howell & Avolio, 1992). Since Ben and Jerry's initiative, many other companies have committed to socially responsible efforts. Examples are The Body Shop, Honeywell Inc., and Bell Atlantic Corp (Kurschner, 1996).

These examples illustrate that modeling by leaders and participants affects the ethical climate of organizations. Another form of modeling is when leaders or participants engage in discussions of ethical issues or bring up ethical dilemmas that can be resolved through an exchange of multiple perspectives.

Moral Talk

How often have you found yourself in an organizational meeting or in a classroom where someone raises ethical or moral questions around a particular issue your group is working on? Leaders and participants would benefit by engaging in conversations that allow people to explore the moral complexities and dimensions of problems or dilemmas. Bird and Waters (1989) provide an interesting notion of modeling or influencing ethical behavior through verbal exchanges or "moral talk" or "dialogic leadership" (Neilson, 1990, p. 765).

The dialogic leader initiates discussions with peers and members about what is ethical and what the material interests of individuals are. Dialogic leadership or moral talk can be used in student organizations as a way to model ethical approaches and to help create and sustain an ethical environment. For example, a student president of an honor society includes on the meeting agenda a discussion of the nature of the group's test files. A member speaks up at the meeting about her concern that a few of the exams in the files have been stolen. She then asks members if maintaining those files is the kind of activity the group should engage in, knowing that this is a violation of the college's honor code. A discussion ensues about whether or not the activity is counter to the organization's mission and the organization's values of academic excellence and integrity.

The relationship between leadership and ethics can be illustrated by the application of enduring values in a system of human relationships (i.e., organizations). This sensitive relationship is made difficult by the fact that value systems vary from individual to individual.—Luciano C. Oviedo is an electrical and computer engineering major at the University of Wisconsin-Madison. He is president of the Society of Hispanic Professional Engineers and a volunteer tutor with a bilingual middle school.

A real-life example of how a student government member used dialogic leadership to inspire leaders and members of the group to discuss values and ethics occurred when the student used the game of Scruples at a retreat. Although it appeared as if the members were just playing a game, in reality they were participating in conversations about how they would approach a series of dilemmas posed by questions on the cards. At the end of the game, the student government member asked others to reflect on what had just happened and how they, as a group of elected officials, should work together to confront complex issues back on campus.

While the topic of ethics is encountered by individual leaders and participants, little discourse about ethics takes place among group members. This lack of discussion about ethics is referred to as "moral muteness" (Bird & Waters, 1989).

Unfortunately, individuals often hesitate to participate in moral talk or discussions about ethical dilemmas (Bird & Waters, 1989). Reasons for this include the avoidance of complex problems with moral overtones, protection of the positional leader's own managerial flexibility in solving problems, and avoidance of dealing with varying ideological or moralistic perspectives—all of which potentially inhibits the problem-solving process. Group members might also avoid discussion of ethics and morals due to their own ethical illiteracy. The potential harm caused by not modeling this through conversations or discussions is the neglect of moral abuses or an environment that is indifferent to moral considerations. It is the shared responsibility of members and leaders to initiate moral talk and to avoid moral muteness.

Moral expressions have the potential to arouse feelings of connection with moral action. The language in moral talk has to be connected with experiences and expectations of people involved in the organization for the modeling effect to occur. Moral talk can be used as a type of modeling influence when the dialogue is used to identify problems, consider issues, advocate and criticize policies, and justify and explain decisions (Bird & Waters, 1989; Pocock, 1989). Leaders and participants can use moral talk to influence others to carefully consider their perspectives and positions on issues.

Dennis Gioia (1991), in a paper entitled, "Pinto Fires and Personal Ethics: A Script Analysis of Missed Opportunities," describes an ethical dilemma in which moral muteness prevailed. In the early 1970s, it was discovered that accidents from low-impact, rear collisions to the Ford Pinto automobiles caused these cars to catch fire and in some cases explode, leading to serious injuries and even deaths. Gioia described the dilemma he faced when working at Ford Motor Company. He had to decide whether to recall the Ford Pinto due to poor safety reports or to denounce the recall based on the low numbers of cars affected. Other corporate managers exhibited moral muteness on the ethical and moral aspects of the safety problems and potential dangers to consumers by refusing to acknowledge that this automobile posed hazards because of a poorly designed fuel system.

Gioia admits that his own thoughts lacked ethical dimensions, which led him to overlook the key elements of the Pinto case. In addition, his superiors and colleagues avoided moral talk about the ethical dimensions associated with the case and focused solely on the bottom line. Leaders and managers at Ford provided negative modeling, which influenced Gioia to overlook critical safety factors associated with the Pinto. Gioia focused mostly on the bottom line and succumbed to financial pressures of the cost-benefit analysis of upgrading the fuel system. Changing the fuel system would have cost the company too much money. Little consideration was given to the public safety issues of the Pinto. Had Gioia encountered an ethical model or mentor during his tenure at Ford or heard other leaders and managers discuss ethical implications of various solutions to this problem, perhaps he would have made a different decision. A vicarious learning experience through a model or the presence of dialogic leadership could have caused him to think of an alternative action.

Ethical Decision-Making Models

The leadership process is filled with daily ethical dilemmas and problems that do not have readily identifiable solutions and that leaders and participants need to confront and resolve. It is not *solely* the responsibility of the leader to address these dilemmas or confront unethical behavior. The Relational Leadership Model, with its emphasis on inclusive and process-oriented leadership to achieve results for the common good, suggests that leaders and members both be included in addressing ethical dilemmas. Leaders and participants together need to be reflective, challenging, caring, purposeful, and consultative when working through ethical issues.

There are several approaches you can use to resolve ethical dilemmas. Some situations might call for using a professional code of conduct. For example, lawyers' and physicians' professional conduct is guided by standards upheld by their respective professional associations. Religious and counseling professionals are guided by a strict adherence to client confidentiality unless a client is a potential harm to self or others. Many campuses have sexual harassment and nondiscrimination policies that also guide behavior. Fraternities and sororities have rituals that serve as statements of organizational standards and values. Students may follow an honor code in classroom testing practices. Student governments are often bound to constitutions and by-laws that assist in decision-making processes related to funding and student organization recognition.

Like leadership, ethics is not a neat and tidy concept. Not all situations can be resolved by the application of professional codes or organizational standards (Beauchamp & Childress, 1979; Kitchener, 1984). It requires human judgment and analysis to even determine whether a situation represents an ethical dilemma or something else, like a personality conflict between two members.

"I rely on my own ethical base. If I am having trouble coming to a resolution, chances are the issue or decision is not clear cut. I take time to think things through. I may not always know the answer, but I do know where to get assistance."—Matthew J. Biaoi is a member of the student senate, president of his fraternity, and involved with orientation at Alfred University.

Although one of several models could be used to guide ethical decision making, the following section includes three models that can be used as practical tools in resolving ethical dilemmas. All of these models should be used by leaders and participants together to collaboratively work through problems. The models should be applied with careful analysis rather than with a rigid application of any particular model; reflection and a careful consideration of other factors are needed. These models call for the use of your moral imagination, that is, visualizing new alternatives to old or unsolved problems; otherwise, the frameworks cannot stand on their own.

Practical Applications

Imagine this scenario. You attend a college that has a strict honor code calling for community members to turn in anyone who violates the code. You are also the president of the interfraternity council.

During an exam, you notice a fraternity brother, who is also one of your best friends, cheating from another classmate. How do you go about confronting this situation? Do you follow the code and turn your fraternity brother in to the judicial office? Or do you try to influence him after the exam not to cheat in the future because you will have to turn him in and it would look bad for your fraternity? Or do you begin to initiate a decision-making process that will guide you from the stage of interpreting the situation—if I respond in a certain way, how will it affect others?—to the final stage of *acting* with your convictions and moral purpose in mind? Or do you do nothing, acting without moral purpose?

Ethical decision-making models encourage people to work through dilemmas with a moral purpose in mind and provide frameworks in which to guide decision making and analysis. Rather than react quickly to dilemmas, you should carefully consider various steps, including ethical analysis, toward making sound decisions.

Rest's Four-Component Decision-Making Model

James Rest (1986) provides a practical decision-making model based on moral reasoning and an ethic of care. This hybrid model includes four components of a decision-making process that can be applied, especially when faced with a problem that poses no clear solution.

According to Rest, moral development or moral behavior is composed of four distinct functions. It is not the result of a single process. Although one process might interact or influence others, the four processes have distinct functions. Rest's model describes the processes involved in the production of a moral act, not general traits of people. The four components are not presented as four virtues that make the ideal moral person but as major units of analysis in tracing how a particular course of action was produced in the context of a particular situation. The model is not a linear, time-bound sequence. There may be complicated interactions between the various components. For example, a person's way of defining what is morally right (Component 2) might affect the person's interpretation of the situation (Component 1). The model presented in Exhibit 9.1 should be thought of as depicting a logical order for the development of a moral act to occur (Rest, 1979, 1986).

Consider the following situation. You are the president of the college's Young Political Club. Your group has discovered that an unflattering article about the club will be printed in the next day's

---

EXHIBIT 9.1 Rest's Four-Component Decision-Making Model

Component I: Moral Sensitivity
                (interpreting the situation as moral)
  A. Being aware of the situation's moral dimension, that is, that the welfare of another person is at stake
  B. Recognizing how possible courses of action affect all parties involved

Component II: Moral Judgment
                (defining the morally ideal course of action)
  A. Determining what should be done
  B. Formulating a plan of action that applies a moral standard or ideal (for example, justice)

Component III: Moral Motivation
                (deciding what to do)
  A. Evaluating the various courses of action for how they would serve moral or nonmoral values (for example, political sensitivity, professional aspirations)
  B. Deciding what to do

Component IV: Moral Action
                (executing and implementing a moral plan of action)
  A. Acting as one intended to act; following through with that decision
  B. Assisted by perseverance, resoluteness, strong character, core values, the strength of one's convictions, and so on

campus newspaper. Club members begin planning a scheme to steal all the newspapers before students get them in the morning. Using the four-component model, how would you approach this situation? What are the moral dimensions of this situation? Is it a violation of a constitutional right to freedom of the press, or a violation of the school's honor code? (Component I). Would you convince members not to execute their plan because they might get caught and the club might loose its charter? Or would you threaten to turn them in if they proceed? Or would you influence them not to do this because it is wrong to steal these papers and an obstruction of the constitutional right of freedom of the press? (Component II). If the group proceeds to steal the newspapers, would reporting them to the campus judicial office result in their expulsion from school and possibly prevent them from ever having the chance to complete their college degrees? If you did nothing, would you be modeling behavior to others that condones an illegal act? What *should* you do? What are all your alternative courses of action? How will your decision affect the ethical environment of your organization? (Component III). What *would* you do if members actually stole the papers? (Component IV).

In the helping professions, several scholars have adapted Aristotle's ethical principles, which serve as the foundation for living an ethical life and as principles or standards to guide physicians, psychologists, and counselors in particular (Beauchamp & Childress, 1989; Kitchener, 1984). Beauchamp and Childress (1979) proposed five principles of biomedical ethics, which were later adapted by Karen Strohm Kitchener, a professor of education, for the counseling psychology field. These five ethical principles are (1) respecting autonomy, (2) doing no harm, (3) benefiting others, (4) being just, and (5) being faithful. As a leader or member, you can use these five principles as a critical evaluative approach to moral reasoning and ethical decision-making processes (Beauchamp & Childress, 1979). Using the critical evaluative approach allows leaders and members "to illuminate our ordinary moral judgment and to redefine the bases for our actions" (Kitchener, 1984, p. 45).

EXHIBIT 9.2 Five Ethical Principles in Decision Making

1. *Respecting Autonomy*: providing leaders and members with the freedom of choice, allowing individuals to freely develop their values, and respecting the right of others to act independently. Autonomy, like constitutional rights and liberties, has conditions and does not imply unrestricted freedom. A major assumption of autonomy is that an individual possesses a certain level of competence to make rational and informed decisions.

2. *Doing No Harm (Nonmaleficence)*: providing an environment that is free from harm to others, both psychological and physical. Leaders and members refrain from "engaging in actions which risk harming others" (Kitchener, 1984, p. 47).

3. *Benefiting Others (Beneficence)*: promoting the interests of the organization above personal interests and self-gain. The notion of promoting what is good for the whole of the organization or community and promoting the growth of the group is upheld in the principle of beneficence.

4. *Being Just (Justice)*: treating people fairly and equally. This principle is traced to Aristotle's work on ethics.

5. *Being Faithful (Fidelity)*: keeping promises, being faithful, and being loyal to the group or organization. Being faithful is a principle premised on relationships and trust. If you as a leader or member violate the principle of fidelity, it is difficult or impossible for others to develop a trusting relationship.

There are many applications of these five ethical principles in leadership and in organizational settings. In Exhibit 9.2, the principles are described in an organizational context. Using these principles should help you determine the correct course of action and should have a bearing on how your decisions will affect others.

Using the five principles, imagine that you are the chair of the homecoming committee and that the promotions subcommittee designed a homecoming t-shirt that you find to be offensive to ethnic groups. The committee spent $10,000 on the shirts, which are being sold by organizational members. The $10,000 must be replaced in the budget by the t-shirt sales. Which of the five principles would you use in working through this dilemma? Do any of the principles clash with one another, such as respecting the autonomy of the committee and doing no harm to others who might be hurt by the symbolism on the t-shirt?

"I handle ethical dilemmas by examining the situation, weighing the pros and cons, and evaluating the situation against my personal ethics, morals, and values. I believe the most helpful thing in handling ethical dilemmas is to know yourself well. Know what your morals, values, and ethics are and gain some 'practice' in handling ethical dilemmas . . . that way you will have the courage to stand by what you believe in when ethical dilemmas occur."—Andrew Ho is a finance major at the University of Maryland, College Park and is active in College Park Scholars in Public Leadership and the Intervarsity Christian Fellowship.

Nash (1987) proposes a model of questions to use when faced with a problem or dilemma. As with the five ethical principles, these twelve questions are designed to be used before you commit to an action or a decision. The questions in Exhibit 9.3 engage you in a thoughtful process as you address a dilemma.

Using Nash's questions, imagine that you are the captain of your college's varsity sports team. The team decides to put the rookie players through a series of hazing activities. One of the players nearly dies from alcohol poisoning. Your coach discovers this and asks you to share with him the list of players who participated in the hazing activities. The story is leaked to the media, and the campus newspaper is calling you for information about this incident. Responding by using the twelve questions, what do you do?

EXHIBIT 9.3 12 Questions to Ask When Making Ethical Decisions

1. Have you defined the problem accurately?

2. How would you define the problem if you stood on the other side of the fence?

3. How did this situation occur in the first place?

4. To whom and to what do you give your loyalty as a person and as a member of the organization?

5. What is your intention in making this decision?

6. How does this intention compare with the probable results?

7. Whom could your decision or action injure?

8. Can you discuss the problem with the affected parties before you make your decision?

9. Are you confident that your position will be as valid over a long period of time as it seems now?

10. Could you disclose without qualm your decision or action to your boss, the president of the board of directors, your family, society as a whole?

11. What is the symbolic potential of your action if understood? If misunderstood?

12. Under what conditions would you allow exceptions to your stand?

Source: Nash, 1987, p. 36. Copyright November 1987, *Training & Development*, American Society for Training and Development. Reprinted with permission. All rights reserved.

These ethical decision-making models can help you reach a more informed and carefully analyzed decision before you take any action. Too often, we are tempted to quickly put out fires or react to pressing dilemmas without engaging in a process that would provide some assurance that the right decision was made. These models alone will not necessarily help you resolve every dilemma you encounter. They provide a framework to guide your decision making. They do not provide the moral imagination and creative thinking that are needed to address complex situations.

Chapter Summary

Leading with integrity is a complex process that includes the moral development of an individual, the influence of role models, values-driven leadership, and the organizational environment. You can decide whether you want to set the temperature in the room or be the thermostat (Sorenson, 1992) in creating and sustaining an ethical organizational climate and leading with moral purpose.

The process of developing into an ethical participant and creating ethical environments does not occur overnight. Groups and organizations are made up of humans who can and do make mistakes, which is part of the learning process. Raising questions around ethical issues is a fundamental component of leading with integrity. People who lead with moral purpose often have as many questions as answers. Leading from the Relational Leadership Model means leading with moral purpose: empowering others to lead by example, including other participants in resolving ethical dilemmas, acting ethically to positively affect the public good, and using a process to approach problems that do not offer clear solutions.

Our society is calling for leaders and participants alike who can be trusted and who are committed to doing the right thing. Despite the turbulent and fast-paced nature of our world, leading with a moral purpose is central to the leadership process. Imagine what an organization, community, or the world would look like if everyone would strive to create and sustain an ethical environment by rewarding ethical acts, to engage in moral talk, and to carefully work, as a group, toward resolving dilemmas by using decision-making models.

What's Next?

The preceding chapters have shown how important the nature of relationships is in leadership and how complex it is to lead with moral purpose. This is clearly hard work. The last section of the book presents the idea that organizations (as groups of people) and individuals (the leaders and participants within organizations) need renewal. The book ends with an emphasis on staying fresh, growing, and forever learning to be organizationally and personally renewed.

Chapter Activities

1. Reflect on this question and the ones that follow: What are your positive and negative beliefs about ethical leadership or ethical leaders?

2. Think of a national, historical, or local person who you believe is an ethical leader. What skills, behaviors, attitudes, or characteristics does that person exhibit? Think of a national, historical, or local person who you believe is an unethical leader. What skills, behaviors, attitudes, or characteristics does that person exhibit?

3. Think of a person who has served as a role model to you. Why did you choose that person? What skills, behaviors, attitudes, or characteristics does that person exhibit?

4. How can or do you serve as a role model to others in your group or community?

5. How would you approach someone in your group or community who is behaving unethically or violating the group's standards?

6. Think of an ethical dilemma you have faced or somehow were involved with. Work through that dilemma using one of the three ethical decision-making models. How would you initiate moral talk with others in your group?

7. Think of a time when you or someone else served as a transforming leader. What was that experience like? How did the leader or members inspire each other to higher levels of morality?

8. Think about an organization in which you are currently a member and answer the following questions.

How would you describe the ethical climate in this organization?

What does the organization do to encourage members to do what is right?

What does the organization do that may encourage inappropriate behavior?

What happens when someone violates the ethical standards of the organization?

How could the organization become more supportive of ethical behavior? List the ways you could reward ethical behavior in your organization. Develop an action plan to put these ideas into place.

9. List the ways you could reward ethical behavior in your organization, residence hall, place of employment, and so forth. Develop an action plan to put these ideas into place.

Additional Readings

Chaleff, I. (1995). *The courageous follower. Standing up to and for our leaders*. San Francisco: Berrett-Koehler.

Ciulla, J. B. (1995). Leadership ethics: Mapping the territory. *Business Ethics Quarterly, 5*, 5–28.

Walton, C. C. (1988). *The moral manager*. New York: Harper & Row.

PART FOUR

Leadership and Renewal

The leadership journey presented in this book started with the inward journey into yourself. Having a consciousness of yourself is the most essential step toward relating effectively to others (*A Social Change Model of Leadership Development*, 1996). Throughout the pages of this book, you explored leadership as a process engaging you and others in communities, groups, organizations.

It would be a mistake to end with something like "six steps in becoming an effective leader" or "ten principles of leadership for all times." Such postulates would be suspect, even ludicrous. While we have promoted your thinking about *relational leadership* to strongly emphasize the importance of *people working together*, we encourage you to develop a personal philosophy of leadership grounded in the principles and values that will work for you in your uplifting relationships with others toward shared purposes. Heider (1985) in sharing the reflections of Lao Tzu, writes:

Beginners acquire new theories and techniques until their minds are cluttered with options.

Advanced students forget their many options. They allow the theories and techniques that they have learned to recede into the background.

Learn to unclutter your mind. Learn to simplify your work. As you rely less and less on knowing just what to do, your work will become more direct and more powerful. You will discover that the quality of your consciousness is more potent than any technique or theory or interpretation.

Learn how fruitful the blocked group or individual suddenly becomes when you give up trying to do just the right thing. (p. 95)

We want to end this journey by coming back to our commitment that to stay effective in rapidly changing times, our organizations must stay renewed and must value people learning together. Further, we as individuals must connect our mind, body, and soul to stay renewed.

Renewal literally means to "make new again." "Re-new" is a dynamic process of individuals and their groups and organizations learning together. No matter how busy, no matter how stressed, no matter how discouraged, no matter how joyous, no matter how satisfied, no matter how happy, no matter how effective—individuals, groups, and organizations regain balance and stay fresh by making renewal processes an essential focus. This section ends with a chapter on the renewal of groups and organizations and a chapter on personal renewal.

10

Why Renewal Is Vital to Groups and Organizations

No matter how effective or exciting a group or organization may be for its members, it will inevitably find itself in need of renewal. Renewal must be an on-going function but may be an obvious need in periods of inactivity when the organization seems stagnant or in times of frenzied activity when the members seem stressed. This is natural and is not something to fear. It is, however, something that must be addressed. As a participant, you have the obligation to recognize when things are not going right and to work to change them.

Richard Farson (1995) discusses organizational renewal in Management of the Absurd:

> Most often what gets organizations into trouble are faulty
> leadership styles, poor internal relationships, and managerial
> blind spots. The delusional hope of a troubled organization is
> that it will be saved without having to make changes in these
> highly personal areas. (p. 86)

Farson goes on to note, "Individuals are very strong, but organizations are not" (Farson, 1995, p. 90). With these prophetic words, he focuses on one of the basic issues facing groups, organizations, and communities as they try to remain healthy and productive—that *relationships* ultimately determine the actions taken. These relationships, when broken or never fully formed, can lead

groups, organizations, and communities to a point of being unproductive and even destructive to its members.

Chapter Overview

This chapter addresses the issues that can cause problems for groups
and organizations as they attempt to continually renew themselves.
These issues include a lack of attention to mission, vision, and core
values; poor relationships; not taking responsibility for actions; lack
of involvement by members; lowering of ethical standards; and
lack of attention to process. As we explore these various concerns,
we show how the Relational Leadership Model, with its stress on
the role of *purpose, inclusion, empowerment, ethics,* and *process,* can
serve as a useful guide in your renewal efforts. We discuss the
renewal process, the impact of the human spirit, and the concept of
transition—how it can be used to help leaders and members renew
themselves and their organization.

The Renewal Process

Gardner (1990) notes that continuous renewal is necessary in
groups and organizations in order to renew and reinterpret values,
liberate energies, reenergize forgotten goals or generate new goals,
achieve new understandings, and foster the release of human potential. Gardner notes further that "leaders must understand the interweaving of continuity and change" (p. 124). Continuity means
taking the best of how the group or organization is and carrying it
forward under conditions that require new approaches.

According to Gardner, the most critical step in the renewal
process is "the release of talent and energy" (p. 136) from within the
members. As he notes, "Nothing is more vital to the renewal of
an organization than the arrangements by which able people are
nurtured and moved into positions where they can make their
greatest contribution" (1990, p. 127). This process begins with the
recruitment of new members and continues with their on-going

development. What do you do to tap into the talents and energy of the members of your groups, organizations, and communities? How could you do this even better?

Gardner (1990) makes a number of other suggestions that can help the renewal effort for organizations. We believe these suggestions can also apply to groups and communities. Groups, organizations, and communities can reassign their leaders to expose them to new challenges; take steps to increase the motivational level of leaders and participants alike; foster at least some diversity and dissent in order to encourage the development of new ideas; refocus on the original reasons that the groups, organizations, and communities were formed; ensure that both internal and external communication are easy and open; keep focused on the vision of a desired future; and finally, reorganize. Some of these steps may require the use of an outside evaluator because people become used to the status quo and can find themselves resistant to any significant change efforts.

Gardner's ideas are important because they give us some ideas about where we need to go when things are going poorly. His work also reflects the relevance of the basic concepts of the Relational Leadership Model. By paying more attention to issues of *inclusion*, *empowerment*, *purpose*, *ethics*, and the *process orientation*, groups, organizations, and communities can remain productive places for all members. When things are going poorly, returning to these basic principles can provide an excellent starting point for efforts aimed at renewal.

Common Purpose and Renewal

In Chapter Seven we explored the importance of mission, vision, and core values, which combine to form the common *purpose* component of the Relational Leadership Model. The concept of being *purposeful* plays a critical role in the renewal of groups, organizations, and communities. In fact, we believe that when things are going badly, going back to the basics of mission, vision, and core values is a great place to begin your renewal efforts.

James Collins and Jerry Porras (1994) examined eighteen extraordinary companies— extraordinary in their longevity and in their productivity. Collins and Porras found that these great companies did not do things as you might expect. Instead of relying on charismatic leaders, they had leaders who were concerned more about building great organizations than about being visible and out-front. Instead of complex strategic planning, they tried a lot of things and kept doing what worked. Instead of changing constantly, they relied on a set of core values that had remained relatively constant over the years. And although these organizations might sound like great places to work, the authors found that a good fit was needed for a member of the organization to thrive. This emphasis on strong core values and on action, experimentation, risk taking, and "big hairy audacious goals" (Collins & Porras, 1994, p. 9) is something that groups, organizations, and communities need to constantly keep in mind.

"Organizations change for the better when members
are selflessly helping to achieve or stand up for the
organization, by having a good leader and members
that collaborate, and when everyone in the group
takes ownership and responsibility for the group.
They change for the worse when members stop caring
about the organization and when everyone is just
looking after his or her own self-interests."—
So-Young "Amy" Choi is president of the Korean
club at Occidental College.

The importance of vision is also articulated by Albrecht (1994); Jaffe, Scott, and Tobe (1994); Senge (1990); and others. Albrecht encourages leaders to do some scanning: scan the environment to discover what is going on, and scan the various opportunities that are available to determine what the possibilities are. Jaffe, Scott, and Tobe cite the importance of self-responsibility, empowerment, purpose, commitment, and partnership. Senge notes the necessity of a "shared vision," of empowerment accompanied by members pulling in the same direction.

This connection between common purpose and renewal is especially evident in student groups, organizations, and communities; members need to know why they are doing what they are doing. When things are not going well, it is often because members have lost touch with what has made their group or organization unique or special. In essence, they no longer remember why the organization exists. Renewal requires members to reaffirm their common purpose.

Getting experienced members to "re-embrace" this common purpose can be very challenging. A retreat can be a powerful opportunity for renewal. Upon leaving for a weekend retreat, some members will complain about having to give up a weekend when they could be socializing and having fun back on campus. But often, at the end of a well-designed retreat with a focus on renewal, members will return uplifted, energized, and glad they spent their weekend on this growth-producing activity. The challenge then becomes how to maintain back home the momentum that was developed at the retreat. In any event, a retreat is a popular method for reconnecting to the common purpose that brought the participants together originally.

Retreats and other structured opportunities that are created for the purpose of renewal provide a forum for all members to come together to share their thoughts and feelings about the group or organization: where it is now and where they would like it to go. Revisiting the vision through this kind of "group conversation" is necessary to keep it fresh for the membership. Of course, meetings like this can also reveal that the vision needs to be changed or shifted. Knowing when to maintain a current vision and when to change the vision is a critical aspect of leadership and renewal. Having a vision that is meaningful to the members is absolutely necessary if it is to guide their plans and actions.

"A group can become strong through working toward a common goal and vision. Many things can bring a group down, creating chaos, such as miscommunications, dishonesty, or disrespect (just to name a few). But, if the group keeps their vision *throughout the chaos*, the group can become stronger than was ever thought possible. In this way, chaos can energize the group above and beyond previous assumptions."—Tiffany Leger, from California Polytechnic State University, is a member of a sorority and a major in psychology.

Another way to maintain a vision works well with new members. It is an easy and enjoyable exercise called The Five Whys, developed by Rick Ross (1994a, p. 108). Ask yourself the most simple of questions such as, Why does your organization (or group or community) exist? This question is relevant whether it is asked about student government, a service organization, the chess club, a residence hall floor or house government, a fraternity or sorority, or a club related to your major. Probe deeply. Now take the reason you have given and ask why that answer is important. Take the answer to that second Why? and ask Why? again. Do this until you have asked Why? a total of five times. Doing this helps you get closer to the essence of why the group exists. See Exhibit 10.1 for an example of the way this technique would apply to an organization.

Although the final line in Exhibit 10.1 about working for the alumni association is humorous, the conversation does get us to a deeper understanding of why we have campus entertainment—to retain students. With this as a reason for the existence of such an organization, the activities they sponsor must appeal to a broad range of students.

Consider the differences between a student government group whose primary reason for existence is to provide social, recreational, and physical activities for the campus community and another

EXHIBIT 10.1   The Five Whys

Consider this imaginary conversation with the chair of a campus entertainment committee:

Why does your organization exist?	To provide campus entertainment for the students.
Why is that important?	So they'll have something to do and have fun.
Why is that important?	So they'll enjoy going to school here and stay out of trouble.
Why is that important?	If they like going to school here and stay out of trouble, they'll stay in school and hopefully graduate.
Why is that important?	If they graduate, hopefully they'll go out and be successful, make a big salary, and contribute money to the school.
So, you really work for the Development Office?	I guess so!

student government group whose purpose is to be the voice of student opinion to the campus administration. These two groups have very different focuses. No group or organization can be all things to all people. Decide what is at the core and return to this core at every opportunity. The core defines why your group or organization exists. It is why people originally started it and why others decided to join. As leaders and active participants, it is your duty to help make this core come alive for the membership.

Inclusion: Tapping into the Energy of Others to Renew the Organization

As we outlined in Chapter Three, inclusion involves developing the talents and ideas of all members in the group or organization, building on differences and commonalties, and being pluralistic. Although embracing this perspective presents a challenge for leaders, it provides valuable information as we consider the renewal process. Of particular importance in this process is developing the talents of members and using the energy that new members can bring with them.

An obvious way to make any group or organization better is to help its members become more aware, knowledgeable, and skilled. By developing the talent of the people who are already members, tasks can be accomplished in a more timely and efficient manner. Knowledgeable members such as these will also provide an experienced core of individuals who have a historical perspective and know about past accomplishments. This will also provide a solid foundation of individuals who are committed to the common purpose, vision, and core values.

When people realize that a group or organization has helped them become more knowledgeable and skilled, they usually feel a reciprocal allegiance. We see this all the time in groups of students. For instance many RAs, student government leaders, and members of volunteer agencies will talk at great length about what they have gained both personally and professionally from their experiences. These same students are also very loyal to other members and dedicated to the common purpose, vision, and core values. They should be selected to play an active role in any renewal effort.

One way to continually renew the group or organization is to invest in developing the talents of all of your members. This can take on a variety of forms: providing workshops on various topics; encouraging attendance at conferences; discussing a pertinent article; asking people to perform a task or duty they have not previously done; and developing the leadership potential in new members. These, and countless other methods, can be used to develop the awareness, knowledge, and skills of the members. Your efforts on behalf of the members will be returned many times over.

Remember to focus your efforts on the members who are on the fringes—people who are sometimes viewed as outside the core group. There may be great energy and creativity in these often-ignored individuals (Kelly, 1994). Such students may be so thrilled at the new-found attention that they become active, involved members.

Empowerment: Helping Members Become Involved

Albert Bernstein and Sydney Rozen (1994) address the concept of empowerment in *Sacred Bull*. In this book, they identify ten "sacred bulls" that prevent people from reaching their potential as members of corporate organizations. The sacred bull is a metaphor for an assumption we make and do not question. "They are the ideas that nobody checks or questions because 'We've always done it this way'" (p. 7).

Many of us would note that using denial, blame, and excuse making are relatively immature ways of coping with mistakes or with results that did not turn out as you had hoped. These ways of coping are examples of sacred bulls. But some of the other examples are less obvious. In fact, they include aspects of our lives that we may define as being very positive, such as being nice, being a perfectionist, and always viewing our way of doing things as the right way. Being nice can mean avoiding conflict. Being a perfectionist can mean seeing your efforts, or the efforts of others, as either being perfect or being nothing. Being right can mean that others never have the right answer or approach.

These bulls can be lethal in that they encourage us to avoid taking responsibility for our actions and for the result of our actions. As such, they can keep us in the quagmire of organizational life where mistakes are always someone else's fault. Leadership is about the task of solving problems—big problems and little problems, significant problems and seemingly insignificant problems—so that the group or organization can better meet its core purpose and be a good place for its membership.

Think for a moment how this concept of empowerment and taking responsibility is essential for renewal. When things go wrong, our first inclination is to say something like, "Well it wasn't my fault. I did what I was supposed to do." We try to find the person responsible so blame can be placed and our lack of responsibility can be proven. Yet, "there is no blame" (Senge, 1990, p. 67). In a group, organizational, or community system, we are all involved in every aspect of the system—in all of its successes and failures. Just as on a true team, winning and losing are treated as outcomes shared by the entire group. The group dynamic changes in amazing ways once we quit trying to lay blame. This can be a key step in renewal.

"An organization is a community when the members feel a sort of connection and bond with one another. The members need to feel that they have an investment in the organization in order to feel that they are a part of a community. They also need to know each other on a more personal rather than 'professional' level."—Joyce Steiner is active in volunteer organizations and student government at the University of Florida.

Let us look at a familiar organizational example. In any organization, recruiting new members is everyone's responsibility. However, the reality of the situation may be quite different. Many times, recruiting may be viewed as the job of a specific officer. Sure, other members are willing to "do their part," but they may see their part as being friendly to prospective members who may come to visit. If membership decreases, members may blame the officer because they, having done their part, could not possibly deserve blame. This is a very different dynamic from members who see their part as bringing prospective members to meetings, making sure they feel welcomed, and engaging them in conversation. These members are truly sharing the responsibility of recruitment and are much less likely to lay the blame for declining membership on any one officer. They understand the role that all participants have in making the recruitment of new members a success. They know that for an event to be a success, everyone must share responsibility and feel a need to make it work.

When this becomes an organizational reality and a "web of shared responsibility" is developed among the membership, truly dynamic results can occur. But this is far easier said than done. A good way to begin the process is to forge a strong sense of connection among the members. This helps each person feel like a part of the whole, like a part of something bigger than herself or himself. Next, involve as many different people as possible in the various aspects of the life of the group or organization. When asked to participate in something meaningful and important, and given some sense of input into how the situation is to be approached, most people will respond with their best efforts. People like to be part of something that is successful and believe that success now will lead to success later. As you can see, all of this begins with shared responsibility—from the leader taking the responsibility of helping the individual members be part of something important, to the individual members taking responsibility for doing their very best to make the group or organization successful in everything it does.

As a leader, taking responsibility for your actions is essential. Encouraging others to take responsibility for their own actions can be an essential part of renewal. Once members agree to take on more responsibility for various activities and functions, they inherently become more involved and feel a greater sense of commitment to themselves and to the other members. Taking responsibility can also help members receive compliments for jobs well done and can also help them realize that efforts that come up a bit less than anticipated are not the end of the world.

Being Ethical: How Doing the Right Thing Can Help Renew the Organization

Being ethical is a proud commitment to justice, care, and socially responsible actions. Maintaining a high standard of ethical behavior helps create a proud membership and provides some guidelines to help leaders do the right thing. Being ethical is not easy. It involves hard work, on-going conversations, and dedicated organizational leaders and members. Yet all of these efforts will benefit the group or organization in the long term by making it attractive to new members.

Consider two different Greek chapters. The first Greek organization truly embraces its founding principles and the policies of the institution, even when these policies create tensions within the membership. Leaders of this group take the time to explain policies to new members and do everything they can to hold the membership to the high ideals upon which the group was founded. Scholarship, service, and sisterhood or brotherhood are stressed, and every effort is made to encourage the membership to be ethical in every way. The second Greek organization has realized just how difficult it is to truly embrace the ideals of scholarship, service, and sisterhood or brotherhood and has chosen to take the easy way out by lowering the expectations they have of each other. Although this may seem beneficial in the short term, it will hurt the organization dramatically in the long term. Each organization will attract new members who have similar goals, beliefs, and interests to the present membership. The group that stresses ethical behavior in its members will attract new members who have similar beliefs and standards. The group that has lowered its standards will attract new members whose behavior may be questionable. Which organization will grow stronger over time?

While this example may seem simplistic, we all know of organizations that fall into each of these two categories. We also have seen that in the long run, the group or organization that treats its membership well and holds its members to a high standard of ethical behavior will continue to grow and develop, whereas the other organization will struggle to survive. An organization that has ethical leaders and is committed to justice, care, and socially responsible actions will attract a membership that is committed to similar ideals. These new members will both renew and strengthen the organization in an on-going manner.

Being Process-Oriented: Using the Concepts of TQM to Renew the Organization

Being process-oriented means that individuals and the group or organization as a whole are reflective, challenging, collaborative, caring, and communal. The main way of accomplishing this is to create opportunities for on-going dialogue and discussion about what is happening within the organization. It is also possible to use some of the approaches from the total quality movement (TQM) to enhance these processes in a way that will aid renewal efforts.

In his book *Out of the Crisis*, W. Edwards Deming (1986) outlined his famous fourteen points that organizations need to follow in order to enhance the quality of their operations. Two of these points are especially important as we consider the topic of renewal: number eight (Drive out fear) and number nine (Break down barriers). Both of these points challenge the "command and control" paradigm that defined leadership for many years. We will look at each of these two points in some detail and show how they can be useful in the renewal process, not only for organizations but for groups and communities as well.

By *driving out fear*, Deming meant that members of groups or organizations need to feel free to speak their minds and share their ideas with peers and with the leaders. Deming thought that the people best able to improve performance are those who do the work. For instance, the persons best suited to make suggestions about improving the method for putting a door on an automobile would be workers whose job it is to put the door on, not some engineer in an office away from the assembly-line floor. Although this idea makes perfect sense, it is not often embraced. Conventional leaders can feel threatened by members who know more about a specific part of the group or organization than they do. Rather than listening and learning from these members, leaders may tune them out and decide that they—the leaders—know best.

This process of alienation of the membership happens every day on every college campus. Leaders are elected or selected because they are popular and seem to know what they are doing. In becoming leaders, some people slowly separate themselves from those who elected or selected them to lead. Comments like, "What happened? She used to be one of us," can often be heard, and members become hesitant to bring up issues they are concerned about; they fear not being heard or understood. This can quickly lead to the groups or organizations being run by one person or a small group of people who no longer have the support of the membership. Ineffectiveness and a lack of care by those who are not involved in leadership may soon follow. It is only by listening and truly hearing the voices of all of its members that groups or organizations can remain strong and renew themselves.

Rituals have been developed that encourage members to speak about what is on their hearts and minds. Groups may hold informal or formal sessions where members share their thoughts and feelings about the group. Some organizations will periodically invite all members to form a circle and pass a candle or gavel around the group. When holding the candle or gavel, the member is free to say anything she or he wishes to say. Other organizations ask that members comment on one thing that is going poorly in the group and one thing that is going well. This is an excellent method of soliciting feedback from all members of the group, including those who are usually quiet. Communities hold open forums or town meetings for a similar purpose. Whatever method is used, the leaders need to be sure that they know what the membership is thinking and feeling. They also need to strive to create an atmosphere in which members feel free to express their thoughts and feelings without fear of repercussions.

Deming's other pertinent point—that barriers should be broken down—is becoming increasingly important as resources are becoming more and more scarce. By this point, Deming meant that the barriers, both real and imagined, need to be broken down. Different factions should work together toward a common purpose. Deming's examples usually involve two different divisions of an organization such as manufacturing and sales. If these two areas do not communicate and work closely together, the organization suffers drastic consequences.

While communicating and working together make organizational (and common) sense, they do not always exist. Consider how a major event on campus is formulated. Various groups and organizations are identified and contacted to help sponsor and fund the event. Those that are interested meet to discuss possible ways of presenting the event, with each group advocating its particular agenda. Sometimes an amiable solution is reached, and everyone leaves the negotiations feeling good about the final agreement. Other times, those with the most resources are able to force their particular ideas on the others who have less money. The end result is an event that may or may not be successful; some groups may not feel their needs and agendas were considered.

The idea of cross-functional teams has become popular in business and, yet, a college campus offers a wonderful opportunity for approaches like this to happen frequently. Consider the issue of tuition and fees. Is this a concern of only a few students? Obviously not. Yet it is almost exclusively the role of the student government organization and possibly the student member of the board of trustees to champion the cause of students to the institution's administration and state legislature. Wouldn't it be truly amazing to see every student club and organization express its opinion when a matter of importance like the tuition and fees was raised? Wouldn't it be even more amazing to recruit parents, supportive members of the state legislature, and even some concerned alumni? In this way the advocacy group crosses several borderlines that often seem to separate people with similar concerns. Another example currently being used on many campuses involves a campuswide approach to addressing the issue of alcohol and drug abuse. Campus health, intercollegiate athletics, Greek organizations, residence life, student activities, judicial programs, and even some academic departments have united to work on this issue.

How does this concept relate to renewal? It relates because power and energy result from the efforts of different groups like these to address a common purpose, even if that purpose is only a temporary one. Students make new friends and see their particular group or organization in a new light. An energy is created through efforts such as these, and this energy is a force of renewal that benefits everyone involved.

This model has much to offer leaders. Think about how a group or organization is born. Individuals sharing a common interest get together and decide to formalize their association. This could be a backpacking club, a renter's association, or an intramural team. In any case, the early days or years are marked by a core of founding members, an informal structure, and a clear understanding of why the group or organization exists. All aspects of the Relational Leadership Model will be visible in this early stage. The founding members have formed around a common *purpose*. *Inclusion* will be high because most of the members will be the group's founders or a few very interested members. *Empowerment* and *process* will also be visible because that is how things get done when a group has no history and little structure upon which to rely. While a high level of *ethics* may or may not be embraced, it is much easier to establish this as a priority early than to introduce its importance later.

The Importance of the Human Spirit

An aspect of leadership and group and organizational life that is receiving more and more attention lately is the importance of the human spirit. In *Leading with Soul: An Uncommon Journey of Spirit*, Lee Bolman and Terrence Deal (1995) take readers on an interesting journey, describing the trials and tribulations of a corporate executive named Steve who is having trouble finding fulfillment in his work. Maria, the woman who acts as Steve's guide on this journey, helps him explore his leadership style in an unconventional manner. She poses questions instead of providing answers. Through this experience, Steve learns the importance of spirit and soul in leadership, that is, of leading from the inside out—from the core of who you are. He also learns the importance of giving and sharing.

Although this may sound like another form of religion, it really is not. The human spirit is the core of your being that gives life its meaning. It is what helps you get out of bed in the morning and look forward to the new day. As such, it needs to be nurtured. This approach is certainly different than what you would expect from a leadership book, yet is found in a growing number of books addressing this topic (for example, Conger & Associates, 1994; Fox, 1994; Hawley, 1993).

The soul-searching that is the basis of Bolman and Deal's book is as important, and probably even more important, than all the how-to-run-a-meeting books you will ever encounter. Certainly, knowing how to run a meeting is important. You probably have some experience doing that or have seen others do it. But have you ever asked yourself why you want to be a leader or what motivates you to want to make a difference? You may not have done that before, nor have you ever seen others try to answer the question. By exploring questions like this, you will find out a lot about yourself. The best leaders know themselves very well—their strengths and the areas in which they need work. You will find that exploring the tough questions and tough issues can be difficult, but it is necessary if you are to find meaning in life and, by doing so, to renew yourselves and your organization.

Although renewing your own spirit is important, helping members of your organization renew their spirit is essential if you are to be a successful leader. You must help others identify their own reasons for being associated with this particular group or organization and try to strengthen these reasons. You can also help provide an environment in which people feel passionate about being members. Being upbeat, positive, and optimistic is infectious. If you do not believe it, just try it. The human spirit is a renewable resource that can prove to be invaluable in all forms of renewal efforts.

The Concept of Transition

Change is localized in time and space. It is easily identifiable and begins when something old ends and something new begins. Transition is the psychological process that accompanies the change. It is difficult to identify, and it begins with an ending—people letting go of old attitudes and beliefs. In his book *Transitions: Making Sense of Life's Changes*, William Bridges (1980) explores the concepts of transition and change. Bridges notes that changes require people to make transitions, and it is the transitions that make life difficult. An example of this would be when a new slate of student government officers takes office. At the time new officers officially take office, they become the representatives of the student body. The out-going officers are no longer in office. This is a change that can be said to take place at the time the oaths of office are given. For the new officers, the feelings that come with having the power and responsibility that go with their offices may be uncomfortable at first. For the outgoing officers, having afternoons and evenings free from meetings may seem very liberating, but adjusting to the new freedom will take some time.

Transitions have three components: ending, neutral zone, and beginning (Bridges, 1980). The ending is a time of disengagement, disidentification, disenchantment, and disorientation. This is followed by the neutral zone—the most difficult period because it is a time of emptiness, disorganization, and despair. Only by being in this psychological state, however, can we prepare ourselves for a new beginning, but it is often difficult to decide how long to stay in it. New beginnings will be successful only if you have stayed long enough in the neutral zone. Because new beginnings take physical and psychological energy, they will often be troublesome.

As a leader, you can use this information in a number of ways. If you have recently taken a new position, realize that it might take the group or organization (and you) a while to get used to your being in the role. This will be especially true if there are many others who were officers or members under the previous leadership. If you have recently ended a term of office, realize that it may take the group or organization (and you) a while to get used to your not being the leader any longer.

This can be an exciting time. Enjoy your new-found free time. Do some of those things you have been too busy to do. Get reacquainted with your friends. While having this much free time may sound nice, you may also find that you were much more productive (and a better student) when you were busier. Many students find that their grades are best when they hold offices or positions of responsibility. This makes sense when you think about it. If you only have two hours a night to do your homework, you will be productive and will not goof off. If you have all night to do the same amount of work, you may find that what begins as an hour of watching television turns into an all-night marathon. This makes no sense intuitively but has been found to be true by many former leaders. If you monitor your time, you can use it in ways that benefit you.

Groups and organizations go through a similar process when they are undergoing a change or transition. The psychological process of understanding and accepting change can range from easy to difficult. Knowing that there will be a time of uncertainty as the new way of doing things gets established is an important concept for leaders. Change and transition can certainly renew a group or organization. In fact, from a systems perspective any act of renewal really does change everything. Understanding how these processes work can help a leader be effective in these kinds of situations.

The concept of transition has much to offer all participants in groups, organizations, and communities. By considering the psychological processes outlined by Bridges (1980), new and old officers can gain a better understanding of their feelings as they enter into or leave their offices. These feelings—joy, anxiety, excitement, nervousness—are all natural reactions to being placed in new situations. In addition, knowing about the stages of ending, neutral zone, and beginning can help participants feel more comfortable in their current situation and help them anticipate what might be coming next.

Chapter Summary

Groups and organizations are a lot like human beings in that they need continual sources of energy to fuel their minds, bodies, and spirits. We know that we need nutritious food and liquids to sustain our bodies, that we need new ideas and information to stimulate, challenge, and intrigue us and keep our minds sharp and flexible, and that we need something to love and something that will give our existence meaning. Without those things, it is difficult to remain upbeat. Groups and organizations are similar in that having a common purpose provides a reason for being. Having a purpose stimulates new ideas, new thoughts, and new approaches to old issues, and provides a guide toward greater achievement.

Energy comes with something new; without this energy, groups and organizations become complacent. They begin to value style over accomplishment. It takes participants with foresight and good judgment to see things that may be wrong but appear to be right, and vice versa. Groups and organizations will not automatically renew themselves. They become renewed when their members become renewed. This sounds simple and maybe it is. Maybe it is as simple as asking, What would it take to make this organization great?—then joining with the other participants and running with the answers as far as you can go.

What's Next?

After this discussion of group and organizational renewal, it is also important to focus on the individual renewal of participants like you. The last chapter of the book reminds us of the importance of attending to the mind, body, and soul of all participants.

Chapter Activities

1. *The Five Whys:* Use your group or organization as the example and repeat the exercise in Exhibit 10.1.
   a. Ask yourself the following question: Why does your group or organization exist?
   b. Now take the answer to that question and ask yourself, Why is that (the answer to part a) important?

   c. Now take the answer to that question and ask yourself,
      Why is that (the answer to part b) important?
   d. Now take the answer to that question and ask yourself,
      Why is that (the answer to part c) important?
   e. Now take the answer to that question and ask yourself,
      Why is that (the answer to part d) important?

How was your answer to "e" different from your answer to "a"?
Do you notice an evolution to your answer as you peeled away
the layers of understanding?

2. *Things Were Going Well:* Think back to a time when
things were going very well for your group or organization.
Get a good strong mental image of this time. Make it vivid in
your mind's eye. Now jot down some answers to these questions.

   a. What was your group or organization doing?
   b. Why were you doing these things?
   c. With what other groups, organizations, communities, or
      individuals were you doing things?
   d. What was your group or organization doing to take care of
      its members? (for example, recognition or awards)
   e. Compare your group or organization now to how it was
      when things were going very well. How are things differ-
      ent? How are they similar? What changes could you make
      to help return to the time when things were going well?

3. *A Retreat:* Design a retreat for a group or organization that
is in need of renewal. What will be your goals for the retreat?
Where will you go? What activities will be included? Design a
town meeting for a community. What will be your goals for
the town meeting? How will you plan, advertise, and run it?

4. *Recruiting New Members:* Design a plan to recruit new
members. Make the enlistment of persons from campus popu-

lations that are underrepresented a priority. Try to incorporate several different approaches.

5. *Cross-Functional Teams:* Identify an important issue that is a major concern on your campus. To address this issue would obviously involve a number of different groups, organizations, communities, and individuals working together effectively. Design a plan to address this major issue. Who would be involved? How would they all work together? What problems do you anticipate? How could you overcome these problems?

6. *Transition:* Identify a major transition that your group or organization has experienced. Describe it in terms of Bridges's model. What was each phase—ending, neutral zone, beginning—like? What was difficult about each phase? What was exciting about each phase?

7. *Spirit:* Plan a way to renew the spirit of your group or organization. What will you do? Who will do it? How will you do it?

Additional Readings

Bridges, W. (1980). *Transitions: Making sense of life's changes.* Reading, MA: Addison-Wesley.

Jaffe, D., Scott, C., & Tobe, G. (1994). *Rekindling commitment. How to revitalize yourself, your work, and your organization.* San Francisco: Jossey-Bass.

11

The Mind, Body, and Soul of the Leader

Any leadership process can be rewarding, exciting, and developmental as well as exhausting, challenging, consuming, and stressful. Most active participants would agree that others in their organizations expect a great deal from them, sometimes at the sacrifice of their personal time or commitments. Political leaders are challenged to meet the demands of dissatisfied constituents yet at the same time to maintain personal balance in their lives. Students often are confronted with the demands of their leadership and membership roles leaving them feeling like they are doing all the work, or everyone's work, on top of their academic responsibilities. How many times have you felt overwhelmed by all your responsibilities, tired by trying to juggle too many things, and said to yourself, "I can't wait until my obligations in this organization are over so I can have a life again!"

Many leadership publications and seminars talk about how leaders can provide renewal to their organizations, members, and communities, which was the focus of Chapter Ten. Equally important is the intentional renewal that leaders should bring into their lives. Achieving renewal can be a challenge when leaders have a tendency to be preoccupied with the daily activities of leading a group or community balanced by school, family, and other responsibilities.

Chapter Overview

This chapter focuses on the renewal of the leader or participant and stresses the importance of being a healthy, renewed individual. Leaders can be more effective and beneficial to their respective organizations and groups when they are energized by what they are doing and balanced by finding personal time. They need to spend time in reflection and to do things unrelated to their organizations while fulfilling their obligations and performing the tasks of leadership.

The health of a leader or participant is as important as the organization's goals and outcomes. A leader who is stressed, unbalanced, physically exhausted, or overwhelmed is not likely to be as effective as a leader who is balanced, renewed, and physically and mentally healthy. It is critical for all participants to pay attention to their mental and spiritual being, as we discussed in the previous chapter. Leaders tend to take care of others and to put their personal needs aside as they advance the needs of their group and its members. Although this is noble, the leader's health is sometimes sacrificed or compromised for the good of others. A balanced approach would suggest that the leader's needs, such as personal time away from the organization without feeling guilty, time to reflect, and other opportunities for personal renewal, be balanced with organizational needs and priorities.

"The common misperception is that we [as student leaders] have all of the answers. Another misperception is that we are only responsible for the organization that we are leading when in reality, we have other aspects of our lives to deal with at the same time."—Cody Nash, majoring in agriculture communications, is a member of the Tarleton State University student government and the Future Farmers of America.

Personal or individual renewal can be viewed as a proactive strategy, in that a person works intentionally to bring new perspectives and energy into a task or role. Conversely, renewal can be approached in a reactive way or as a means to correct an already unhealthy or unbalanced lifestyle. Some students, unfortunately, realize too late that working fourteen hours a day, six or seven days a week nonstop results in burnout, broken relationships, serious health problems, and ultimately, a negative effect on their organizations. These cases have been chronicled in our daily newspapers by stories of university presidents, congressional leaders, or athletes who step down from their roles because they need to spend more time with family or to pursue other interests. They may state that their jobs did not permit them to find balance in their lives. Women and people of color may also feel pressure to work twice as hard to achieve the same recognition and credibility as their male counterparts (Morrison, 1996). This added stress can lead to burnout, dissatisfaction, or disappointment.

We also have positive role models in leaders and members whose lifestyles enable them to be productive in their roles. Perhaps they learned the hard way that there is more to life than a career on the fast track or working harder to get more recognition and material rewards. Some leaders possess a philosophy that they need daily or regular time for personal or spiritual renewal, and they work to avoid leading a stressful, unhealthy life that can lead to burnout.

Personal renewal means different things to different people, but we understand renewal when we experience it. Some people escape or take a week or so away from their organization to recycle, be alone, rest, get refreshed, or simply to have fun and enjoy the company of friends or family. Others regularly take long walks, exercise, garden, paint, dance, hang glide, listen to soothing music, take a bubble bath, or find quiet, uninterrupted time for reflection. To start each morning feeling rejuvenated, some people meditate or exercise, or engage in some other habitual, renewing activity; others find time later in their day for renewal.

> "Renewal for me comes in taking some downtime away
> from others. In school, I was always required to work
> with many people, running from class to sports, to
> meetings, and so on. The only way I could keep this
> pace was to spend time by myself. It really didn't
> matter what I did—either read a book, talk to my
> parents on the phone, take a warm bath, watch a
> cheesy romantic movie, pray, and so forth."—Vanessa
> M. Helsing is a recent graduate of the Jepson School
> of Leadership Studies at the University of Richmond
> working in Washington, D.C.

A former president of Carlow College was about to retire, and her secretary of many years stepped into her office to ask a question that had been on her mind for quite some time. She inquired of the president, "During all of these years that you've been president, you've had a standing appointment every day at four o'clock in the afternoon with someone named Mrs. Jones. In all my time as your secretary, not only have I never met Mrs. Jones but I never once saw Mrs. Jones enter or leave your office. Now that you are getting ready to step down from the presidency, can you tell me who this mysterious Mrs. Jones is?" The president explained that Mrs. Jones was a fictitious person whom she scheduled every day on her calendar for one hour because if people knew that what she really was doing for that hour was reflecting quietly in her office, the hour would be frivolously taken up by appointments, phone calls, or meetings. The president went on to say that probably the most productive time of her day while she was in office was that time she had with Mrs. Jones.

This chapter is entitled "The Mind, Body, and Soul of Leaders" because we see these three entities as interrelated. Tending to your mind, body, and soul as a leader is a part of the renewal process. When your body is tired or you feel mentally exhausted, your spirit may lack enthusiasm. If you have overcommitted yourself by agreeing to do dozens of projects and tasks, you might drift aimlessly, not knowing where to begin. However, when you feel refreshed and energized, and approach your work with spirit and zest, you achieve entirely different results. Your critical task as a leader is to pay attention to your "inner voices" (Bolman & Deal, 1995, p. 38), focus on your purpose or mission, continue your search, and find meaning in your endeavors. Like most aspects of the arduous work of leadership, this is easier said than done. The bottom line is that leaders must take good care of themselves physically, mentally, and spiritually, in order to effectively lead with others.

As you approach all your communities in practice, learn to view the people and processes with new lenses, which is part of the renewal process. This book attempts to guide you to understand and accept a new meaning of leadership. To be an effective community member or leader, you need to continually develop your capacity to understand how the systems around you are "mutually related and interacting and continually changing" and how they affect you as a person.

Self-Renewal

One way to assess your self-renewal is to ask, Am I exhausted, existing, or excited? Which of these attributes describes you most of the time? Each of these three questions identifies a different status of renewal and describes various aspects of the mind, body, and soul of a leader.

Am I Exhausted?

Busy people who face many responsibilities and much stress may think they feel exhausted. Your body can give you physical signals that you have abused it. Like an engine, it will shut down until it gets the repairs it needs. You may indeed need to maintain some balance and set some priorities on your activities. If the source of your exhaustion is guilt, however, it may become a slippery slope because you can never be good enough, or do enough, or work hard enough. This Superman-Superwoman syndrome can wear you down. We know a woman with a sign on her refrigerator door that reads "Don't *should* on yourself today." Think of all the "should" messages you deliver to yourself (I should be thin; I should be done with this paper; I should be cheerful when someone comes to my room at 3 A.M.). It is overwhelming, if not impossible, to try to be all things to all people all of the time. At the end of each day, do you find that you have spent the entire day doing for others to the extent that you are too exhausted to do anything for yourself?

You might also identify a source of your exhaustion as worry. You may live in the world of "what ifs?" and spend a great deal of energy worrying about things that might never happen. Even if they did (or did not) happen, it might not be so terrible. Life will go on. An excited person may also feel fatigued, but this is very different from mental depression or exhaustion. Experiencing anxiety or depression to the degree that it becomes debilitating needs some professional intervention or at a minimum, self-renewal.

Am I Existing?

Perhaps you are pausing and need some time out. You may need some time to pull yourself back together after breaking up with someone close to you, to handle the death of a family member, or to manage some other energy-draining crisis. Pausing in this way—existing—can be a useful psychological state that allows you time to pull parts of your life back together. Your mind may be in need of developing new or positive perspectives.

But perhaps you feel like you are existing because you are plateauing (Bardwick, 1986). You are stressed—you have simply done all you can in the organizations of interest to you. Or perhaps you see your parents stagnating in their jobs because there is not enough newness to challenge them. Or maybe existing is a way for you to manage a very busy, stressful time in your life. Some people might say that they need to get recentered as a way to move from an existing state to a more focused and exciting existence. When you are in an existing state, it is important to return to, or refocus on, what makes you happy, what will energize you, and what brings meaning to your life.

Am I Excited?

If you are an excited person, you are open to new experiences and seek out new opportunities. And not all excited people are outgoing and energetic. You may be low-key and thoughtful, but your friends can tell from the twinkle in your eye that you love what you do. Excited people are continuous learners; they can identify something they know this year that they did not know last year. They know they are always growing and learning. Excited people feel some control over their own sphere instead of completely powerless to do anything. They tend to be initiating instead of waiting for others to tell them what to do. Excited people are often very tired, but being a tired, excited person is different from being an exhausted one. Excited people draw on internal energy—they draw from their spirit—and operate from a philosophy based on optimism and a focus on what is possible for a fulfilling future. Their soul is ablaze with their purpose or mission in life, which is the fuel that keeps their engines going. Being in touch with your personal values, seeking congruency between those values and actions, and being in touch with your inner core are ways to stay energized throughout your leadership journey.

Continuity and Transition

Self-renewal is not something you put off until Thanksgiving or wait until summer break to start. Renewal is the endless "interweaving of continuity and change" (Gardner, 1990, p. 124). It is the best of how you are now and what you want to be in the future, woven together with the new challenges and opportunities you face. Renewal is a way of viewing every day of your life so that you stay as fresh as possible.

"I have a bad habit of forgetting [personal balance] sometimes, but when I do remember, I take a hot bubble bath while reading one of my favorite books."— Luchara R. Sayles, from the University of North Carolina at Chapel Hill, views renewal as essential.

Renewal also means keeping your priorities in perspective and knowing when you need to do something differently to regain balance. Renewal requires you to pay attention and tend to your mind, body, and soul.

As part of your leadership development, you will be making many transitions along the way—transitioning into a new role or position, transitioning out of a leadership role, graduating from college, starting a new career, going back to graduate school. The list goes on. At times, you might feel overwhelmed or stressed as you go through transitions in your life. Transitions also can be a source of renewal. In *Overwhelmed: Coping With Life's Ups and Downs*, Nancy Schlossberg (1989a) proposes a model of transition. In her model, the significance of a particular transition will depend on four factors: how it changes your roles, your relationships, and your routines, and how it affects your assumptions about yourself and the world. The more factors that the transition changes, the greater the impact of the transition. Think about the newly elected student government officer. Certainly that person's role, relationships, and routines will change dramatically. It is also quite possible, even probable, that the person's assumptions about self and the world will also change. Feelings of importance and significance may be enhanced, and the world may now be viewed as full of previously unseen opportunities.

Potential resources for helping a person deal effectively with these transitions are called the four S's by Schlossberg (1989a) and include your overall situation, your self, your supports, and your strategies for coping. Again, consider the newly elected student government officer. The position itself will include many resources such as other officers and advisers. Certainly, anyone who has been elected to office has exhibited some talents to the electorate. Exhibit 11.1 illustrates that many of these strengths, including the ability to connect with other people, a sense of self-confidence, a record of previous achievement, will also be helpful in working through the transitions being faced. Obviously, supports for a new officer are evident in the people found in and around the student government itself. Finally, the strategies the new officer develops for working through the transition will also be useful. These could include a new officer retreat away from the business of campus to plan what will happen during the first few days and weeks of the new administration.

The sources of support offered by Nancy Schlossberg (1989a) can assist you in identifying the various people, processes, and resources that may be useful. Another way of achieving renewal is by incorporating the four Ss of support into your leadership approach.

Leadership Development as Renewal

No matter what career you choose, you can make a difference by being effective with others in a leadership or group setting. Whether you become an engineer or a high school French teacher, professional and work-related issues will benefit from the relational leadership processes presented in this book. Whether the focus of your leadership activity is your work, your neighborhood, your team, your place of worship, or community services, you can be an effective agent of change in collaboration with others.

The relational leadership principles presented in this book emphasize being process-oriented, seeking common purpose with

EXHIBIT 11.1 Sources of Support

Situation	Excited about new responsibilities; looking forward to forming new relationships; anxious to begin new activities; able to make plans in advance for assuming a new office; previous leadership experience; feelings of optimistic excitement; good timing.
Self	Challenging nature of new leadership role; confidence based on previously successful leadership experiences; feelings of optimistic excitement.
Support	Staff advisers; other officers, previous officers, members; trusted friends; mentors; printed resources; teachers; family members.
Strategies	Take action; seek advice; assert yourself; create structures (meetings, and so forth); practice relaxation skills.

Note: Some ideas drawn from Schlossberg, 1989a, pp. 33–91.

others, being inclusive, empowering, and ethical. As we noted earlier, being the kind of person who practices this philosophy of leadership is being what Covey (1991) calls a principle-centered leader. Covey relates values and beliefs to leadership by identifying characteristics of principle-centered leaders. They are continually learning. They are service-oriented. They radiate positive energy. They believe in themselves and in other people. They lead balanced lives. They see life as an adventure. They are synergistic. They exercise for self-renewal (pp. 33–39). Consider several interventions or practices to keep you engaged in the opportunities of leadership while keeping yourself renewed:

1. *Stretch yourself to learn and to do new things.* Learning and confidence are built by experiencing new situations that require you to use your skills and values to adapt or to make changes. The first woman commandant of the U.S. Naval Academy was asked about her experience and her advice to others in a similar situation. In

describing how she best learned, her reply was "to find your comfort zone, and then stay out of it." Think of all the exciting possibilities for you and your organization with "a healthy disregard for the impossible" (LeaderShape Institute, 1996).

2. *Develop the realization that what you are doing matters.* People who know that their contributions make a difference somehow or that there is value in their work have a sense of purpose and confidence that sustains them through many difficult times. In a study of sixty thousand Americans, Gail Sheehy (1981) sought to identify characteristics of well-being and life satisfaction. She found the ability to say "My life has meaning and direction" was the most salient factor distinguishing happy adults from those who were not.

3. *Keep a sense of personal balance.* Find time to enjoy not only leadership endeavors but personal interests and pursuits that bring satisfaction and happiness to your life. It is important to avoid being consumed by your leadership or membership responsibilities or to become addicted to your organization or work. What you do to find and maintain balance in your life may change over time, which in itself is renewing. When you take time for yourself, do not let yourself feel guilty because you think you should be doing something for someone else or your organization. Your morale will be better when you feel balanced and renewed, which should positively affect the morale of your organization or group.

4. *Make time for peaceful reflection and centering.* Most major problems and dilemmas do not have easy and quick solutions. One of the best strategies for resolving a dilemma is to step back from the situation after you have gathered the necessary information and consulted with the appropriate people and carefully think through all the dimensions of the situation. Reflect on what is actually happening and identify all your possible alternatives for action. On a personal level, constant reflection is needed to stay in touch with your inner core and to stay centered with your values and principles, and with knowing what is really important to you.

5. *Maintain healthy, supportive relationships.* This means relationships within your group and outside of your group. Develop

relationships with mentors. Leaders often mentor others in the organization. Leaders also need the rich support and empowerment that can be derived from a mentor, someone who has your best interests at heart and can help you stay centered, renewed, and balanced while leading others.

6. *Prioritize your tasks and responsibilities.* Use your judgment to determine what must be accomplished by the end of the day and what realistically can wait until tomorrow, or next week, or next month. If your daily to-do list goes on for pages, then you have to decide what is achievable in the time you have each day. And make sure that you build in time for yourself or time to take care of yourself, whether that means having a daily appointment with Mrs. Jones, exercising, or spending time with friends or family.

"When things become so crazy that you can't hear yourself think, *stop* and laugh, because laughing can aid in refocusing."—Annester Taylor-Brown, from Metro State College in Denver is chair of the Metro Activities Council.

Your personal leadership development can be a source of renewal-seeking opportunities to develop new skills and to find various avenues (careers, community service, recreational activities, and so forth) for exercising your leadership.

Staying Renewed

Lappé and Du Bois, authors of *The Quickening of America*, talk about the importance of understanding ourselves better as we interact with diverse people, being patient with ourselves, growing through learning, knowing that change and paradigm shifts bring some levels of discomfort, and finding ways to be creative in a sometimes messy and ambiguous world. These are the traits of what Lappé and Du Bois (1994) call our "democratic selves" (p. 288).

These are also characteristics of individuals who work to seek renewal in their lives and who work from the Relational Leadership Model.

Following is a chart of qualities adapted from Lappé and Du Bois's work on developing our democratic selves. Exhibit 11.2 illustrates that any of these qualities, along with others we included, show a contrast between leading from an exhausted and existing state (left-hand column) to leading from an exciting and renewed

EXHIBIT 11.2 Developing Ourselves for Leadership

Exhausted State	Excited, Renewed State
Pessimistic	Prudently optimistic
Easily defeated	Persevering
Despairing	Hopeful
Self-pitying	Self-respecting
Feeling unappreciated	Mattering
Simply blaming action	Accepting responsibility for action
Intolerant of uncertainty	Expects the unexpected
Fearful of embarrassment	Takes discomfort in stride
Mistrustful	Critically aware
Unthinking	Strategic
Passively frustrated	Actively engaged
Stuck	Always growing
Intolerant	Values diversity
Shut off	Seeking connections with others
Satisfied with the status quo	Making a difference
Exhausted	Balanced
Existing	Excited
Dysfunctional relationships	Healthy relationships
Unfocused	Having clear priorities
Stagnant	Learning
Reactive thinking	Reflective thinking

Source: Lappé & Du Bois, 1994, p. 294. Copyright 1994 by Jossey-Bass. Adapted with permission of Jossey-Bass, Inc., Publishers.

approach (right-hand column). Following Lappé and Du Bois's exercise, circle the qualities most important for you to develop in order to get, or stay, renewed.

Chapter Summary

In Chapter One a few essential questions were raised: What is your purpose? Who are you? What do you stand for? These questions are central to the self-renewal process. Understanding yourself, being aware of your inner core, paying attention to the signals your mind, body, and soul give you, and being comfortable with yourself are elements of self-renewal. Your journey to self-renewal will have no end destination. The process of renewal is cyclical.

Be careful not to fall victim to thinking that you are renewed when in fact you are not. Renewal affects your entire being. On your journey to renewal, make sure your mind, body, and soul together benefit from this process. Gardner (1990) observes, "The consideration leaders must never forget is that the key to renewal is the release of human energy and talent" (p. 136). When your mind, body, and soul are in harmony, you will feel good about yourself as a leader or contributing member and become a greater asset to your organization.

Chapter Activities

1. Reflect on this and the following questions: What does self-renewal mean to you?

2. Right now, do you feel renewed? Why or why not?

3. Make a list of all the activities you are involved in currently. Then, next to each activity designate which activities you do for *other* people and which you do for *yourself*. Are you spending enough time on you?

4. What would you like to do every day that would cause you to feel renewed? How could you make this a habit?

5. How do you know when you are feeling stressed? Do you become irritable, stop eating right, avoid exercise, fail to get enough rest? List ways in which you can reduce or avoid the stressors in your life (for example, exercise daily, prioritize tasks).

6. Think of an individual who you believe leads a healthy life, is balanced, and intentionally seeks renewal. What does this person do that allows him or her to be balanced? (If possible, arrange an interview to ask questions to explore this.) What is there about this person that you can adapt to your life?

7. Evaluate where you are in your own state of renewal and balance. Develop an action plan that would include all the characteristics you circled from the box to allow you to stay the course of a balanced and renewed person. What will you do to ensure that you are always growing and balanced, and have self-respect?

A Final Reflection

Through eleven chapters, we have taken a journey through the world of leadership. A theme throughout this book has been our belief that leadership means change—change for the greater good of the people in your group, organization, community, and world. We hope that you have found the Relational Leadership Model to be a useful guide when you work with others to accomplish change.

We ended each chapter with a series of reflections and activities. The activities are over, but we did want to end with a few questions for you to reflect on as you consider what you have learned and what the future might hold for you as a leader.

- How have you been able to apply what you have learned about leadership?

- How are you more aware of yourself?

- What things do you now see differently? How are you changing?

- How will you continue your learning about leadership?
- What is your own philosophy of leadership?

As Michael Sarich and Reena Meltzer, both students at the University of Maryland, College Park noted, "While the theories and concepts included within this text do work, they are not a substitute *for* work." Now it is time for you to continue on this incredible journey—into your own world of people and ideas—into your own future. We hope you have been challenged and maybe even inspired to see how you can make a difference.

We wish you well in this hard work. We know there will be rough seas ahead, but we hope you will navigate the permanent white water successfully and with a sense of passion, joy, and wonder, and with a commitment to the relationships you will have along the way. Stay well!

Additional Readings

Bolman, L. G., & Deal, T. E. (1995). *Leading with soul: An uncommon journey of spirit*. San Francisco: Jossey-Bass.
Gardner, J. W. (1981). *Self-renewal* (Rev. ed.). New York: Norton.
Schlossberg, N. K. (1989a). *Overwhelmed: Coping with life's ups and downs*. Lexington, MA: Lexington.
Vaill, P. B. (1996). *Learning as a way of being: Strategies for survival in a world of permanent white water*. San Francisco: Jossey-Bass.

References

Adizes, I. (1988). *Corporate lifecycles: How and why corporations grow and die and what to do about it.* Englewood Cliffs, NJ: Prentice Hall.

Alberti, R. E., & Emmons, M. L. (1974). *Your perfect right: A guide to assertive behavior.* San Luis Obispo, CA: IMPACT.

Albrecht, K. (1994). *The northbound train.* New York: AMACOM.

Alinsky, S. (1971). *Rules for radicals.* New York: Vintage Books.

Allen, K. (1990a). Making sense out of chaos: Leading and living in dynamic systems. *Campus Activities Programming, May,* 56–63.

Allen, K. E. (1990b). *Diverse voices of leadership: Different rhythms and emerging harmonies.* Unpublished doctoral dissertation. University of San Diego, San Diego, CA.

Angelou, M. (1994). *The complete collected poems of Maya Angelou.* New York: Random House.

Armour, M., & Hayles, R. (1990, July). *Managing multicultural organizations.* Paper presented at the Summer Institute for Intercultural Communications, Portland, OR.

Bandura, A. (1977). *Social learning theory.* Englewood Cliffs, NJ: Prentice Hall.

Bardwick, J. M. (1986). *The plateauing trap: How to avoid today's #1 career dilemma.* New York: Bantam Books.

Bass, B. M. (1981). *Stogdill's handbook of leadership: theory and research* (2nd ed.). New York: The Free Press.

Bass, B. M. (1990). *Bass & Stogdill's handbook of leadership: theory, research, and managerial applications* (3rd ed.). New York: The Free Press.

Beauchamp, T. L., & Childress, J. F. (1979). *Principles of biomedical ethics*. New York: Oxford University Press.

Beck, L. G., & Murphy, J. (1994). *Ethics in educational leadership programs: An expanding role*. Thousand Oaks, CA: Corwin Press.

Benne, K. D., & Sheats, P. (1948). Functional roles of group members. *Journal of Social Issues, 2*, 42–47.

Bennett, M. (1979). Overcoming the Golden Rule: Sympathy and empathy. In D. Nimmo (Ed.), *Communication yearbook 3* (pp. 407–422). New Brunswick, NJ: Transaction Books.

Bennis, W. (1989). *On becoming a leader*. Reading, MA: Addison-Wesley.

Bennis, W., & Goldsmith, J. (1994). *Learning to lead*. Reading, MA: Addison-Wesley.

Bennis, W. G., & Nanus, B. (1985). *Leaders: The strategies for taking charge*. New York: Harper & Row.

Berman, S., & La Farge, P. (Eds.). (1993). *Promising practices in teaching social responsibility*. Albany, NY: State University of New York Press.

Bernstein, A., & Rozen, S. (1994). *Sacred bull: The inner obstacles that hold you back at work and how to overcome them*. New York: Wiley.

Bird, F. B., & Waters, J. A. (1989). The moral muteness of managers. *California Management Review, 32*, 1, 73–87.

Block, P. (1993). *Stewardship: Choosing service over self-interest*. San Francisco: Berrett-Koehler.

Bok, D. (1982). *Beyond the ivory tower: Social responsibilities of the modern university*. Cambridge, MA: Harvard University Press.

Bok, D. (1990). *Universities and the future of America*. Durham, NC: Duke University Press.

Bolman, L. G., & Deal, T. E. (1995). *Leading with soul: An uncommon journey of spirit*. San Francisco: Jossey-Bass.

Bothwell, L. (1983). *The art of leadership: Skill-building techniques that produce results*. New York: Simon & Schuster.

Bridges, W. (1980). *Transitions: Making sense of life's changes*. Reading, MA: Addison-Wesley.

Broome, B. J. (1993). Managing differences in conflict resolution: The role of relational empathy. In D. J. D. Sandole & H. van der Merwe (Eds.), *Conflict resolution theory and practice: Integration and application* (pp. 97–111). New York: Manchester University Press.

Brown, I. (1963). *Understanding other cultures*. Englewood Cliffs, NJ: Prentice Hall.

Bryson, J. M., & Crosby, B. C. (1992). *Leadership for the common good*. San Francisco: Jossey-Bass.

Buber, M. (1958). *I and thou*. New York: Scribner.

Burns, J. M. (1978). *Leadership*. New York: Harper & Row.

Carnegie Foundation for the Advancement of Teaching (1990). *Campus life: In search of community*. Princeton, NJ: Carnegie Foundation for the Advancement of Teaching.

Carse, J. (1986). *Finite and infinite games*. New York: Ballantine.

Cartwright, T. (1991). Planning and chaos theory. *APA Journal*, Winter, 44–56.

Cathcart, R. S, Samovar, L. A., & Henman, L. D. (Eds.). (1996). *Small group communication: Theory & practice* (7th ed.). Madison, WI: Brown & Benchmark.

Chaleff, I. (1995). *The courageous follower: Standing up to and for our leaders*. San Francisco: Berrett-Koehler.

Chrislip, D. D., & Larson, C. E. (1994). *Collaborative leadership: How citizens and civic leaders can make a difference*. San Francisco: Jossey-Bass.

Ciulla, J. B. (1995). Leadership ethics: Mapping the territory. *Business Ethics Quarterly, 5*, 5–28.

Clifton, D. O., & Nelson, P. (1992). *Soar with your strengths*. New York: Delacorte Press.

Cohen, M. D., & March, J. G. (1974). *Leadership and ambiguity* (2nd ed.). Boston: Harvard Business School Press.

Collins, J., & Porras, J. (1994). *Built to last: Successful habits of visionary companies*. New York: HarperCollins.

Conger, J., & Associates. (1994). *Spirit at work: Discovering the spirituality in leadership*. San Francisco: Jossey-Bass.

Conner, D. R. (1993). *Managing at the speed of change*. New York: Villard.

Covey, S. (1989). *The seven habits of highly effective people*. New York: Simon & Schuster.

Covey, S. R. (1991). *Principle-centered leadership*. New York: Summit Books.

Crum, T. F. (1987). *The magic of conflict*. New York: Simon & Schuster.

Davidow, W., & Malone, M. (1992). *The virtual corporation: Structuring and revitalizing the corporation for the 21st century*. New York: HarperBusiness.

Deal, T., & Kennedy, A. (1982). *Corporate cultures: The rites and rituals of corporate life*. Reading, MA: Addison-Wesley.

De George, R. T. (1986). *Business ethics* (2nd ed.). New York: Macmillan.

Deming, W. (1986). *Out of the crisis*. Cambridge, MA: MIT.

De Pree, M. (1989). *Leadership is an art*. New York: Doubleday.

De Pree, M. (1992). *Leadership jazz*. New York: Doubleday.

Donaldson, T. (1989). *The ethics of international business*. New York: Oxford University Press.

Drath, W. H., & Palus, C. J. (1994). *Making common sense: Leadership as meaning-making in a community of practice*. Greensboro, NC: Center for Creative Leadership.

Etzioni, A. (1993). *The spirit of community*. New York: Crown.

Fairholm, G. W. (1994). *Leadership and a culture of trust*. New York: Praeger.

Farson, R. (1995). *Management of the absurd: Paradoxes in leadership*. New York: Simon & Schuster.

Festinger, L. (1962). *A theory of cognitive dissonance*. Stanford, CA: Stanford University Press.

Fitzgerald, C., & Kirby, L. K. (1997). *Developing leaders: Research and applications in psychological type and leadership development*. Palo Alto, CA: Davies-Black.

Fox, M. (1994). *The reinvention of work: A new vision of livelihood for our time*. New York: HarperCollins.

French, J. R. P., & Raven, B. H. (1959). The bases of social power. In D. Cartwright (Ed.), *Studies in social power* (pp. 150–167). Ann Arbor, MI: Institute for Social Research.

Gardner, J. W. (1993). The antileadership vaccine. In W. E. Rosenbach & R. L. Taylor (Eds.), *Contemporary issues in leadership* (3rd. ed., pp. 193–200). Boulder, CO: Westview Press. (Original work published 1965)

Gardner, J. W. (1981). *Self-renewal* (Rev. ed.). New York: Norton.

Gardner, J. W. (1990). *On leadership*. New York: The Free Press.

Gioia, D. A. (1991). Pinto fires and personal ethics: A script analysis of missed opportunities. *Journal of Business Ethics, 11*, 379–389.

Goodman, N. (1992). *Introduction to sociology*. New York: HarperCollins.

Gozdz, K. (1993). Building community as a leadership discipline. In M. Ray & A. Rinzler (Eds.), *The new paradigm in business: Emerging strategies for leadership and organizational change* (pp. 107–119). Los Angeles: Jeremy P. Tarcher/Perigee.

Greenleaf, R. (1977). *Servant leadership: A journey in the nature of legitimate power and greatness.* New York: Paulist.

Greenwood, R. G. (1993). Leadership theory: A historical look at its evolution. *The Journal of Leadership Studies, 1*(1), 4–19.

Grenier, R., & Metes, G. (1995). *Going virtual: Moving your organization into the 21st century.* Upper Saddle River, NJ: Prentice Hall.

Gudykunst, W. B. (1991). *Bridging differences: Effective intergroup communication.* Newbury Park: Sage.

Haas, H. G., & Tamarkin, B. (1992). *The leader within.* New York: HarperCollins.

Handy, C. (1996). *Beyond certainty: The changing worlds of organizations.* Boston, MA: Harvard Business School Press.

Harriger, K., & Ford, M. (1989). Lessons learned: Teaching citizenship in the university. In S. W. Morse (Ed.), *Public leadership education: Preparing college students for their civic roles* (pp. 22–28). Dayton, OH: Kettering Foundation.

Hart, L. B., & Dalke, J. D. (1983). *The sexes at work: Improving work relationships between men and women.* Englewood Cliffs, NJ: Prentice Hall.

Hawley, J. (1993). *Reawakening the spirit in work.* New York: Fireside/Simon & Schuster.

Heider, J. (1985). *The tao of leadership: Lao Tzu's tao te ching adapted for a new age.* New York: Bantam.

Heilbrunn, J. (1994). Can leadership be studied? *WQ,* Autumn, 65–72.

Helgesen, S. (1990). *The female advantage: Women's ways of leadership.* New York: Doubleday.

Helgesen, S. (1995). *The web on inclusion: A new architecture for building great organizations.* New York: Currency/Doubleday.

Helms, J. E. (1992). *A race is a nice thing to have.* Topeka, KS: Content Communications.

Henderson, V. E. (1992). *What's ethical in business?* New York: McGraw-Hill.

Hodgkinson, C. (1983). *The philosophy of leadership.* New York: St. Martin's Press.

Hofstede, G. (1980). Motivation, leadership, and organization: Do American theories apply abroad? *Organizational Dynamics,* Summer, 42–63.

Hollander, E. P. (1993). Legitimacy, power, and influence: A persepctive on relational features of leadership. In M. M. Chemers & R. Ayman

(Eds.), *Leadership theory and research: Perspectives and directions* (pp. 29–47). San Diego: Academic Press.

Hoopes, D. S. (1979). Intercultural communication concepts and the psychology of intercultural experiences. In M. D. Pusch (Ed.), *Multicultural education: A cross cultural training approach* (pp. 10–38). Chicago: Intercultural Press.

Hoopes, D. S., & Pusch, M. D. (1979). Definition of terms. In M. D. Pusch (Ed.), *Multicultural education: A cross cultural training approach* (pp. 1–8). Chicago: Intercultural Press.

Horwood, B. (1989). Reflections on reflection. *Journal of Experiential Education, 12*(2), 5–7.

Howell, J. M. (1988). Two faces of charisma: Socialized and personalized leadership in organizations. In J. A. Conger, R. N. Kanungo & Associates (Eds.), *Charismatic leadership: The elusive factor in organizational effectiveness* (pp. 213–236). San Francisco: Jossey-Bass.

Howell, J. M., & Avolio, B. J. (1992). The ethics of charismatic leadership: Submission or liberation? *Academy of Management Executive, 6*(2), 43–54.

Hughes, R. L., Ginnett, R. C., & Curphy, G. J. (1993). *Leadership: Enhancing the lessons of experience.* Homewood, IL: Richard D. Irwin.

Jackson, B., & Holvino, E. (1988). Developing multicultural organizations. *Journal of Religion and Applied Behavioral Science, 9,* 14–19.

Jaffe, D., Scott, C., & Tobe, G. (1994). *Rekindling commitment. How to revitalize yourself, your work, and your organization.* San Francisco: Jossey-Bass.

Jensen, G. H. (1987). Learning styles. In J. A. Provost & S. Anchors (Eds.), *Applications of the Myers-Briggs Type Indicator in higher education* (pp. 180–206). Palo Alto: Consulting Psychologists Press.

Johnson, D. W., & Johnson, F. P. (1994). *Joining together: Group theory and group skills* (6th ed.). Boston: Allyn & Bacon.

Johnson, D. W., Maruyama, G., Johnson, R., Nelson, D., & Skon, L. (1981). Effects of cooperative, competitive, and individualistic goal structures on achievement: A meta-analysis. *Psychological Bulletin, 89*(1), 47–62.

Jones, P., & Kahaner, L. (1995). *Say it and live it: The 50 corporate mission statements that hit the mark.* New York: Currency/Doubleday.

Jones, S. R., & Lucas, N. J. (1994). Interview with Michael Josephson. *Concepts & Connections: Rethinking Ethics & Leadership, 2*(3), 1, 3–5.

Jung, C. (1923). *Psychological types*. New York: Harcourt Brace.

Kanter, R. M. (1989). *When giants learn to dance*. New York: Simon & Schuster.

Keirsey, D., & Bates, M. (1984). *Please understand me: Character & temperament types* (4th ed.). Del Mar, CA: Prometheus Nemesis Books.

Kelley, R. E. (1988). In praise of followers. *Harvard Business Review*, (66)6, 142–148.

Kelley, R. E. (1992). *The power of followership*. New York: Doubleday/Currency.

Kelly, K. (1994). *Out of control: The rise of neo-biological civilization*. Reading, MA: Addison-Wesley.

Kidder, R. M. (1993). Ethics, youth, and the moral barometer. In *The Public Perspective*, 4(6), 22–25.

Kidder, R. M. (1994). *Shared values for a troubled world: Conversations with men and women of conscience*. San Francisco: Jossey-Bass.

Kiefer, C. F., & Senge, P. M. (1984). Metanoic organizations. In J. D. Adams (Ed.), *Transforming work: A collection of organizational transformation readings* (pp. 68–84). Alexandria, VA: Miles River Press.

Kitchener, K. S. (1984). Intuition, critical evaluation and ethical principles: The foundation for ethical decisions in counseling psychology. *The Counseling Psychologist*, 12(3), 43–55.

Kline, P., & Saunders, B. (1993). *Ten steps to a learning organization*. Arlington, VA: Great Ocean.

Knowles, M., & Knowles, H. (1959). *Introduction to group dynamics*. New York: Association Press.

Kohn, A. (1992). *No contest: The case against competition* (Rev. ed.). Boston: Houghton Mifflin.

Komives, S. R. (1994). Increasing student involvement through civic leadership education. In P. Mable & C. Schroeder (Eds.), *Realizing the educational potential of college residence halls* (pp. 218–240). San Francisco: Jossey Bass.

Kotter, J. (1995). Leading change: Why transformation efforts fail. *Harvard Business Review*, 73, 59–67.

Kouzes, J. M., & Posner, B. Z. (1987). *The leadership challenge: How to get extraordinary things done in organizations*. San Francisco: Jossey-Bass.

Kouzes, J. M., & Posner, B. Z. (1993). *Credibility: How leaders gain and lose it, why people demand it*. San Francisco: Jossey-Bass.

Kouzes, J., & Posner, B. (1995). *The leadership challenge* (2nd ed.). San Francisco: Jossey-Bass.

Kübler-Ross, E. (1970). *On death and dying*. New York: Macmillan.

Kurschner, D. (1996). The 100 best corporate citizens. *Business Ethics Magazine, 10*(3), 24–35.

Lappé, F. M., & Du Bois, P. M. (1994). *The quickening of America: Rebuilding our nation, remaking our lives*. San Francisco: Jossey-Bass.

LeaderShape Institute Manual (1996). Champaign, IL: LeaderShape.

Leppo, J. (1987). Multicultural programming: A conceptual framework and model for implementation. *Campus Activities Programming, 19*(9), 56–60.

Leppo, J., & Lustgraaf, M. (1987). *Student government: Working with special constituencies*. Programming, Leadership & Activities Network, Memorial Union. Grand Forks, ND: University of North Dakota.

Levine, A. (1993). *A portrait of college students in the 90s: Taking responsibility for educational management*. Paper presented at the Annual Conference of the National Association of Student Personnel Administrators, Boston.

Lewin, K. (1958). Group decision and social change. In E. E. Maccoby, T. M. Newcomb, & E. L. Hartley (Eds.), *Readings in social psychology* (pp. 197–211). New York: Holt, Rinehart & Winston.

Lewis, H. A. (1990). *A question of values*. New York: Harper & Row.

Lipman-Blumen, J. (1984). *Gender roles and power*. Englewood Cliffs, NJ: Prentice-Hall.

Lipnack, J., & Stamps, J. (1993). *The TeamNet Factor: Bringing the power of boundary crossing into the heart of your business*. Essex Junction, VT: Oliver Wight Publications.

Lippitt, G. L. (1969). *Organizational renewal: Achieving viability in a changing world*. New York: Appleton-Century Crofts.

Lippitt, G. L. (1973). *Visualizing change: Model building and the change process*. Fairfax, VA: NTL-Learning Resources.

Loden, M., & Rosener, J. B. (1991). *Workforce America!* Homewood, IL: Business One Irwin.

Lucas, N., & Anello, E. (1995). *Ethics and leadership*. Unpublished paper. Salzburg Leadership Seminar. Salzburg, Austria. November 11–18, 1995.

Manz, C. C., & Sims, H. P., Jr. (1981). Vicarious learning: The influence of modeling on organizational behavior. *Academy of Management Review*, 6(1), 105–113.

Manz, C. C., & Sims, H. P., Jr. (1989). *SuperLeadership: Leading others to lead themselves*. New York: Berkley Books.

Mathews, D. (1994). *Politics for people*. Urbana, IL: University of Illinois Press.

Matusak, L. R. (1996). *Finding your voice: Learning to lead . . . anywhere you want to make a difference*. San Francisco: Jossey-Bass.

McCaulley, M. H. (1990). The Myers-Briggs Type Indicator and leadership. In K. E. Clark & M. B. Clark, (Eds.), *Measures of leadership* (pp. 381–418). Greensboro, NC: Center for Creative Leadership.

McFarland, L. J., Senn, L. E., & Childress, J. R. (1993). *21st century leadership: Dialogues with 100 top leaders*. Los Angeles: The Leadership Press.

McGill, M. E., & Slocum, J. W. (1993). Unlearning the organization, *Organizational Dynamics*, Fall, 67–79.

McIntosh, P. M. (1989, July/August). White privilege: Unpacking the invisible knapsack. *Peace and Freedom*, 10–12.

McMahon, T., Kochner, C., Clemetsen, B., & Bolger, A. (1995). *Moving beyond TQM to learning organizations: New perspectives to transform the academy*. Paper presented at the annual meeting of the American College Personnel Association, Boston, March 18–22.

Meadows, D. (1982) Whole earth models and systems. *Co-Evolution Quarterly*, Summer, 98–108.

Mizrahi, T., & Rosenthal, B. S. (1993). Managing dynamic tensions in social change coalitions. In T. Mizrahi & J. Morrison (Eds.), *Community organization and social administration: Advances, trends and emerging principles* (pp. 11–40). New York: Haworth Press.

Morrison, A. M. (1996). *The new leaders: Leadership diversity in America*. San Francisco: Jossey-Bass.

Murrell, K. L. (1985). The development of a theory of empowerment: Rethinking power for organization development. *Organization Development Journal*, 34, 34–38.

Myers, I. B. (1980). *Gifts differing*. Palo Alto, CA: Consulting Psychologists Press.

Nanus, B. (1992). *Visionary leadership: Creating a compelling sense of direction for your organization*. San Francisco: Jossey-Bass.

Nash, L. L. (1987). 12 questions to ask when making ethical decisions. *Training & Development Magazine*, November, 36.

Nash, L. L. (1990). *Good intentions aside*. Boston: Harvard Business School Press.

National Leadership Symposium (1991). *Proceedings from the 1991 National Invitational Leadership Symposium*, College Park, MD.

National Leadership Symposium (1992). *Proceedings from the 1992 National Invitational Leadership Symposium*. College Park, MD.

Neilson, R. P. (1990). Dialogic leadership as ethics action method. *Journal of Business Ethics*, 9, 765–783.

Nicoll, D. (1984). Grace beyond the roles: A new paradigm for lives on a human scale. In J. D. Adams (Ed.), *Transforming work: A collection of organizational transformation readings* (pp. 4–16). Alexandria, VA: Miles River Press.

Nutt, P. C., & Backoff, R. W. (1992). *Strategic management of public and third sector organizations: A handbook for leaders*. San Francisco: Jossey-Bass.

Palmer, P. J. (1990). *The active life: A spirituality of work, creativity, and caring*. San Francisco: Harper & Row.

Parr, J. (1994). Foreword. In D. D. Chrislip & C. E. Larson, *Collaborative leadership: How citizens and civic leaders can make a difference* (pp. xi–xiii). San Francisco: Jossey-Bass.

Peck, M. S. (1987). *The different drum: Community-making and peace*. New York: Simon & Schuster.

Pedersen, P. (1988). *Handbook for developing multicultural awareness*. Alexandria, VA: American Association of Counseling and Development.

A person of character (1993). Character Counts Coalition. Marina del Ray, CA: Josephson Institute of Ethics.

Peters, T. (1989). Foreword. In C. C. Manz & H. P. Sims, Jr., *Superleadership: Leading others to lead themselves* (pp. xiii–xiv). New York: Prentice Hall.

Petersen, J. (1994). *The road to 2015: Profiles of the future*. Corte Madera, CA: Waite Group Press.

Phillips, J. M. (1995). Leadership since 1975: Advancement or inertia? *The Journal of Leadership Studies*, 2(1), 58–80.

Pickover, C. (1991). *Computers and the imagination: Visual adventures beyond the edge*. New York: St. Martin's Press.

Piper, T. R., Gentile, M. C., & Parks, S. D. (1993). *Can ethics be taught?:*

Perspectives, challenges, and approaches at Harvard Business School. Boston: Harvard Business School.

Pocock, P. (1989). Is business ethics a contradiction in terms? *Personnel Management, 21*(11), 60–63.

Pope, R. (1993). Multicultural-Organization development in student affairs: An introduction. *Journal of College Student Development, 34,* 201–205.

Postman, N. (1992). *Technopoly: The surrender of culture to technology.* New York: Knopf.

Potter, E. H., III, & Fiedler, F. E. (1993). Selecting leaders: Making the most of previous experience. *Journal of Leadership Studies, 1*(1), 61–70.

Provost, J. & Anchors, S. (Eds.). (1987). *Applications of the Myers-Briggs type indicator in higher education.* Palo Alto, CA: Consulting Psychologists Press.

Pusch, M. D. (Ed.). (1979). *Multicultural education: A cross-cultural training approach.* Chicago: Intercultural Press.

The quotable woman. (1991). Philadelphia: Running Press.

Rest, J. R. (1979). *Development in judging moral issues.* Minneapolis: University of Minnesota.

Rest, J. R. (1986). Moral development in young adults. In R. A. Mines & K. S. Kitchener (Eds.), *Adult cognitive development: Methods and models* (pp. 92–111). New York: Praeger.

Rheingold, H. (1993). *The virtual community: Homesteading on the electronic frontier.* New York: HarperCollins.

Rhinesmith, S. (1993). *A manager's guide to globalization: Six keys to success in a changing world.* Homewood, IL: Business One Irwin.

Rogers, J. L. (1996). Leadership. In S. R. Komives & D. B. Woodard Jr. & Associates, *Student services: A handbook for the profession* (3rd ed., pp. 299–319). San Francisco: Jossey-Bass.

Rosenthal, T. L., & Zimmerman, B. J. (1978). *Social learning and cognition.* New York: Academic Press.

Ross, R. (1994a). The five whys. In P. Senge, et. al., *The fifth discipline fieldbook* (pp. 108–112). New York: Doubleday.

Ross, R. (1994b). Skillful discussion: Protocols for reaching a decision—mindfully. In P. Senge, A. Kleiner, C. Roberts, R. Ross, & B. Smith (1994). *The fifth discipline fieldbook: Strategies and tools for building a learning organization* (pp. 385–391). New York: Currency/Doubleday.

Rost, J. C. (1991). *Leadership for the twenty-first century.* New York: Praeger.

Rost, J. C. (1993). Leadership development in the new millennium. *Journal of Leadership Studies, 1*(1), 91–110.

Schein, E. (1992). *Organizational culture and leadership* (2nd ed.). San Francisco: Jossey-Bass.

Schlossberg, N. K. (1989a). *Overwhelmed: Coping with life's ups and downs.* Lexington, MA: Lexington.

Schlossberg, N. K. (1989b). Marginality and mattering: Key issues in building community. In D. C. Roberts (Ed.), *Designing campus activities to foster a sense of community* (pp. 5–15). New Directions for Student Services, No. 48. San Francisco: Jossey-Bass.

Senge, P. M. (1990). *The fifth discipline: The art and practice of the learning organization.* New York: Doubleday.

Senge, P. (1993). The art and practice of the learning organization. In M. Ray & A, Rinzler (Eds.), *The new paradigm in business: Emerging strategies for leadership and organizational change* (pp. 126–137). Los Angeles: Tarcher/Perigree.

Senge, P. (1994). Moving forward: Thinking strategically about learning organizations. In P. Senge, A. Kleiner, C. Roberts, R. Ross, & B. Smith, *The fifth discipline fieldbook: Strategies and tools for building a learning organization* (pp. 15–47). New York: Currency/Doubleday.

Senge, P., Kleiner, A., Roberts, C., Ross, R., & Smith, B. (1994). *The fifth discipline fieldbook: Strategies and tools for building a learning organization.* New York: Currency/Doubleday.

Shaw, B. (1962). *Back to Methusaleh: Complete plays, with prefaces.* New York: Dodd, Mead. (Original work published 1921)

Shaw, W., & Barry, V. (1989). *Moral issues in business* (4th ed.). Belmont, CA: Wadsworth.

Shea, G. F. (1988). *Practical ethics. AMA Management Briefing.* New York: AMA Membership Publications Division.

Sheehy, G. (1981). *Pathfinders.* New York: Bantam.

Simons, G. F., Vazquez, C., & Harris, P. R. (1993). *Transcultural leadership.* Houston: Gulf.

Sims, H. P., Jr., & Lorenzi, P. (1992). *The new leadership paradigm: Social learning and cognition in organizations.* Newbury Park, CA: Sage.

Sims, H. P., Jr., & Manz, C. C. (1981). Social learning theory: The role of modeling in the exercise of leadership. *Journal of Organizational Behavior Management, 3*(4), 55–63.

Sims, H. P., Jr., & Manz, C. C. (1982). Modeling influences on employee behavior. *Personnel Journal, 61*(1), 58–65.

A *social change model of leadership development: Guidebook version III*. (1996). Los Angeles: University of California Los Angeles Higher Education Research Institute.

Sorenson, G. L. (1992). *Emergent leadership: A phenomenological study of ten transformational political leaders*. Unpublished manuscript.

Spears, L. C. (1995). *Reflections on leadership. How Robert K. Greenleaf's theory of servant-leadership influenced today's top management thinkers*. New York: Wiley.

Spence, J. T. (Ed.). (1983). *Achievement and achievement motives: Psychological and sociological approaches*. San Francisco: W. H. Freeman.

Stacey, R. (1992). *Managing the unknowable*. San Francisco: Jossey-Bass.

Stogdill, R. M. (1974). *Handbook of leadership: A survey of theory and research*. New York: The Free Press.

Talbot, D. M. (1996). Multiculturalism. In S. R. Komives, D. B. Woodard Jr., & Associates, *Student services: A handbook for the profession* (3rd ed., pp. 380–396). San Francisco: Jossey-Bass.

Tannen, D. (1990). *You don't understand me: Women and men in conversation*. New York: Morrow.

Taylor, H. L. (1989). *Delegate: The key to successful management*. New York: Warner Books.

Terry, R. (1993). *Authentic leadership*. San Francisco: Jossey Bass.

Tichy, N. W., & Devanna, M. A. (1986). *The transformational leader*. New York: Wiley.

Tjosvold, D., & Tjosvold, M. M. (1991). *Leading the team organization*. New York: Macmillan.

Toffler, B. L. (1986). *Tough choices: Managers talk ethics*. New York: Wiley.

Tubbs, S. (1984). *A systems approach to small group interaction* (2nd ed.). Reading, MA: Addison-Wesley.

Tuckman, B. W. (1965). Developmental sequence in small groups. *Psychological Bulletin, 63*, 384–399.

Vaill, P. B. (1989). *Managing as a performing art: New ideas for a world of chaotic change*. San Francisco: Jossey-Bass.

Vaill, P. B. (1991). *Permanent white water: The realities, myths, paradoxes, and dilemmas of managing organizations*. San Francisco: Jossey-Bass.

Vaill, P. B. (1996). *Learning as a way of being: Strategies for survival in a world of permanent white water*. San Francisco: Jossey-Bass.

Van Fleet, D. D., & Yukl, G. A. (1989). A century of leadership research. In W. E. Rosenbach & R. L. Taylor (Eds.), *Contempoary issues in leadership* (2nd ed., pp. 65–90). Boulder, CO: Westview Press.

Walton, C. C. (1988). *The moral manager*. New York: Harper & Row.

Watkins, K. E., & Marsick, V. J. (1993). *Sculpting the learning organization*. San Francisco: Jossey-Bass.

Webster's ninth new collegiate dictionary. (1986). Springfield, MA: Merriam-Webster Inc.

Weick, K. E. (1979). *The social psychology of organizing* (2nd ed.). New York: Random House.

Wheatley, M. J. (1992). *Leadership and the new science: Learning about organization from an orderly universe*. San Francisco: Berrett-Koehler.

Wheatley, M., & Kellner-Rogers, M. (1996). *A simpler way*. San Francisco: Berrett-Koehler.

Willie, C. V. (1992). *Achieving community on the college campus*. Paper presented to the Annual Conference of the American College and University Housing Officers-International, Boston College, Boston.

Wood, D. J., & Gray, B. (1991). Toward a comprehensive theory of collaboration. *Journal of Applied Behavioral Science, 27*(2), 139–162.

Wren, T. (1994). Interview: H. Norman Schwarzkopf, General, USA. *Journal of Leadership Studies, 1*(3), 1–6.

Yukl, G. A. (1989). *Leadership in organizations* (2nd ed.). Englewood Cliffs, NJ: Prentice Hall.

Yukl, G. A. (1994). *Leadership in organizations* (3rd ed.). Englewood Cliffs, NJ: Prentice Hall.

Zaleznik, A. (1977). Managers and leaders: Are they different? *Havard Business Review, 55*(5), 67–78.

Name Index

Subject Index

A

Academic department communities, 243
Acceptance: of differences, 149, 150; of multicultural diversity, 145, 146
Accountability: and autonomy in coalitions, 239, 240–241; in ethical organizations, 249–251; in groups, 188; and responsibility, 119, 120, 188
Acculturation, 140–142, 143; your own, 144–145, 255–256
Action: coalitions for community, 238–243; five principles of ethical, 267–269; four components of moral, 265–267; making a difference, 16, 309, 312; pausing to reflect before, 55, 155, 190; team or working group, 188; twelve questions for ethical, 269–270
Ad hoc groups, 167
Adaptation, Jung's four core functions of, 122–124
Admiration: of human differences, 149, 150; of other cultures, 146, 148, 217
Adoption of values from other cultures, 147, 148
Adversarial group processes, 168–169
Advisers, organization, 218
Affiliation or active practice, 233–234, 285–287
Affirmations, positive, 134–135
African American student groups, 171–172
Agents, change, 87, 215–216, 217
Aggressive communication, 157, 158
Alcohol and drug abuse, combatting, 291
Alienation of the membership, 182, 185, 229, 289–290

Alliances. See Coalitions
Allowing involvement, 181–182
Alone, doing things, 84, 299
Ambiguity, comfort with, 124
Andness, the concept of, 52–53
Annual reports, slide shows, 51–52
Appreciation: building multicultural, 145–148; of human differences, 149, 150
Art metaphors, 32–33
Artifacts, organizational culture, 209
Assertiveness, in communication, 156–157, 158
Assumptions: about ethical leadership, 252–256; before meetings, 159; conflicting, 178; cultural heritage, 144–145, 255; of leadership theories, 36–37; made by change agents, 215–216, 217; mental models, 98, 218; organizational culture, 209; and problem solving, 57–58, 236; sacred bull, 285
Atom theory metaphor, 34–35
Attendance, meeting, 58
Attitudes. See Beliefs and attitudes
Attractors of meaning, strange, 51, 54–55
Authenticity, action with, 92, 118
Authority: attitudes toward, 152, 242; and decision making, 181–182, 183–184. See also Leaders, positional
Automobile safety case, 262–263
Autonomy: and accountability in coalitions, 239, 240–241; principle of respecting, 268
Awareness: of differences, 148–149; of multicultural diversity, 145, 146; self, 106, 115–116, 137